6-05

S0-AFG-642

HOW TO SET UP YOUR OWN SMALL BUSINESS

VOLUME 1
2005 Edition

ISBN 0939069741

American Institute of Small Business

7515 Wayzata Blvd
Suite 129
Minneapolis, MN 55426
www.aisb.biz

800-328-2906
952-545-7001
Fax   952-545-7020
info@aisb.biz

HOW TO SET UP YOUR OWN
SMALL BUSINESS

Kris Solie-Johnson

Published by
AMERICAN INSTITUTE OF SMALL BUSINESS
7515 Wayzata Blvd. Suite 129
Minneapolis, MN 55426
(952) 545-7001
Fax (952) 545-7020
(800) 328-2906
www.aisb.biz

VOLUME I

ISBN 0-939069-74-1
ISSN 1074-6080
Library of Congress Catalog Number: 94648091

CONSULTATION

CERTIFICATE

If You need help with
your current or new business,
please call our office for a 15
minute consultation.

We will be glad to help
you and way we can.

1-800-328-2906

American Institute of Small Business

7515 Wayzata Blvd
Suite 129
Minneapolis, MN 55426
www.aisb.biz

800-328-2906
952-545-7001
Fax   952-545-7020
info@aisb.biz

What Other Librarians Are Saying about the 2005 Edition

"This comprehensive work offers objective accurate information, including the answers to real-life problems entrepreneurs face. The explanations are clear, and the filled-in-forms, addresses and samples that are included make this work invaluable. **Any public library** whose patrons include start-up or established entrepreneurs **should get their money's worth** from this set. Librarians would find it worthwhile to familiarize themselves with the contents, as it provides practical answers to so very many questions."

- Susan from Cuyahoga County Public Library, Maple Heights, OH

"Starting a business? **Here's all you need** - a 2 volume set, packed with vital information, yet easy to read and understand. What would our Business Resource Center do without it?"

- Linda from Aurora Public Library, Aurora, CO

"Anyone who is considering starting a business should **make this one of the first books they read**."

- Susannah from Norwalk Public Library, Norwalk, CT

"**Our Patrons use** "How To Set Up Your Own Small Business" **frequently.** It really gives the small business owner everthing they need to get their business up and running"
- Krista from Lisle Library, Lisle, IL

"The books are **very comprehensive**, written in language the average person can understand. I anticipate wide usage. **Previous editions have been heavily used** and appreciated by our patrons. I would recommend these books to anyone starting up their own business."

- Janice from Madison County Library, Madison, VA

"A readable introduction to the basics of all aspects of setting up a new business. This is a good general resources for people just getting started."
-Booklist

"Each step of setting up a small business is considered and covered in the two-volume set."
-School Library Journal

TABLE OF CONTENTS

VOLUME 1

About the American Institute of Small Business
Preface
Acknowledgements

Start-Up

How to Start a Business in 27 Days	1
Getting Off to A Good Start	16
Buying a Business	56
Home Based Business	79
Franchising a Business	112
Forming a Company	150
Researching the Market (Initial)	194
Selecting a Location(s)	252

Finance and Accounting

Forecasting Sales	284
Finding Money	307
Using the Small Business Administration	358
Bookkeeping Made Easy	393

TABLE OF CONTENTS

VOLUME 2

Marketing and Sales

Advertising for Success   428
Creating Publicity and Public Relations   466
Selling for Profit   503
Understanding the Internet   567
Setting Up a Web Site   587
Internet Marketing   610

Management and Operations

Insuring Your Future   621
Purchasing the BEST   646
Drafting Effective Business Policies   669
Managing Personnel   693
Small Business Tax Basics   738

The Business Plan

Developing an Effective Business Plan   758

Appendices and Index

SBA Regional Offices   A
SCORE State Offices   B
SBDC State Offices   C
Sample Partnership Agreement   D
Your Secret Riches Exercise   E
Marketing Customer Contact Form   F
The Ultimate Marketing Calendar   G
Marketing/Advertising Tracking Form   H
Recommended Books   I

Index

About the American Institute of Small Business

AISB's™ mission is to teach entrepreneurs the skills needed to successfully start and run a small business by providing resources to librarians, teachers, current business owners, and others who serve as local advocates.

Formed in 1984, The American Institute of Small Business focuses on potential business owners with little or no small business experience.

Our publications are easy to understand and cover a wide variety of topics to help start and run a successful small business. A web site has been created at www.aisb.biz to help librarians, teachers and entrepreneurs find the additional information they may need. If you have comments about the web site, please contact us at info@aisb.biz.

The popular 2-volume set of books, written by Max Fallex, "How to Set Up Your Own Small Business" is currently in its 8th Edition since 1985. These books have been a foundation for many entrepreneurs when setting up their new businesses and a major focus of AISB's™ goals as well. The information is regularly updated to keep small businesses competitive.

> *"A readable introduction to the basics of all aspects of setting up a new business."* — **Booklist** (reviewing the 2-volume set of books "How to Set Up Your Own Small Business")

Owner and President, Kris Solie-Johnson, has been deeply involved with small business consulting since 1989. She received her MBA in Venture Management from the University of St. Thomas in 1996. While serving as a Strategic Alliance Account Manager at Residential Funding Corporation (RFC), she helped small companies receive new technologies in exchange for loans sold to RFC. She continued her career at a small Internet company offering financial reporting to small community banks over the Internet. Ms. Solie-Johnson purchased the American Institute of Small Business and is dedicated to continuing the work and vision of teaching entrepreneurship instilled by AISB's™ founder, Max Fallek.

Max Fallek, original founder, authored several books in the field of small business and entrepreneurship. Mr. Fallek has demonstrated his expertise in small business development by successfully starting and operating eight different small businesses including an advertising agency, a market research firm, a telemarketing company, and a real estate firm. Since his appointment in 1987, he has served as a member of the National Advisory Council to the U.S. Small Business Administration.

Preface

It has been said that there are small businesses but no small people.

The principles that make businesses grow and prosper are the same small or large.

Some people jump into business with no previous experience. They have ideas and enthusiasm and no idea of the difficulties waiting ahead. Unfortunately the experience needed to make the business successful can be costly and financially disastrous.

Getting involved in a new business, especially if you have no previous experience, can bring you face to face with a whole new world of complex problems. It need not be overwhelming if you are prepared.

The only intelligent way to go into a new business venture is with all the knowledge you can get and solid planning.

A careful reading of this book is a worthwhile first step in opening your business. It could save you heartaches and headaches and help protect your investment.

Nothing can replace personal experience but we believe the information we've put together can go a long way toward reducing uncertainty in the small business venture by giving you some ideas of what is to be expected.

It presents in clear and simple terms the basic principles of getting into, operating, and succeeding in small business. It contains specific, detailed financial and operating data for a wide variety of small business opportunities.

This book has been written by people who are actively involved in small businesses. They have faced all the problems you are likely to face as you enter this exciting world.

We hope that our experience and the solid, factual information contained in this volume will help you to make decisions that will lead to a better understanding of small business and help you achieve success in the business you choose.

This manual will teach you:

-        how to select the kind of business that's right for you
-        how to select the right business opportunity
-        how to conduct market research
-        how to find the best location for your business
-        how to hire, supervise and train people
-        where and how to get the money you need
-        how to advertise and merchandise properly
-        how to select, control and track your inventory procedures
-        what the basic management skills are and how to use them
-        how to calculate your actual cost per product
-        plus much more you probably already know but need to learn   better

Acknowledgments

In writing this book, there have been many sources that we have consulted. The list of sources would include parts of the Federal Government, the Small Business Administration and many individuals including:

Andrew Ralston, President
Andy's Playground Web Design and Development
e-mail Andrew@andysplayground.com
www.andysplayground.com

Thomas M. Fafinski   Specializing in Small Business
Benepartum Law Group P.A.   Legal Matters and Asset Protection
860 Blue Gentian Road, Suite 295   For Business Owners
Grand Oaks Business Park
Eagan, MN 55121
651-994-4300

In addition, my employees have been very open in sharing their opinions and thoughts when I needed them. I would also like to thank my husband and children for the patience and understanding in allowing me to follow my dream of owning a small business. I sincerely thank all these people.

Chapter 1

27 Days to Your Own Business

"No one lives long enough to learn everything they need to learn starting from scratch. To be successful, we absolutely, positively have to find people who have already paid the price to learn the things that we need to learn to achieve our goals." - Brian Tracey, Motivational Speaker

In this chapter you are going to learn about what other successful business owners do to jump start their businesses for immediate success. No point in trying to reinvent the wheel, let's just use the techniques that work for others.

Why I Added This Chapter

When people think about starting a business, rarely do they know what they need to do first, second and third. This chapter is for all the struggling entrepreneurs who really want to start a business, but don't know what to do first.

I have been where you are now: reading books about small business. Most of them are written by MBA graduates with more theory than actual down to earth tasks. This chapter has been written just for you.

When I talk to high schools about starting a small business, I tell them that it is a lot like bungee jumping. Some people think about climbing the ladder to get to the platform and never do it. These are the dreamers. They will always dream and never act. The next group is a form of the dreamer, the one that stands on the platform but never jumps. They are always checking the ropes, the height of the platform, their harness – research, research, research, but still never jump. You are never really in small business until you take a step off that platform and have a few minutes of a scary free fall until you believe with every bone in your body that everything will be fine and you can find any answer you need to be successful.

 Our minds control a lot of the success we have. "If you can believe, you can achieve."(Napoleon Hill) Believing is the first hard part.

The smart entrepreneur looks at every situation and tries to figure out how to make the most of it. How can you use your limited resources? My small business education has taken over 20 years and tens of thousands of dollars. I want to pass on the short cuts to small business success through this chapter. I truly believe that everyone should have a side business. A job working for someone else is too uncertain in these economic times.

My Assumptions About You

Before we get started, let's talk about you. I have made a few assumptions about you and your small business dreams.

1. I assume you have (or can find) some money to spend, whether it is your own or borrowed. You will need some money, although not much to start any business. If you can not find "some" money, go get a job, until you have some saved up.
2. You have an incredible "burning desire" to be successful in business. This will take shape in many different ways. Starting a business is not all fun and roses. There will be times that it looks like you should hang it up. That is why you need a deep desire to succeed. If you make a half-hearted effort, you will only get marginal results or no results at all.

After the First 27 Days

This is NOT a get rich quick scheme, it is the process any business owner should go through to start a business. After the first 27 days, you will need to continue to market your products and services and continue to grow your business until it fulfills your personal and lifestyle goals. As you continue to grow your business I know that once you taste success, you will want to devote as much time as necessary to its on-going success.

Day 1 - The Right Frame of Mind

Before you get started, let's schedule time out for the next week to work on your business. Take your TV time at night and devote it to your new business. What you miss in reality TV will not help you as much as an hour spent on a new business.

Let's get started. First you need the right frame of mind. Let's make sure you have "enough" reasons to start a business. Take out a notebook and write at the top of the page "Everything I Want". Then start to list everything that you want to own, everyplace you want to go, everything you want to do that money will allow you to have.

After the first list create a short list of "Why Am I Really Starting A Business".

Next think about what your life is like when you have achieved your business goals. What happens on a day-to-day basis? What do you feel like? How do others treat you differently? Remember those feelings and use them to your advantage. You will meet your goals. You can do it.

Day 2 – Find the Group

The first week is a lot of brainstorming and thinking instead of "doing". The first thing you are going to do is to brainstorm different markets or groups of people that you want to help. Let's take, for example, you think you could help the people in your neighborhood or at your church but maybe you don't know how. That's OK, we will talk more about an actual product on a later day.

We want to think of a group of people that will buy from us. They either know us or have something in common with us. There are also groups that "know" you by association. If you have trouble with this exercise, try

---

thinking of all the groups that you are a part of, like:

1. You have a group at work
2. You have a family and relatives group
3. You have a friends group
4. Maybe you are part of a bowling team or other sport team
5. You may have a church or religious group
6. Maybe a group of small business owners
7. Consider groups by town, state or country
8. Consider different cultural groups
9. Consider groups of income level
10. Same lifestyle groups like 2 kids both parents work, or over 65 years old
11. Consider school groups

Most successful business people would agree on the fact that if you had 2,000 buying customers, you should be able to earn $1 million per year. So it is very important to keep track of each and every customer you have.

Day 3 – Ask the Group

Once you found your group, go and ask them what is their biggest problem. Take out a sheet of paper and keep notes on their comments. This will help us to create a product or service that will fit the needs of your group.

To find your group, go to where they hang out. Read magazines that they read. Start to notice trends for your group.

Let's take an example: I have a community group. My community typically "hangs out" at home at night. So I go door-to-door for a little bit each night  and ask them about their biggest problem they see with your community. Do they want or need any services that are not currently available? If they compared your neighborhood to a perfect neighborhood, what would be different?

The answers that come back may surprise you. Some neighbors may want more communication with each other, some may see a need for a new dry cleaning shop or home delivery of evening meals.

I would keep the notes in my notebook to look at later when I am searching for product ideas. It is important in this step to realize that the most successful businesses will be the ones that address the needs of their customers. If you start with the customer's needs, you have a better chance at success.

One other example. If my group was African American women between the ages of 18-30 because those were my friends and family. In the 1970's I would have heard about the lack of makeup available for ethnic women. This may have been the start of a very lucrative cosmetic line targeted at this market. These women would have gladly paid for makeup made especially for them and their skin tones. The cosmetic industry has gotten better in more recent years, but I think they are still behind the times for Asian skin tones and colors.

Day 4 – Analyze the Answers
The next part of your journey will be analyze the answers that everyone gave us and to come up with some trends. First try to group the answers into common problems. When I did this with my customers, I could group the answers into the different parts of doing business, like marketing, money, operations. But there were other topics that kept coming around, like health insurance.

Make a short list of the most common issues that your research found.

Day 5 – Brainstorm Products or Services
Today is a day I always enjoy. Take the most popular item that was on the list yesterday. Relax and ask yourself silently, "How could I solve this problem for my group?" When you relax it allows your mind to use the power of the subconscious.

Let's work with a couple of examples. Maybe on your list was your church group that you are involved in. The most popular issue was fundraising. Everyone wanted to know how to raise more money for mission trips. It is important when you are doing these brainstorming exercises that you do not throw out any ideas no matter what they sound like when the come to you. So, if you relax and think about solution, you may come up with a list like:
1. Special event to church members
2. Special event for non-church members, but community members
3. Creating a marketing campaign to ask community leaders and corporations for donations or money or supplies

---

4. Creating a product the church could sell to other churches (maybe fundraising ideas)

Sometimes you will think of so many ideas it will amaze you. If you have trouble with this part, create a get together. One of the best ways people brainstorm is in groups. Have your most open-minded friends and family members over for dinner. Before they come to dinner tell them to think of different ideas for your group's most common issue. Be sure to pick only one issue. If you pick more then the conversation gets out of control.

Before dinner, start making a list of everyone's ideas. No idea will be thrown out at this time. You can always throw it out later. Then after dinner, continue with the exercise. This is a really fun way to create product ideas.

Day 6 – Analyze Your Product Ideas

Today is the day you let your mind think about all your ideas. You want to look for one that you can get behind 100%. You want to be passionate about the product/service idea. Which ones do you like more than the others? Start by ranking them in order from 1-10.
The top 5 ideas you will research further. Make your final list of the top 3 ideas.

One caution here: **DO NOT** toss out product ideas at this stage. Even if you feel you could never deliver the product or service that you are thinking about, keep it in your notebook. There are so many resources available that we can always find a way to bring the product to the group. The group and its needs are much more important than your ability to create the product.

Day 7 – Ask The Group Again

Today is the day that you go back to your group. you want to make sure if you are going to put time, energy and resources into a new business that someone will buy from us.

First you want to reconfirm that the issue you identified is really important to your group. Here is a series of questions you want to ask your group:

1) Is this an important issue to you that you will be willing to pay something for it to solve the problem?
2) How much would you be willing to pay?
3) Where would you expect to find this item?
4) Since you are not using it now, what are you doing to solve the issue?

Tally the results in your notebook and look for the most common answers. This exercise will help you to define pricing, true needs of the group and possible marketing strategies.

Day 8 – Back to Day 6 or Forward to Tomorrow
Review your notes from yesterday and see if you need to go back to Number 2 on your product idea list or head on to Tomorrow. If you need to go back, don't get frustrated. Making sure you are identifying the needs of your group will make you more successful sooner rather than later. Spending time on this area is important.

In addition, be sure that your product idea is one that you can be passionate about. That will help you through the tough areas that come with every business.

Day 9 – Product Specifics Brainstorming Day
Once you have a good product idea that has been confirmed from your group, it is time to figure out how to deliver the product or service. Again relax and think about all the different ways to deliver your product or service. You have two ways to do this:

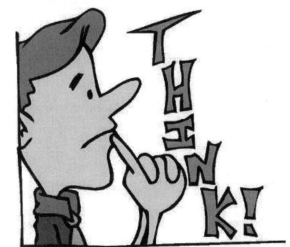

1) You create the product or service
   a. Pros of creating:
      i. You control the product
      ii. It's YOUR baby

   b. Cons of creating:
      i. Typically need more money to create product
      ii. Slower to market and positive cash flow
      iii. Need to create marketing materials and process

2) Someone else creates the product or service – You only USE their product or service
   a. Pros of Using:
      i. Faster to market and positive cash flow
      ii. Marketing materials may already be created
      iii. Need less cash and resources to start

   b. Cons of Using:
      i. You do not have control of product features, pricing etc
      ii. Success of your business relies on someone else

There is no right or wrong way of doing business. Both options are very successful business models when used in the right situation with the right partners. In addition, just because you start doing business one way in the beginning does not mean that you are permanently stuck in that way of doing business.

If you have limited resources, I would suggest USING someone else's product or services until you have enough resources to do it on your own. Let's go through some examples:

Let's say, my group talked about the need for a dry cleaner in the community. Starting a dry cleaning business is very expensive. You have the costs of the building, the equipment, employees and much, much more. But, you could always provide a delivery service for your community to a dry cleaner in the next town. You could pick up and drop off. When you have enough money you could always build a dry cleaner in your town.

 In the makeup example from before, you could find a current cosmetic manufacturer that is producing this type of product. Maybe it is overseas in Asia. You could then agree to sell their products in the United States. You would buy the products at a discount and then mark them up when selling to your customers. Depending on your resources, you could sell them door to door or to larger accounts like major department stores. Either way would be USING someone else's product.

In creating your own product, you would need to do more research on the exact costs it will take you to start that type of business. Before you invest thousands of dollars, it may be beneficial to do some more market research with your group before you commit dollars.

Day 10 – Research Day

If you are Creating a product, start researching everything you need for your product or service. Start creating a business plan for your business to make sure you address all the important issues.

If you are Using a product, this is a day to research different vendors that you could use. In your previous examples, you would want to look for dry cleaners. Who has a good reputation? Who does the best work? Who may help you promote your business? Remember in a Using relationship, both parties win. You win by making money selling their products and the vendor wins because they sell more without having the headaches of employees.

If you are looking at the cosmetic example, you will want to head down to your local library and start searching on the Internet for possible vendors. Once you find them, you need to contact them about selling their products. If you contact a company and said, "I want to help you sell more product", it would be a very foolish company to turn you away. But sometimes businesses are not very smart in marketing and sales. Don't be surprised if you get turned down, just move on to the next possible vendor. Someone will be smart about your offer.

Day 11 – The Name Is The Game

Today you will focus on naming your business. Names come in all different shapes and forms. Some companies use the owner's name (Levi Strauss) some have made up words (Microsoft), while others use a word to mean something else (Apple). Whatever you chose, think about the following considerations:

1. Easy to say
2. Tells something about you and your product
3. Can you get the www (Internet) address
4. Should convey reliability, creativity, or your image

Brainstorm as many ideas as you can. Try for 20 minutes to list all your ideas. If you get writer's block, just keep writing anything such as: blah, blah, blah until your thoughts start again. It is important to keep your pen moving. That will help your mind to keep moving.

Day 12 – Filing Your Name and Business

The next thing you need to do is file your business with the state and federal agencies. First you need to decide what form of business yours will be: sole proprietorship, partnership, LLC or corporation. Consult the LEGAL Chapter for more information in deciding.

Typically you will then need to contact your Secretary of State office for an "Assumed Name" form. This form will need to be filled out and the fee paid (around $40, unless incorporating) before your state will let you do business.

The Secretary of State will send you a confirmation form in the mail.

Next is Tax ID numbers and sales tax numbers. Ask the Secretary of State office which numbers you will need for your business. You can file you Federal Tax ID by phone, mail or Internet.

Day 13 – Office Set Up

Even if you do not have a formal office for your business, you need to set some space aside for your business. This may be a drawer in a desk or even a dresser. Keep a couple of folders in there to keep your information together. Start with simple folders labeled: Sales - Done, Receipts, Orders to be Filled and any other that would be helpful.

Day 14 – Your Personal List
Today is the day you start your marketing efforts. Take out a blank sheet of paper and start making a list of everyone you know.

Use the following categories:

- Family
- Friends
- Neighbors
- People I Worked With
- People That Worked for Me
- Vendors I Know
- Old Friends from School
- Groups that I am In (sports, church, etc.)
- And any others that you can think of.

Be sure to keep the following information on people you know:
- Name
- Company they work for
- Address, City, State, Zip
- Phone Number
- Fax Number (for business to business sales)
- Email (if they have one)

The majority of these people want to support you in your new venture. It will be important to tell them what you are doing at a later time.

Concentrate today on making the list of everyone you know.

Day 15 – Your Group List
Today you will add to your list. Now it is time to list everyone that you think would be interested in your product or service that is not on your previous list.

In the previous examples, the delivery for dry cleaning would consist of a geographic area. How could you get the names and addresses of each person? For business to business products, you could use the yellow pages. Time to take another trip to the library. Ask your librarian to help you find the information you need for your group. They have some wonderful resources and would be glad to help.

At the end of Day 14 and Day 15, you should have a large list of prospective clients. The larger the list the better as long as the list includes people that will typically buy from you.

Day 16 – Estimate Start Up Costs

Make a list of all the items you need to start your business. These are probably one-time expenses only at start-up. Be sure to include computer, new phone installation, Internet costs (if you use it), office supplies, or other equipment (car?) etc.

Have it listed on a piece of paper as follows:

Start-Up Costs
Car (use my own)	$0
Computer	$500
New Phone	$35

If you have a few minutes and are really tight on cash, brainstorm how you could get each item without paying for it. For example, most libraries have computers that you could use for a short while if you needed it. Maybe you know someone that owns a business that would be willing to let you use their office computer at night when they aren't using it. The smart entrepreneur is going to find ways to meet their goals, even if they have to do business a "different" way in the beginning from everyone else. Really think about who has the resources you need and how could you "borrow" them.

Day 17 – Cost Of Doing Business

Now it is time to start doing some projections for your business. In all of your responses to group questions from Day 3 and Day 7, try to determine how much of your product you can sell. One way to do that is take how much people thought they would buy and cut it in half. Some people will tell you they will buy, but then never do.

Estimate how much it will take you to either produce that product or buy that product from your vendor. You should have something like this:

Sales	$500
Expenses	
Cost of product (50%)	$250

Next determine what other monthly expenses you will incur including: phone, fax, Internet access (AOL), supplies, gas etc.

Be sure to add in a dollar amount for marketing. This number is typically 3-5% of your sales. In the above example, the amount for marketing would be $15- 25. It will be important that you spend that each month on marketing, because you can never stop marketing. Even if you have too much business you should raise your prices instead of stopping your marketing.

This list becomes your first projection for your business. It tells you what you think you will make. It also gives you a benchmark to achieve on an ongoing basis.

Day 18 - Setting Your Price

Pricing can be tricky. You have a choice at this point that you need to decide before pricing your product or service. Do you want to be the highest price option or the lowest priced option? Some considerations in thinking about this choice would be your service level, additional things you can offer that the competition does not, and where you feel comfortable. Most entrepreneurs and typically women entrepreneurs tend to price their products too low. It is important to understand your costs of doing business. Luckily you calculated that above. You need to make sure that you cover all the expenses of the business in your pricing.

Brainstorm some prices and see how the work with your projections.

Day 19 – Unique Selling Proposition (USP)

Today you will focus on your USP. A USP is a statement about you that tells a customer why they should buy from you rather than any other option available to them. Domino's Pizza had great success with their USP: "Hot Pizza in 30 minutes or less, guaranteed." Before Domino's, pizza delivery was slow that many people received cold pizza for dinner. What is your unique selling proposition? What makes you different for every other option available? Why should a customer do business with you? This will help us to develop your first marketing message.

Brainstorm many ideas and then decide which one fits your business the best. Focus on the biggest benefit that you bring to your customers.

Day 20 – Marketing – The Offer

Today is the day you start your marketing process. Even if you only have $5, you can market you business, but first you need an offer. What are you going to offer your first customers? Will it be a discount, free delivery with a paid month, or free samples? There are lots of things you can offer them. When you determine your basic offer, try to add items that are inexpensive for you to add it, but valuable to the customer. For instance in the dry cleaning example, you could add in a coupon for a discounted car wash from the local car wash. Or how about a restaurant coupon or a small gift.

In our business, at the American Institute of Small Business, we give our clients small gifts like chocolate, cookies or other small goodies. Food items are very well received. There are really endless possibilities where you could offer value, where it does not cost you much.

Day 21 – Marketing – The Sales Medium

Now that you have a good, solid, valuable offer, let's chose a sales medium. A sales medium could be anything that gets your message to your customer. Some examples would be flyers, postcards, newspaper advertising, yellow page ads, Internet ads, billboards, telemarketing, or faxing. There are almost too many sales mediums to list. What is easy for you to get in front of your customer? If you had the dry cleaner delivery or a landscaping business, flyers may be the best way to get in front of clients.

The cosmetic business may be best by door-to-door sales. Pick a sales medium to try. Remember to chose one that will be easy an inexpensive to get your message in front of your customers.

Day 22 – Marketing – Writing Your First Sales Letter

Today is creation day. Start with a blank piece of paper and start jotting out your marketing piece. Start with your offer. Place it on the page to get the most visibility. Then create a headline for your piece. Think of a compelling reason that your customer should continue to read your marketing piece. This is the same for almost any marketing piece you create.

Finally, create an action step. Tell your customer exactly what you want them to do: Call you, mail you, email etc.

To get your customers to act more quickly, put in a deadline, a time when the offer will no longer be available. Or you can make the offer only available to the first 25 clients that call. You can choose any number, but I used 25 as an example.

Review what you have created. Change items as necessary to help it read better or easier.

Don't forget to include information on how your clients can contact you. It is very important. I have seen some messages that never had contact information. So even if I was interested in the offer, I couldn't take advantage of it anyway because I won't search them out.

Day 23 – Marketing Piece #2

Since you have gotten so good at writing marketing pieces, you should write the second one. This will help to solidify in your mind that marketing is a process, not just a one-shot deal. After you have used a marketing piece you must create another one.

Day 24 – Delivery of Marketing Piece

Send out/deliver your marketing piece to your prospective customers. The next step will separate you from almost all other struggling entrepreneurs. You need to track your responses. To do this, make a chart in your notebook that looks like this:

Description of Piece	How many pieces sent?	How many responded?	How much did it cost me?	How much did I make in sales from piece?

Why do you want to do this? Many small business owners have no idea if their marketing efforts are paying for themselves. I see so many expensive yellow pages ads that never pay for themselves. If they do, the entrepreneur does not know that they do and then cancels the ad because it is so expensive. You need to track your marketing pieces and their effectiveness.

Also make a list of things you would do differently in the next marketing piece. We have learned by trial and error some very valuable mistakes. The first mailing we did was too wide for standard postage. The main post office called us to come re-stamp about 200 letters. What a waste of time and money.

Day 25 – Update Marketing Piece #2

With everything you have learned from the first piece, make changes to your second piece and schedule a time to mail it.

A good second piece may have some information teasing the customer with quotes like:
> "Did you lose my original offer?"
> "Did you need it to potty train your puppy?"
> "Did you forget?"

Sometimes people do forget and the reminder is just what they were looking for.

The second piece should go out within 15 days of the first. You can do a third mailing with a "Last Chance" type of offer. This is very effective.

Day 26 – Growing Customer Lists

One of the most valuable assets of your new company is your customer list. This is another aspect that separates successful business owners with the ones that are struggling. Always and I mean always look for new prospects and add them to your list. It may sound goofy, but talk to as many people as possible, at the grocery store, in line at a restaurant. Tell them what you are doing.

Day 27 - CELEBRATE

By this time, you should have some customer calling you for your product or services. Take some time to recap all of the things you have accomplished over the past 27 Days. You will be successful if you follow this process.

Beyond Day 27

As you continue with your marketing efforts you can purchase business cards to give to people when you meet them. There are thousands of ways to market your new company, but the most important thing is to prioritize the methods that will make you money quickly.

GOOD LUCK!

Tell us about your progress
info@aisb.biz

Chapter 2

Getting Off To A Good Start

Build a bridge, and then take it

This chapter is about getting you off on the right foot. It's about decisions that have been made up front **before** you actually get into the thick of running your business.

In this chapter you will learn:

1. *Characteristics that make up the successful entrepreneur.*
2. *How to measure your own success potential.*
3. *How to arm yourself with the tools of success.*
4. *How to select the business that's right for you.*
5. *How and where to get the help you need to start and operate your own business.*

You may have already selected the kind of business you want to go into. **We urge you to read this chapter anyway.** If you have gone through the selection process properly, this chapter will confirm in your mind that you're off to a good start. Knowing you're off to a good start, that you've done things right, will boost your confidence and help you succeed.

If you have not selected your business opportunity yet, this chapter will show you how to examine your thinking and weigh the many alternatives available to you. Better to pause now than plunge ahead in the wrong direction.

This chapter is probably the most important one in the manual, because it is concerned with getting you started in the right direction. Take your time.

Do all the exercises and quizzes. This is one of your first giant steps on the road to success.

Fasten your seatbelts and hang on, because you're about to start on one of the most exciting journeys available in life. Your destination is a business of your own.

There is a special brand of opportunist known as the Entrepreneur or, the

Small Businessperson. A dictionary definition of an entrepreneur is "one who manages, organizes and assumes the risk of a business or enterprise." The entrepreneur represents freedom: freedom from the boss, freedom from the time clock and - with a lot of hard work and more than a little luck - freedom from the bank.

Now, if America is the land of the free and the home of the brave, too few of us are brave enough to venture out on the road to freedom. But, those of us who have ventured, very few of us would choose to go back.

The road to success in small business ownership is full of potholes, bumps, and pitfalls. But if you have the motivation and the will to succeed, you're off to a good start. This manual, written by fellow entrepreneurs **who have achieved success**, will give you the information you need to plot your own course for success. You'll understand how and why things happen ... and how to apply that knowledge to ANY business you choose.

PREPARING FOR THE JOURNEY

Most people spend more time planning a vacation than they do planning their lives. Many float aimlessly through life, taking its ups and downs as they come, getting by, living from day to day. If they become even moderately successful, or even comfortable, it's more by accident than by plan.

Achieving success in small business, however, is not a matter left to luck or chance. You may know of successful entrepreneurs who were "lucky" or "in the right place at the right time" -- but it's not something you can count on, nor will luck or good timing carry you through years of operating a business successfully.

You wouldn't think of starting out on a vacation trip without knowing where you're going, how you're going to get there, and having adequate money and provisions to see you through to your destination. In other words, you must **plan and prepare** for your journey.

That's what this chapter is all about. You select your destination; but we help you make the choices. You plot your own course, but we show you how to avoid the dead ends, the rough roads, and obstacles in your way. In short, we show you how to get there successfully.

PROFILE OF AN ENTREPRENEUR

American entrepreneurs number in the millions. Of the approximately 20,000,000 small businesses in this country, more than 12,000,000 are operated as sole proprietorships - in other words, "entrepreneurs in the business for themselves."

So, who are these people we call entrepreneurs? While there are no absolutes, there are some general observations you can make about entrepreneurs:

1. **We love to make money.** With some, it's the things that money can buy. With others, money is just a way of measuring success.

2. **We have bigger dreams than other people.** We challenge ourselves to do more because we want more. More of the money, freedom and status that accompany entrepreneurship.

3. **We are very success oriented.** We have a need ... sometimes a burning desire ... to succeed. We need to prove ourselves to everyone who knows us, to our families, and to our toughest critics ... ourselves.

4. **We work harder than most people.** Some of us even think working eighteen hours a day is fun. We don't mind putting in extra effort when we get to reap the rewards. What we don't like is working hard so someone else can reap the rewards. Maybe that's why - as a group - we don't like working for other people.

5. **We are better at something than most people.** Some of us have great artistic talent; some are brilliant marketeers. Many of us have a natural gift for organizing; most are born leaders. We all have something extra that helps us succeed. And we're smart enough to make the most of it.

6. **We look at risks differently than most folks.** We understand the basic risk and reward ratio of life: the greater the risks, the greater the rewards. In other words, no guts, no glory. We can't win if we're not in the game. But, it's not just rolling the dice. Our risks are almost always carefully calculated, and supported by confidence and belief in ourselves. We reduce the risk by knowing what we're doing.

7. **We are proud.** Proud of our abilities and our achievements. Our success proves to us that we are not average or mediocre. Success

gives us great satisfaction - and pride!

8. **We respond to challenges in a positive way and learn from our mistakes.** We never give up! Challenges are exciting and we feel the need to conquer them.

9. **High Level of Integrity**. Entrepreneurs know that every person holds a success key for the future. Treating people like they were your biggest client can dramatically influence your business. The billionaire Oprah Winfrey says it best, "Real integrity is doing the right thing, knowing that nobody's going to know whether you did it or not."

Joseph Mancuso, President of The Center for Entrepreneurial Management, in a recent survey, came up with the following additional common traits and profiles or successful entrepreneurs:

1. **One or both parents were self-employed.** The child who grows up in a home where at least one parent is self-employed is more likely to try his hand at his own business than children of salaried parents.

2. **They have been fired one or more times.** The entrepreneur's brashness and almost compulsive need to be right often leads to dismissal, usually by a superior who wants less conflict and/or less competition. But, this need to be right often turns rejection into courage and courage into authority.

3. **They were in business at a young age.** Mowing lawns, shoveling snow, or peddling papers - the enterprising adult first appears as the enterprising child.

4. **They are in their 30s.** The age range is down from the late 1950's and early 1960's, when it was found to be between 40 and 45. The younger generation seems to be doing almost everything sooner.

5. **They are usually the oldest children in a family.** Perhaps it has something to do with being a leader rather than a follower.

6. **The majority are married.** A spouse can be an asset by providing support, encouragement, love and a possible second income. Also, bankers and venture capitalists look more favorably on entrepreneurs who are married because they regard it as a sign of stability and commitment. Fair or not, that's the way it is.

7. **Most have a bachelor's degree,** and the trend seems headed toward the M.B.A. Few entrepreneurs have the time or the patience to earn a doctorate.

8. **They are very sociable people,** and more often than not, charming as well. Which better equips them to charm the right banker or supplier and get what they want.

9. **They are super-organized.** Organizational methods and systems may differ, but you'll never find a successful entrepreneur without one.

10. **They are highly competitive.** Entrepreneurs tend to be participants, not observers; players, not fans. They like challenge, and they like to win. The greater the challenge, the more glorious the victory.

HOW DO YOU MEASURE UP?

After reading the profiles of entrepreneurs described above, how do you stack up against them? If you can say "Yes, that's me", then you're feeling pretty good right now. But, if your profile is vastly different from the people we've described - don't let it get you down. There is no absolute profile of the successful business owner, it only means that you may have to balance it with other strengths, or that you may need the help of others who have certain talents that you lack.

Many high achievers become entrepreneurs, but it is not a requirement by any means. Most people have a good amount of hidden entrepreneurial instincts in them - and most people want to make a lot of money, too. What you do with what you have will make the difference.

Take the following Entrepreneur's Test:

	ALWAYS	SOMETIMES	NEVER
I am persistent.			
When I like a project I am working on, I tend to			
I have clear, written goals.			
When I make a mistake, I can learn from it.			
I achieve my goals when I create them.			
I want to succeed above everything else.			
I am creative and have new ideas.			
I can find a path to solve a problem.			
I am interested in how things work.			
I am insightful.			
I can always find a solution to a problem.			
I see problems as opportunities & challenges.			
I take risks.			
I don't need all the answers before I start. I will			
I like learning about things I don't know about.			
I can continue after setbacks.			
I believe in myself and my abilities.			
I'm a positive person.			
I experiment until I find a solution.			
I'm willing to endure hardships for possible long			
I usually do things my own way.			
I tend to question authority.			
I often enjoy working by myself.			
I like to control things around me.			
I can be stubborn.			
Totals			
	X 3	X 2	X 1
Total Score			

Multiply the number of times you chose column one, by 3 to get your first column total. Then do the same for column 2 and 3. Then add your three columns together to get your final score. If you scored between:

60-75   You should start your business. You have the traits of a successful small business owner.

48-59   You have the potential, but you need to keep yourself focused and on task. You may want to take some classes to improve your skills in your weaker areas or look to hire someone with these skills.

37-47   You may not want to start a business by yourself. Look for someone who has skills that would complement your knowledge.

Below 37   Small business is very challenging and may not be for you at this time. Work toward getting some experience that your don't currently have and learning more about how small businesses succeed.

MOTIVATION - THE FUEL THAT KEEPS YOU GOING

You may have just recently **discovered** that you have the clear-cut desires and ambitions to succeed as an independent business owner. But, the personality trait or inspiration may well have begun when you were a child. That doesn't necessarily mean that you've wasted all the years in between. Everything seems to happen for a reason, and chances are you'll find a way to apply all the experiences and lessons of the past years.

What's important now is to recognize that, today, you **have** the motivation to start your own business and to succeed. Hang on to that determination that you're feeling now and use it to keep you going through the anxieties and tough times that may come your way. If you have a **good** reason for wanting the life of the entrepreneur today, it will be a good reason tomorrow, next week, next year, five years from now. It may be a time-worn cliché, but **the power of positive thinking really works!**

WHY PEOPLE GO INTO BUSINESS

You may have decided to start your own business after an external event triggered your entrepreneurial abilities. The event may have been a

> An entrepreneur is the kind of person who will work 16 hours a day just to avoid having to work 8 hours a day for someone else.
>   -Anonymous

very positive occurrence, such as inheriting a family business from an uncle. Or, it could be a traumatic event, such as being fired or laid-off. In either case, you should look upon what has happened as an opportunity. Seize it, and make the most of it. This may well be the most significant time in your life.

There are many reasons why people go into business for themselves. But, they usually fall into one of two categories: concrete **practical** or abstract **personal**.

Some of the **concrete, practical** reasons include:
1.   To make a living and/or get rich.

2.   To prepare for retirement. That is "something to do" in retirement, or to provide additional income, or both.

3.   For supplemental income and equity building, such as in real estate.

4.   To use as a tax shelter or business write-off.

5.   To have something to occupy spare time. To relieve boredom.

6.   To create a common cause for the whole family, thereby building togetherness.

Some of the **abstract, personal** reasons include:

1.   For emotional rewards; a realization of self worth self-image, seeing your creativity develop and expand.

2.   To escape working for someone else.

3.   To have flexible working hours - the freedom to do what you please, when you please.

4.   To stop having to take orders.

It's important that you go into business with your eyes open and not kid yourself.   Emotional rewards are certainly worthwhile motives, but you should understand that they sometimes are a long time in coming.   The emotional rewards are worth working towards, but don't expect them right away.

Working for yourself, instead of someone else, may be a welcome change for you. But be prepared to probably work a lot harder and work longer hours. In some businesses, it means doing what your employees don't get done, which often means working on nights and weekends.

Your working hours will certainly be more flexible, but don't count on taking a day off or flying off for a month's vacation any time you please, especially the first year or two. It's not unusual for new business owners to work 70-80 hour weeks, see their golf clubs collect dust in a corner, and postpone their vacation indefinitely.

If you never want to take orders again, then you'll need a business that doesn't involve serving customers. Because customers tell you what they want, and if they don't get it they don't do business with you. So be prepared to jump through hoops just to keep your customers happy so you can stay in business.

EXAMINE YOUR OWN MOTIVES

It's important that you examine your own motives for going into business. Identify them. Make your desires part of your goal plan. But be sure they're realistic. You want to avoid setting yourself up for a letdown early in the game. If you expect too much or expect something not easily attainable, you only run the risk of early discouragement.

Going into business is a lot like going into marriage. If you do it for the wrong reason, or with unreal expectations, you increase the chances that it won't survive. Marrying because of superficial physical attraction, or because it's "convenient," or because one person has a lot of money, practically guarantees failure.

Like marriage, a business needs a firm foundation, realistic expectations, and a total commitment in order to succeed.

WHY DO BUSINESSES FAIL?

Businesses, like marriages, fail for many different reasons. But generally, most of them are related to going into business **unprepared**. Or, put another way, usually a case of **not enough of something.** Not enough money, not enough skill, not enough experience or just plain not enough planning before starting. Many business owners underestimate the difficulty of starting a business. But with patience and hard work and the right planning, most anyone can start a business.

A recent survey of why businesses fail lists the following reasons:

- Lack of experience
- They start with too little money.
- Their industry or market is dying.
- They don't understand their customers' needs.
- They don't know their product.
- They merchandise poorly.
- They merchandise the wrong products.
- They're poorly managed (accounting and personnel are the most common trouble areas).
- Their inventory is out-of-date.
- They don't know their true costs of selling a particular product.

-      Their businesses grew too fast to control.
-      Poor locations.

You have already taken perhaps one of the smartest steps to avoid all the problems people will warn you about: you have recognized the need for this manual, to teach you what you need to know. Together, we will build a well-thought out, carefully constructed plan for your business.

Businesses do fail, but there is no reason why you should fail if you know what you're doing.   Success will come through knowledge, proper preparation, and perseverance.

If you want to see a future successful entrepreneur, look at yourself in the mirror.   Know thyself and be honest about your true needs and desires. Unless you genuinely feel a deep motivation to go into business for yourself, you are better off doing something else. But if you want the life of the successful business owner, we'll help you prepare so that you will not fail.

WHAT MAKES A SUCCESSFUL ENTREPRENEUR?

One of the "formulas for success" is the 5 D's that makes an entrepreneur successful.

The Five D's are:

- Desire
- Diligence
- Details
- Discipline
- Determination

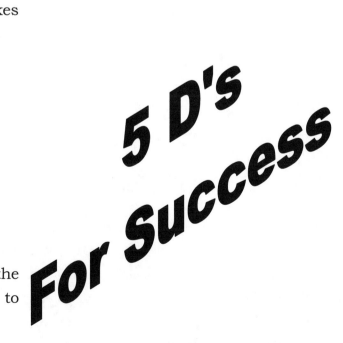

Without these five qualities, the entrepreneur is not going to reach his full potential.

Desire is the carrot out in front of you. Desire is the vision that burns in the heart of the entrepreneur. If your desire is strong enough, it will point you toward success and provide the fuel to get you there. Desire is the vision that you see in your mind about what life is like when you have achieved your small business dream.

Diligence is making the most of your opportunities and options. It's developing your strengths and overcoming any lack of skill, education, space, or money. You learn what you need to learn, do what you have to do, to get the job done. This takes diligence.

Details, especially focusing on details, is a special skill of most entrepreneurs, who are usually excellent organizers. Some can do it with a simple "To Do" list on their desk. Others employ a battery of computers and electronic or paper organizers. Organizational systems may differ, but you'll never find a truly successful entrepreneur without one.

Discipline is the sister of detail because it's hard to have one without the other. One of the nation's most successful salesmen attributed his success to doing the things that other salesmen don't want to do in other words, doing things that are difficult, or uncomfortable, or that require some sacrifice. Your success will require that you discipline yourself to do the tasks you'll be tempted to put off or avoid altogether.

Determination is closely related to Desire and Diligence. But it's more than the two combined. Determination is what keeps you going when the going gets tough. Determination is a measure of your character. It's seeing your dreams through to completion and not letting others get you down.

The entrepreneur-in-motion is a joy to watch. He exploits the products and services he offers. He is unrelenting in his attack. He goes after the exposure he needs. He builds bridges between clients, suppliers, business contacts and other entrepreneurs.

The entrepreneur also trains himself for success by getting into everyday success-oriented habits:

1. Get to bed early, get to work early, and keep yourself physically fit and mentally alert. Ben Franklin was right!

2. Manage your personal finances properly. Keep accurate checking and savings account balances.

3. Dress to do business. Keep a neat appearance; you never know when you're going to meet a customer.

4. Keep your appointments and always be on time.

5. Call everyone you say you are going to call; keep all other promises, too.

6. Strive to be happy in your work and friendly, fair and honest in your personal and business dealings. Running your own business is a highly personal matter, and people will judge your business by how you conduct yourself.

7. Learn to love your hard work and achieve your goals.

8. Set goals and create a plan to achieve them.

You learn these habits through practice; you go over them in your mind and imagine yourself becoming better and better. Whatever you do, work them into your system in such a way that they become second nature to you.

Making money is only part of the success formula. Feeling good about your business is part of it, too. At the beginning, that may be all you have. In the end, it is not enough to sustain you and your family, but if you believe you will succeed, you stand a good chance of making it happen.

Drawbacks of Small Business Ownership

Along with the opportunity to gain control of your destiny, to make a difference in a cause that is important, to reach your full potential, to reap unlimited profits, to contribute to society and be recognized for your efforts, and to do what you enjoy, there are some disadvantages of small business ownership. These include:

1. **Unknown Income** – Owning a small business is no guarantee that you will earn millions of dollars in the next year. To reach your financial goals, careful planning is necessary.
2. **Risk of Losing Your Own Money** - Almost every financing source will require you to put money in for initial costs. Your initial money shows them that you are serious enough to invest in yourself and that you have something to lose if the business is not run well.
3. **Long Hours and Hard Work** – Most small business owners will agree that they put in more time than they ever did working for someone else. The work is also more difficult with many more decisions to be made. You may even have to clean the bathrooms.
4. **Changed Life** – Because ownership takes longer hours and more work, many of the typical duties with being a mother, father, wife or husband get put on the "back burner" until the business gets started.
5. **Higher Levels of Stress** – The higher stress level comes from

longer hours, harder work and your new work lifestyle. These can all take a toll on your mental attitude and your physical well-being.

6. **Complete Responsibility** – This is also an advantage. But with complete responsibility comes more pressure to make decisions faster and with less information.

WHICH PATH SHOULD YOU TAKE?

Making the all-important decision to go into business for yourself is only the beginning. Whether running a small operation in your own home or managing a giant corporation being in business involves constant decision-making. Right off the bat, there are decisions you must make just in getting started. And there are many paths. Getting you on the right path is what the rest of the chapter is all about.

WHAT BUSINESS IS RIGHT FOR YOU?

Selecting a business that's right for you really involves two questions:

1.   What **kind** of business to choose?

2.   What **business** opportunity to choose?

At first glance, these two questions may appear very similar. But they are quite different.

What kind of business means: What is the **nature** of your business? What goods or services will you offer? Where and how will your business operate? Small businesses typically fall into one of three types: personal services, retail merchandising, and light manufacturing. And no two businesses are the same; each has its own requirements for capital investment.

31

What business opportunity is concerned with **how** you are going to get into your particular business? Will you start from scratch? Or will you buy an existing business or franchise?   Where and how will you get the money?

These are questions you don't answer by flipping a coin, or drawing them out of a hat. This chapter will show you how to arrive at the right answers, how to choose the right business, and the right opportunity. You'll see how to arrive at sound decisions logically and systematically, using a proven method of gathering and analyzing data. The techniques you'll learn will help you to continue making sound decisions in your business during the months and years ahead.

CHOOSING THE RIGHT BUSINESS

Choosing a business is one of the most important decisions of your life, yet many people do it by chance or coincidence. Some get lucky and succeed. Some even get rich. Those are the stories you hear about.

But for every lucky break success story, there are hundreds of disillusioned people who've gone broke, or sold out, or are still struggling just to make ends meet. Too often, these are people who started the wrong business, in the wrong neighborhood, at the wrong time, in the wrong way.

Too often, the eager entrepreneur chooses a particular kind of business that's right for someone else, but totally wrong for them.

For example, you may have a friend or relative who's making a bundle as an independent sales rep, and so you're tempted to give that a try. But unless you really enjoy meeting people, and enjoy selling, and don't mind traveling, your career as a sales rep would likely fail or be an unhappy struggle at best.

There are four types of commonly accepted businesses including:

1. Retail or Product companies
2. Service companies
3. Combination of retail and service companies
4. Manufacturing companies

Retail companies sell physical products to end-users like consumers or business for their own use. Product companies can either be a retail or wholesale establishment. Examples of retail businesses include stores such as clothing, giftware, hardware, sporting goods, drug stores, or grocery stores. Wholesale establishments such as plumbing supply, electrical supply, or medical equipment.

Service companies are the second type of business. For example, restaurants, dry cleaners, insurance agents, automotive repair, consulting companies and tree trimming firms. These companies offer a service rather than the sale of a specific product or group of products.

Combination companies offer products and service to end users. Examples include landscape and garden centers, computer sales and service, gasoline service stations, import and export companies, and swimming pool companies.

Manufacturing companies includes any type of company that builds a finished product that is ready for sale, or takes a product, adds value to it for resale to another company that may possibly use it in their making of a finished or semi-finished product. Examples of products made by such companies include computer casings, electric motors, plastic components, and construction materials.

One day we were having lunch with a friend, Jane, and it was obvious she was wrestling with some problem. When we asked what the trouble was, Jane replied: "Oh, I've just had it up to here with working for somebody else.

I'm tired of company politics, and being controlled and exploited by my boss, and waiting for an annual raise. I've got to get out on my own, start my own business, be my own boss."

When we asked Jane what type of business she was considering, she answered: "Well, I really haven't made up my mind yet. Maybe a pizza place ... or a McDonalds ... or maybe manufacturing of some kind, if I can raise the money. What do you think?"

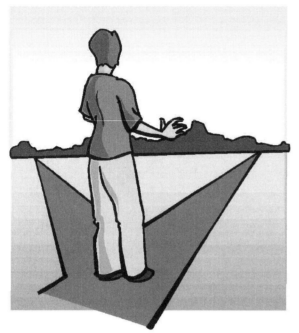

We could have pointed out that Jane knows nothing about the food business or about manufacturing. But, instead, we thought of a business more suited to his background and interest. You see, Jane is an avid sports "nut." She was an all-around athlete in school and is still active in many sports. For three or four years she's been a volunteer coach in Little League Baseball and PeeWee Football. "How about a sporting goods store?" we suggested. Jane admitted she hadn't considered that idea, but said it sounded interesting. In a few minutes we had a list of about ten more types of businesses that might be right for Jane. We arrived at our list of possible businesses by discussing Jane's interests, her background and experience, and her skills. We also discussed her personal goals and the kind of life style she envisioned for herself. And whenever we came up with an idea that Jane shrugged off with obvious lack of interest, we immediately discarded it. Our "top ten" were all ideas that Jane could consider with **enthusiasm**.

It's extremely important to select a business that satisfies your personal goals, that suits your life style, and that involves the kind of work you like to do and are good at doing. If you enjoy and find fulfillment in your work, you are much more likely to do an outstanding job. And if you do an outstanding job, you are much more likely to succeed.

Up to now this chapter has dealt mainly with personal qualities and traits, motives, success formulas, and good habits. Consciously or unconsciously, you've been "taking inventory" of your own personal qualities, motives, and mental attitude. You've been sizing yourself up as to whether or not you have what it takes to go into business. We'll assume the answer is definitely **"yes."**

Now we want you to get down to the nitty gritty about "who you are" in a different kind of self inventory. We're going to select the business **that's right for you** based upon who you are and what you are. Our objective is to come up with businesses you're likely to succeed at, and rule out those in which you'd be more likely to fail.

Using the questionnaire below, prepare your own "resume" of experience, hobbies, interests and acquired skills. In a way, you're "hiring yourself" for a career job. So take care that you don't lie to yourself or exaggerate the truth. Be honest and objective.

> - What skills do you have?
> - What knowledge do I have in finance, accounting, marketing, sales, and management?
> - What experience have you acquired that could be applied to your own business?
> - What are your three most satisfying accomplishments?
> - What are your hobbies and interests?
> - What knowledge expertise have you acquired from schools, seminars, and special training?
> - What do I like to do with my time?
> - What do others say I am good at?
> - Do I have hobbies or interests that are marketable?
> - Will I have the support of my family?
> - How much time do I have to run a business?

Armed with the information from your resume and the above questionnaire, you now have a good picture of your strengths, your skills, and your acquired knowledge. It should be fairly evident what you can bring to your new business and where your interests lie. Keep this inventory handy, for it will be an important tool in selecting your business. For areas that you do not feel comfortable, find someone who can teach you about those areas.

WHAT DO YOU WANT FROM THE BUSINESS?

It's important to know what you can give to the business. It's equally important to know what you expect the business to give you. You may be thinking, "That's easy". I want independence, wealth, and status. But which of the three is most important to you?   How important is personal satisfaction? How about creative expression? And how about the impact your business may have on your family? These considerations, and more, are all important when selecting a business that's right for you.

You'll want to look at both business goals and personal goals. You may find a business goal contradicts a personal goal, and you'll have to make a choice between them, or at least modify one or both.   For example, you may list "spend more time with my family" as a personal goal and "build a national franchise operation" as a business goal. Chances are, your business goal of developing your operation nationwide will involve considerable travel and working longer hours. Thus, you would likely be spending less time at home, not more. So you may decide, instead, to develop a local business close to home and perhaps even choose one that gets the family involved in its operations.

WHAT ARE THE BUSINESS POSSIBILITIES?

Now it's time to go shopping. First, we need a shopping list. What are the **kinds** of businesses you might consider? Now, we don't want you to start **evaluating** the possibilities yet, except in a very general way. What we want you to do is come up with a **long** list of businesses you could possibly consider, eliminating only those that are obviously not for you. In other words, rule out the ones that: (a) demand obvious talents or qualifications you don't have; or, (b) ones you would definitely **not** enjoy being associated with.

Where do you look for types of possible business candidates? Here are some of the places you might look:

1. Your telephone yellow pages.

2. Your own neighborhood business community or shopping center.

3. Your SBA business library.

4. Your public library. Consult Thomas Register, and other business directories. Also, a directory of FRANCHISES is available and may give you some ideas. But remember, you're just looking for **kinds** of businesses at this point, not specific business opportunities.

5. Entrepreneurial magazines, such as "Income Opportunities," "Entrepreneur," "Inc.," "Fortune," "Small Business Opportunities," "Success," "Money" and   similar publications. Some of the magazines are only available on the Internet.

6. Networking with friends, associates, neighbors, relatives. What businesses are they in?

7. Inside yourself. You may have an original idea for a business that no one has thought of, or for a product that doesn't exist. But don't limit your thinking only to this new business or product. You want to see how your idea "stacks up" against other possible businesses.

8. Search the Internet. Search "small business" or "home based business" on www.google.com or www.yahoo.com or other search engine.

THE CRITERIA RATING SYSTEM

Ever notice how Consumer Reports goes about rating a product? Notice they don't come right out and say a product is excellent, good, fair, or poor and expect you to take their word for it. Instead, they take a systematic approach to rating products by considering certain criteria they feel are important to consumers. They then compare products to each other based on the selected criteria, and allow readers to make evaluations of their own. Readers can select their own criteria the things most important to them and select one product over another accordingly. In other words, Consumer Report researchers recognize that you may give different value points to one feature or another based on what's important to you.

We're recommending that you follow a similar process in selecting the kind of business that's right for you, and apply the process again later in selecting the specific business opportunity for you. You want to find a business that "fits" with you. You don't want to open a coffee shop if you can't get up in the morning. Even if everyone is making lots of money at coffee shops, you will end up hating it and not doing very well. You want to find a business that fits with your personality, family and financial limitations.

GIVING VALUE POINTS TO YOUR CRITERIA

The first thing you should do is take 20 minutes and write down all of your goals. Try to write 50 goals the first time you try this exercise. You should try to get up to 100 goals. After writing down your goals, break them into Personal Goals and Business Goals. With the summary of the things you're looking for in a business; your personal goals, and your business goals, now you can rate these goals in order of importance and assign a point value to them.

Use the following procedure:

1.   Reduce your list of personal goals to the top six or less goals, and list them in order of priority.

---

2. Do the same with your business goals.

3. Divide your lists in half and assign a rating scale to the upper half that is twice the range of the scale applied to the lower half.

For example: Items 1-3, (upper) rate on a scale of 1-6.
Items 4-6, (lower) rate on a scale of 1-3.

Personal Goals	Rating
1. Use my creative talent	(1-6)
2. Use My past experience	(1-6)
3. Enjoy my work	(1-6)
4. Meet people	(1-3)
5. Spend more time with my family	(1-3)
6. Get more exercise	(1-3)
Business Goals	Rating
1. Limited investment needed	(1-6)
2. Good growth potential	(1-6)
3. Non-seasonal business	(1-6)
4. Total independence of management	(1-3)
5. Minimum government	(1-3)
6. Local outreach	(1-3)

Thus, a number three goal with a four rating (on a scale of one to six) would outweigh a number four goal with a three rating (on a scale of one to three). (See example illustration.)

Using this rating method, higher priority items will usually count for more than lower priority items. You will better appreciate the importance of this distinction when you work out your rating chart and add up the scores.

MAKING YOUR OWN RATING CHART

Following the example in the illustration below, make your own rating chart using the following procedure:

1. In the left column, list the business possibilities you've come up with. There's no limit to the number of businesses you might consider. They can be listed in any order. Don't try to prioritize them.

2. Make vertical columns to the right of your list of businesses, one for each of your personal and business goals. (Maximum of twelve columns.)

3. List your personal and business goals across the top, along with their assigned scale. (one to six or one to three.)

4. Evaluate each of the businesses you've listed according to the criteria you've listed across the chart, rating how they measure up on a scale of either 1-3 or 1-6. Enter the score in the appropriate box to the right of each business.

5. Add up the points from left to right horizontally after each business listing. Enter the total score in the far right column.

6. Narrow your possible business candidates down to the top five which will be the five that scored the highest totals.

SAMPLE CHART OF GOALS & RATING SCALES

	PERSONAL GOALS							BUSINESS GOALS						
	#1 (1-6)	#2 (1-6)	#3 (1-6)	#4 (1-3)	#5 (1-3)	#6 (1-3)		#1 (1-6)	#2 (1-6)	#3 (1-6)	#4 (1-3)	#5 (1-3)	#6 (1-3)	Total
Business A	5	4	2	3	1	2		6	5	5	3	1	2	39
Business B	6	5	2	2	3	1		5	4	6	2	3	2	40
Business C	2	4	5	2	2	1		3	4	4	2	1	2	32
Business D	6	6	5	3	3	2		5	6	3	3	2	2	46
Business E	3	2	2	2	1	1		4	3	2	2	0	1	23
Business F	4	3	4	2	3	1		4	5	2	2	1	1	32
Business G	5	6	5	3	3	2		6	5	6	3	2	2	48

How did your selections come out?   Did you have some surprises? Did you eliminate some that you considered favorites? If you did, take a good look at your list of goals again and the way you prioritized them.   Maybe you left some important goals off your list.   Or maybe you underestimated the importance of some.   If you end up changing your list, or their order of priority, you'll have to go through the rating procedure all over again.   It's worth doing until you feel your rating system is accurate, objective, and "feels right."

This type of rating system can help you evaluate different areas of your business.   But in the end, you must also listen to your "gut feeling" in addition to the cold, hard facts.   There's something mysteriously powerful about our intuition sometimes.

MAKING THE FINAL SELECTION

You may not end up going with the kind of business that scored the highest. You may select number four or five on your list. The rating method is not totally conclusive. But what you have done is eliminated those businesses that only stand a remote chance of being "right" for you when considering your priorities.   Now that you have narrowed the possibilities down to five good candidates, you can go about the selection process in more depth. Here's the procedure we recommend in making your final selection:

1. **Talk to people in the same or similar business.** Seek out people who are operating businesses like or similar to the ones you're considering. Most people love to talk about their businesses. Select people outside of the area in which you are considering locating your business. Be frank and honest with them. Let them know you're considering a business similar to theirs and you would value their advice. Usually, these contacts will be flattered and willing to share their experience and advice. Meeting at their place of business is best, unless your presence will inhibit their operation or the activity would not allow for a relaxed conversation. You may want to consider meeting the business owner for lunch or for coffee or dinner after hours. **Note**: While talking with these people, you may conduct some market research. Be sure to come prepared with written questions and take notes of responses.

2. **Check success and failure reports.** Articles are written each year on small businesses, and most of them list the ones most likely to succeed and those most likely to fail, based on recent data. These articles are usually available at your public library. If you know of businesses like the ones you're considering that have failed, try to contact former officers or employees of the company and inquire about **what happened.**

3. **Ask professional advice.** There are three professionals you should get to know if you are to succeed, and you might as well start now. The professionals are: Lawyer, Certified Public Accountant (CPA), and Banker. These people work with business owners every day, and have a good knowledge of the ins and outs of most of them. Share your thoughts with them. Tell them what businesses you're considering and why. They will likely point out factors you haven't thought about or share with you specific knowledge about the particular businesses. You'll want to consult these same people later when you come to select your specific business opportunity.

4. **Share your thoughts with your family, friends, and associates.** Your family members, friends and associates may point out some considerations you never thought about. They may come up with significant thoughts that would discourage you from one idea, or, they may offer real encouragement for pursuing another idea. An added benefit is the comfort you feel in getting others who are close to you involved in your big decision.

5. **Make the final decision yourself.** If you've followed all the steps faithfully and carefully, and thoroughly investigated the "top five", you've done all that you could to prepare yourself. You have given yourself the benefit of ample data, advice, and knowledge from which to make your decision. The rest is up to you. You're on your own. If, for a specific business type, you can answer yes to all three of the following questions, you're ready to make a commitment:

1. Does the business satisfy most of my wants and desires? (That is, business selection criteria.)
2. Do I know how to be successful in this type of company?
3. Do I have, or can I develop (or hire), the attributes and capabilities that are required for success in this business?
4. Is the current condition and outlook for this type of business favorable?
5. Am I and my family willing to make sacrifices to achieve business success?

If you can answer yes to all five questions, you're in great shape. But what if the best you can do is two out of three and one maybe? Or, what if all five rate the same? What then? At this point, it boils down to going with your "gut feeling." Remember, there probably is no perfect business. None will suit you exactly; you're going to make some compromises. But if the choice is between remaining a frustrated and unhappy employee, or making a few compromises so you can be in your own business, then you will probably be much happier in the long run if you make the compromises.

When you've made your commitment, you're halfway home. You've finished Step One of the business selection process. Congratulations! Now you can go on to Step Two: Selecting your Specific Business Opportunity.

SELECTING YOUR SPECIFIC BUSINESS OPPORTUNITY

You've selected the kind of business you want to go into. That is, you know what product or service you want to market.   But now what?

Basically, you have three options

1.   You can buy a franchise business.
2.   You can buy an existing business.
3.   You can start your own business from scratch.

Each is a different kind of venture.   Each has its own advantages and disadvantages, its own risks and rewards, and its own financial requirements.

WHERE TO LOOK FOR BUSINESS OPPORTUNITIES

Whether looking for independent ongoing businesses or for new franchise opportunities, you need to know where to look. Generally, there are three main places to look for a new business opportunity.

1.   **Business Professionals.** Your bank is a good place to start.   Your **banker** deals with people in business every day and would be one of the first to know if an owner is considering selling his

business. Your **lawyer**, if he is a business lawyer, would also know of business opportunities and would be in a position to advise you on which ones are worth considering. Other good contacts include investment brokers, marketing consultants, and other entrepreneurs.

2. **Directories**. Your **public library** can provide you with a current catalog of franchise opportunities. These catalogs are published each year, and include descriptions of the franchises, the approximate investment dollars required, and how to get in contact with the franchiser. (Your local **SBA Office** also has an extensive library of directories, as well as dozens of various business brochures and pamphlets that provide excellent reference for the new business entrepreneur.)

3. **Newspapers and Magazines**. Your local newspaper is a good place to start. Check the classified section under "Business Opportunities" as well as the display ads, which may be found either in the classified section or in the business news section.

4. **Industry and Trade Contacts.** You can find a wealth of information from trade shows and association meetings. It is also a good way to examine potential competitors, meet distributors, learn of product and market trends and identify potential products.

Other publications include:
- Wall Street Journal
- Entrepreneur
- Income Opportunities
- Opportunity
- Popular Mechanics
- Selling Direct
- Mechanics Illustrated
- Money Making Opportunities
- Money
- Success
- Ladies Home Journal
- Work Bench

Of course, we haven't listed all the magazines where you'll find opportunities. There are many others, and new ones seem to show up all the time. If you're considering a very selective market or business, check the trade magazines that reach that market. For example, if you're thinking of raising horses, or training horses, there are a number of magazines that appeal specifically to horse lovers, horse ranchers, horse trainers, and so on.

There are also various business opportunity and entrepreneurial conventions, shows and expositions. These are excellent places to make business contacts and talk to other entrepreneurs. Inquire with your SBA Office as to when the next ones are scheduled.

BUYING A FRANCHISE BUSINESS

The great attraction of entering business through a franchise is that all the planning comes prepackaged for you, often at a price far lower than if you were to start fresh. Thus, you avoid the problem of raising large sums of money often the most difficult part of establishing a business.

Another plus is that you receive the right to operate a business under the leadership of a well-known distributor or manufacturer. In return for a fee and royalty payments, you have immediate access to a proven product, a consumer image, publicity, and goodwill. In many cases, the franchiser provides the goods whether they are automobiles or fried chicken as well as the training and techniques for conducting the operation. If the franchise is a sound one, the likelihood of success in your own business is increased. The security and know-how offered by the franchising company, along with the name-brand recognition, lowers the risk of failure for you.

There are, however, disadvantages to franchises: you have to conform to the chain's standards, sell only their product at their price, share in the problems of the distributor (though they may be none of your doing), perhaps find that centralized management is unresponsive to your needs, and of course, share the profits.

If freedom and independence is high on your list of priorities, you would probably not be content to operate a franchise. In fact, most franchising companies don't want independent types. One Franchising company representative said something like: "We're not looking for generals who want to do everything their own way, we're looking for sergeants."

When considering a franchise your first concern is assessing the success, reputation, and image of the franchising company. You'll want to know, for example:

1.   What is the reputation of the franchiser? Has it changed (better or worse) recently?

2.   How successful have the franchisees been? Would they do it again if given another chance?

3.   What do competitors think about the reputation and success of the franchiser being evaluated?

4.   How well does the franchiser rate with financial reporting services, banks, and community agencies?

If you are considering buying a franchise, you should visit other franchisees, the Better Business Bureau, and the Chamber of Commerce to investigate the company's reputation and track record. Before you sign any contract you should consult your lawyer, since your agreement will regulate such key items as exclusivity, inventory, royalty rates, purchase requirements, and investment obligations.

There are two publications which list most of the franchises which are available:

A.   Franchise Opportunity Handbook Number 003-008-00191-2 Published by Department of Commerce.

Government Printing Office, Supt of Documents   Washington, D.C. 20402 1988 edition

B.   Info Press located at 736 Center Street, Lewiston, New York   14092. This is a private publishing Company which publishes the Franchise Annual.

BUYING AN EXISTING BUSINESS

In buying an ongoing concern you have some of the same advantages as a franchise:

- an active and loyal clientele
- a known product or service
- goodwill
all the past efforts which went into making the business successful.

In addition, when you buy an ongoing business, you get:

- brick and mortar (an established building and location)

- employees who already know the business
- inventory and supplies
- tax and credit history

Often when you buy a business you are getting more than the "book" value. For example, if you were to start a restaurant from scratch, it may cost you $100,000 for leasehold improvements such as ovens, dishes, and so on. But often a business is sold at below book value so you pick up all the leasehold improvements at a considerable savings. That's why many second or third generation restaurants survive when previous owners have gone belly up.

On the other hand, if you buy a successful ongoing business, you should be prepared to pay the owner a premium for the intangible efforts that go into building a thriving business. That is, its following, customers, trade relations, management efficiency, public acceptance in short, goodwill.

One of the disadvantages of buying an existing business is the problem of not knowing exactly what you're buying. Why is the present owner selling? Are there some hidden problems?

When considering buying an ongoing business, you'll want to know the answers to such questions as:

1.   Are there any changes in the nature of the business or in the character of the neighborhood?
2.   What is the extent of the company's liabilities?
3.   What promises or contracts has the company entered into that might commit the new owner in the future?
4.   Are there any potential lawsuits coming against the company? (For example, for defective products or injury liability.)

We urge you to proceed very cautiously when considering buying an existing business. Just as when you shop for a used car or a home, it pays to check out what you're buying thoroughly before you put your money down and sign on the dotted line. Again, your best friends can be your attorney, your CPA, your banker, your marketing consultant and reference agencies such as the Better Business Bureau and Dun and Bradstreet. Use them to investigate the company's reputation and track record. In addition, try to talk to key employees of the seller's company and also ex-employees. You may uncover facts or factors the seller has been reluctant to talk about.

The danger of hidden liabilities when buying an established business is a strong reason for starting out fresh with your own business.

STARTING YOUR OWN BUSINESS FROM SCRATCH

Starting fresh with a new business certainly permits you the most freedom, since you are not restricted by what has gone before and are not regulated by someone else's rules.

When you start from scratch, you have a clean history, a clean inventory, and the excitement of something new. You get to choose the name of the company, its location, its employees, all the equipment and furnishings. You can, in fact, define its entire personality. If successful, you have one of the biggest rewards of all: the satisfaction of knowing you did it all yourself, from the ground up.

In many cases, starting fresh is your lowest-cost approach of getting into business. This is especially true if your particular type of business lends itself to a small-scale, spare-time start-up. It's possible that you can get started with just a few thousand dollars from your savings or with a small loan from members of your family.

On the other hand, you may be considering the type of business that will require a great deal of money to get started. In this case, the success of your enterprise may rest upon your ability to raise the money. Raising the money may be the most difficult job you have ever faced. However, the process can be made easier by following the guidelines presented in the, Financing Your Small Business chapter.

No two businesses are the same each has its own requirements for capital investment. But generally, they are usually either capital intensive or labor intensive.

Businesses requiring a great deal of money to start up are called capital intensive. A printing house with modern presses, a trucking company with

long-haul tractors and trailers, and a machine shop with numerically controlled equipment are all examples of companies that rely on large amounts of invested capital to purchase or lease equipment, which does most of the work.

Businesses that rely more on people than on equipment are labor intensive. Artists, writers, and consultants, for example, establish their businesses on their talents, techniques and knowledge. Although this type of business requires the least amount of capital to get started, it's often difficult to get a loan (if needed to finance it) simply because you have no fixed assets (inventory, equipment, a building) for the bank to consider as collateral. Also, the independent, skilled professional is often in a business that banks find vague and hard to judge for success potential. In such a business, your Business Plan is often the key to convincing your lender that your business has promise for profitability.

Of course, few businesses are completely "capital intensive" or "labor intensive." For example, retail stores, manufacturing assembly lines, and restaurants all need equipment and people. Knowing the relative importance of each labor and equipment for the business you wish to start will help you determine the amount of money you'll need to start. Then you'll be in a better position to decide how feasible your plan is. If your prospects of raising the needed capital are rather limited, and the new business will not be generating cash quickly, it would be prudent to find an operation which either needs less money or has an immediate inflow of cash.

There are other considerations when you start a business from scratch. They will be covered in detail in later chapters, but you should be aware that the considerations include:

1. Determining both **fixed** and **variable** costs.
2. Projecting start-up costs.
3. Projecting profit and loss for the first year.
4. Projecting cash flow.
5. Projecting year-end net worth (assets minus liabilities).
6. Deciding on the legal form of your organization: Sole Proprietor, Partnership, or Corporation.
7. Where to locate your business.

As you can see, the list above is essentially the reverse of buying an ongoing business, where the advantages include having all or most of those elements in place when you buy it. At first glance, the list of considerations may scare you but keep in mind that you'll **know how** to deal with those challenges after you've completed this manual. So if your heart really lies in starting your own business from scratch, pursue that idea with the confidence that we're going to teach you exactly how to do it. And we will teach you one step at a time so that you will be the master of that step after you learned it yourself.

MARKET RESEARCH

Before starting your own business from scratch, or buying an existing business, you'll want to do a thorough market analysis. In a new product or new business, you'll need to study the market potential in other words, determine the extent of need for your product or service. If you're buying an existing business, you'll need to investigate product quality, price competitiveness, delivery and service reputation, and the image the company has with its current and past customers.

Large corporations usually employ a full staff of marketing people, or, they hire an outside marketing firm or consultant, when launching a new product, starting a new business, or acquiring an existing business. In the next chapter, we will introduce you to the methods big companies use in doing market research, and show you how to adopt similar techniques for your own business venture.

ANALYZING YOUR START UP OPPORTUNITIES

Even after thorough investigation of selected business opportunities, using the expert help of your lawyer, banker, and marketing consultant, you may come up with several "good" possible opportunities in your chosen product/business area. How do you decide which one is best for you? We recommend you go right to your list of business goals and personal goals and see which business opportunity satisfies your priorities best. Use the same kind of chart analysis you used to select the kind of business that's right for you. List the possibilities, rate them according to your priorities, and add up the scores. (But don't forget to listen to your "gut feelings" too.)

THE DECISION IS YOURS

In this chapter you have learned how to build a firm foundation for your business venture, how to select the kind of business that's right for you, and the options available to you in business opportunities. There is no single right way of getting into business. Buying an ongoing business is right for some people in some situations. Starting from scratch is right for other people in other situations. We've pointed out the different options you have and **how to go about** selecting what's right for you. But the final decision is yours. The important lesson here is that you take a careful, logical, systematic approach to making your decision, giving yourself the benefit of as much information as you can gather. With the proper information, self-analysis, and the principles you'll learn in this manual, we are confident that you will succeed if you have the desire to succeed.

Here are a couple of other thoughts on how to create a truly successful business:

---

1. **Know your business inside and out before you start**. The more you learn the better you will be to handle the different decisions that need to be made. Contact anyone that you can think of in the industry to gain more education.

2. **Prepare a Business Plan**. This will help you understand the areas of your business that you may need more help from outside advisors or consultants. If you have trouble creating the financial statements, and this is very important to running a successful business, you will need to take a class or get help from someone to understand financial statements before you jump into your own business. This is a major reason for failure in small businesses.

3. **Manage your money**. Many entrepreneurs lose sight of the cash in the bank account and the amount that they will need to fund upcoming purchases and bills. It always costs more to start a business than most entrepreneurs prepare for.

4. **Understand financial statements.** You can not learn enough about managing money in a small business.

5. **Learn to Manage Your Employees.** Employees will make or break your business. The best way to make them effective is to train them well and make sure they are motivated to help you reach your goals.

6. **Make Your Business Different than the Competition**. In competing with the large companies, try to give better customer service, better quality, better pricing or whatever will make your customers happy.

7. **Keep Your Mind and Body in Shape**. You can not perform at the level you need to on a daily basis if you are constantly run down,

drinking too much or too stressed. The decisions you will make will not be in the best interest of the company.

In this chapter you have learned:

1. *Entrepreneurs come in all shapes and sizes but most have an overriding desire to make lots of money.*
2. *People go into business for a variety of reasons including practical and personal reasons. Understanding your own reasons for starting a business is very, very important for the success of your business.*
3. *Choosing the RIGHT business for you can be an easy task when you use a process for ruling out businesses that do not "fit" with your personal and business goals.*
4. *The final selection of a business is ultimately up to you alone.*

Chapter 3

Buying a Business

BUY A BUSINESS OR START FROM SCRATCH?

This is the $64,000 question! Should I start my business from scratch or, do I find just such a business that is available for sale? Each one has it's advantages as well as it's disadvantages. For those individuals who have a business idea that is new to the market or where their experience is unique should strongly consider starting a business from scratch. Transforming a current business into a new business process is difficult.

But what about the person who wants to go into a business in which the product or service is not new. That is, where competition is plentiful and the type of business has been around for some time. This is the scenario for most businesses. Many experts agree that the safest and most effective way into business is to buy someone else's business.

Buying a Business

When one thinks about buying business that is already set up and running, the first thing that comes to mind is: "Wow, all I have to do is to open the doors and let in the customers!" There are many advantages to buying a business rather starting one up from ground floor. The main reason to buy a business is the incredible reduction in start-up costs of time, money and energy.

Let us look at these advantages. They all do not apply to every business that is purchased, but, in many situations, several of these advantages do apply.

ADVANTAGES TO BUYING A BUSINESS

1. Name Recognition. A going business has a name. It is recognized by both customers and suppliers. In some instances, one cannot put a value on a name. Large franchises are a good example of name recognition. Take for example **"McDonalds"**-what comes to mind immediately? If you answered Hamburgers, you are correct! Or take the name of **Roto-Rooter.** What first comes to your mind? If you thought of: "Clogged plumbing or sewer lines", you would be correct.

2. History. History is defined as an "account of what has happened." This is equally true when applied to a business. It is reflected in every aspect of a business over a period of time including such important areas as start-up, sales, profits, product lines, and relationships to customers, employees and suppliers. It has often been said that history repeats itself. Thus one can learn much from studying a company that has been purchased and learn from it's past experiences and operations.

3. Customer base. One of the major advantages in the purchase of an ongoing business is that it has established customers. For without customers there can be no business. One can have the greatest product, or it may offer the greatest service, but without customers the business would be unable to survive.

Likewise one can have adequate financing and can have top management. Again, without customers, the cash register does not ring.

4. Distributor Base. If your business works through distributors, many of the agreements and contracts have already been negotiated for you. This may be good or bad for your company. So make sure you check out the agreements before you finalize the purchase.

5. Employees. Elmer Smith, the father and pioneer of the oxygen acetylene welding and cutting equipment industry in this country was once asked by a business reporter from the **Wall Street Journal:** "What do you attribute your success to?" He responded by saying: "I surrounded myself in each area of my business with employees who were smarter then me!" Often when purchasing a business, a key element may be that it comes with good employees.

For example employees who understand the business and the industry. Those employees who are conscientious loyal and faithful. Or those who have good rapport with customers and have solid product knowledge.

6. Known product line. There is nothing like getting up in the morning and looking into your pantry closet and having a choice of your favorite cereals for breakfast. The same can be true for a company that has been in business selling a product or service that has name recognition within the community. In some instances, it may have taken years to establish this  recognition. Regardless of the time length, having a product line that both customers and prospects are familiar with, has considerable value.

7. Company assets. The assets of an ongoing business fall into two main groups. They are tangible assets and those which are intangible. Examples of tangible assets include such items as inventory, cash, accounts receivables, equipment, supplies, and real estate. Examples of intangible assets include goodwill, business name, logos, company history, and employees. All assets have value. Thus when one purchases a business, he or she is able to see a value to part of their cost of buying the business. Some assets take not only money, but lots of time to create. A logo can be very valuable but take a long time to create.

8. Banking history. One of the more difficult problems for a person going

into business, and particularly for one not having been in business, is to establish a banking relationship with a banker. This problem is greatly alleviated especially when one purchases an ongoing business. Whoever has been the seller's banker, is quite familiar with the history of the business and especially the financial history. Such familiarity facilitates the buyer in continuing on with the banking relationship.

9. Supplier relationships. We have already seen where one of the advantages to purchasing a business is that of the "known product line." Tied in with this is: who are the suppliers to this product line?" For it usually will insure that there will be an ongoing source of supply for the products being sold. It also means that the suppliers have confidence in the business and have an opportunity to open up a new relationship with their new customer. Considerable time and energy can be used up locating new sources of supply for a new business and in establishing a relationship.

10. Location familiarity. There is an old saying: "There is no place like home." That is because one is familiar with it and it's surroundings. Likewise, when a business has been in a specific location for a period of time, customers and prospects automatically know where to come. If the business is a store, they know where to go to find certain merchandise. Knowing the

---

location comes from using the business which in many instances leads to familiarity with employees and even owners.

11. Equipment in place. Most businesses require the need for certain types of equipment. If it is a manufacturing firm, depending upon what is being produced will determine the type of machinery needed to produce what is being made. If it is a service company, then tools are usually the important equipment to run the business. A major advantage to buying a business is the fact that the necessary machinery, equipment and tools are in place.

12. Office furniture and supplies. When one thinks about starting a business the emphasis on cost is placed on inventory, if products are being sold, the location and leasehold improvements, employee salaries, and if it is a manufacturing firm, necessary equipment. Office furniture and supplies are generally last on the list unless the business deals with "walk-in customers." Obviously, when one purchases an operating business, most likely any needed office furniture and supplies will be in place.

13. Inventory. Imagine being able to open the doors to one's new business, such as a sporting goods store, for the very first time, and not having to order a single item that is going to be sold. Imagine having a customer enter your store, walk down the aisles putting tennis balls, athletic shoes, shorts, a tennis racket and shirts into a shopping cart. The customer then come directly to your cash register. What thought would be going through your mind?

Better still, what do you think you will feel when the customer puts his or her charge card or cash in your hand to pay for the purchase? This is what comes when you purchase an ongoing business such as the sporting goods store. Simply put, you open the doors and are ready to go.

14. Relationship with community. Often the success of a business rests with having a good relationship with the community. This includes the local government, such as the city council, licensing departments within the city, and possibly the city purchasing department. Likewise, certain groups of customers within the community may be important such as contractors, schools, or fraternal organizations. These relationships are already in place by an existing business which makes them a valuable asset to the next owners.

15. Historical image-advertising. What comes to mind when you hear the name of a business? **Walmart?**-Discount Store. **Home Depot?**-Hardware store. **IBM?** Computers. **Allstate?** Insurance. These names are all on the national scene. But in each and every community, small or large, certain business names in each and every field or industry stand out over and above all others. Likewise, when one purchases a business, he or she is purchasing a name which hopefully has high recognition in the community where it is located.

16. Consultants and advisors in place. One of the advantages of purchasing a business, is that it may come with invaluable advisors who may have assisted the business over a long period of time. Examples of these include consultants in advertising, insurance, banking and finance. Or if the business has an uncommon mission, such as a publisher of software, then having the right copyright attorney and software developers in place could

---

61

prove to be invaluable.

17. Business policies. Business policies come in all forms. They cover a broad range of the operations of the business. Policies may include how to handle return goods to when to charge for delivery or gift wrapping. Other policies on employee personnel policies such as sick leave, vacation, overtime, working hours, dress code and review procedures are already written. It is easier to update current policies than to create new ones.

Another type of business policies are in the area of products and services such as warranties and guarantees. Business policies are usually in written form in order to be meaningful both to consumers and employees. Considerable time and effort is saved in this area when purchasing a business. In purchasing a business, be sure to ask for all the written policies.

18. Using the business to buy the business. One of the leading advantages to purchasing a business over that of "starting from scratch" is the possibility of using the assets of the business as collateral in the actual purchase of the business. Assets of an existing business can be in the account receivables, real estate, machinery and equipment, inventory, even good will (business name or logos).

For example, let us assume that you are giving consideration to the purchase of a sporting goods store. The seller's price is $150,000. You have only $25,000 in cash. If the store has $75,000 in good clean inventory, one can use this inventory and pledge it as collateral to the bank for a loan. Or, if the store has $25,000 in account receivables, such as from schools and athletic teams, this too can be used as collateral in obtaining the loan.

In finance language, this is called "assigning the asset" to the bank or organization that is making the loan." In most instances, banks will require collateral or something which has corresponding value or importance, to cover the amount of the loan. This is protection that the bank requires in the event that one is unable to repay the loan.

19. Cash flow. To the owner of a business, there is no better music to one's ears then hearing the cash register ring. The "feel" of money is like instant gratification. Therefore, when purchasing an ongoing business, the buyer can experience this instant gratification as the cash register rings over and over again.

This is important since it is a direct reflection of what is considered positive "cash flow" for a business. Unlike opening a new business from starting at it's very beginning, one that is already operating produces cash from day one.

20. Availability of owner's knowledge and advice. One advantage of buying a business is the opportunity to learn from the experiences of the past owner. The owner can represent a wealth of knowledge particularly if he or she started the business or has been operating it over a relatively long period of time. The buyer can learn from both mistakes that the previous owner has made as well as the successes of the business.

Probably the most important areas that any new owner can learn from the seller, is what mistakes were made in the past. What advertising and marketing programs should be avoided? What are the important sources of supply? What products

---

63
2005 Copyright of the American Institute of Small Business

sold better than others? In plain and simple words, what works and what does not work?

21. Reduced Time. Many of the tasks associated with starting a business from scratch are time consuming. Constant decisions need to be made on products, policies, hiring, site selection, tax filings, banking relationships and supplier negotiations. When buying a business so many of these items have already been done for you. You always can update them over time, but at least they are set up in the beginning. Creation always takes longer than modification. One more advantage would be the time saved in creating financial projections. It is much easier to create projections if you have past figures to use. This reduces the amount of time you need to spend on your projections.

WHAT TO LOOK FOR IN BUYING A BUSINESS

It is important to make a good decision in buying your own business. Remember this can be one of the safest and most effective ways to have your own business. Here is what to look for:

1. Look for something you enjoy – Fit with your business is incredibly important. It doesn't make sense to purchase a profitable business if you hate what you are doing. Every day will be harder and harder to get out of bed. It is difficult to keep up with changes in the industry and helping customers is stressful.
2. Seasoned small business – This is a business that has 3-5 years of financial records and tax filings that coincide with the financial statements. Failure rate of businesses that have been around for 5 or more years is very low.
3. Growth pattern – These businesses are keeping up with the trends and moving in the right direction.

4. Trained employees – Monitor the employees and the number of years they have been with the business. The longer they have been employed, the more they can teach you about the business.

5. Good customer base – Review the customer database and determine how often customers are contacted. A current database of customers is much more valuable that an out-of-date database. Also make sure the customer data is an electronic format.

6. Proper Equipment – Check with other businesses in this field and make sure you have equipment that is current. For example, in buying a restaurant, you need to know how old the refrigerators are, because they only last a few years.

7. Established Inventory – Having inventory already purchased and in stock makes selling easier. As you get more knowledgeable about your new business you can add products as they become available.

WHERE TO FIND BUSINESSES FOR SALE

There are approximately 6 million businesses in the United States that have under 20 employees. Most of these businesses would be perfect to purchase, if they meet the criteria above. The majority of businesses for sale are found in five different areas:

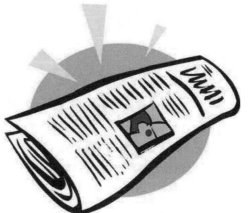

1. Local newspaper in the Classified section. Look under "Business Opportunities" or "Business Opportunities for Sale". Some local communities also have a section in local business magazines.

2. Search the Internet through the Wall Street Journal site or other business for sale sites.

3. Find an experience business broker. You can find a listing of brokers in your local yellow pages or contact the International Business Brokers Association for a referral. Many states require brokers to be licensed. Make sure the broker you work with has fulfilled the appropriate requirements.

4. Call local Certified Public Accountants. These individuals prepare the taxes for many small businesses. They may know of a client that is interested in selling their business.

5. Call the owners of businesses that you frequent or look like you would enjoy owning. Ask the owner if they would like to sell. Be careful in this approach, because you may pay too much for the business if you look too eager.

VALUING A BUSINESS FOR SALE

Coming to agreement with the owner on the price for the business is one of the most difficult negotiations in the whole transaction. The main part of the price is based on the value of the business. Typically an owner will value the business for more than it may be worth because the business has been such an integral part of their lives. The value of any business is based on what someone is willing to pay for the business. Here is a quick and dirty method for determining value. This does not take into account the quality of intangible assets like customer database and updated equipment.

First add together all the cash benefits the owner receives from the business. This may include owner's salary, perks (trips & meals), non-business expenses, non-business use of vehicles and insurance, or owner's kid's salaries. Then add to it depreciation, interest, amortization, excessive and over market expenses.

Next, add this number to the net profit number from the financial statements. If the company had a loss, subtract the loss from the amount in A. This number should be about 10-20% of the gross sales.

Many businesses sell for 2-4 times net profit plus owner's benefit. After you have calculated net profit plus owner's benefit, multiply it by 2 and 4 to see one value of the business.

For example:

Company X

Gross Sales	$375,000
Owner's Benefit	$ 50,000
Net Profit	$ 25,000

Net Profit + Owner's Benefit = $75,000

Multiplier

$75,000 X 2 = $150,000

$75,000 X 4 = $300,000

The business should be priced with this methodology somewhere between $150,000 and $300,000.

This is only one way of many to value companies. Be sure to consult an attorney and an accountant before you make a bid for a company. Both the attorney and accountant can make sure you have covered all the financial bases before making a decision. Paying too much for a business is one of the leading causes of business failure after businesses change owners.

DISADVANTAGES TO BUYING A BUSINESS

As with any business situation, there are disadvantages. The following is a list of disadvantages of buying a business.

1. **Reduced Reward**. Because you normally will have a debt payment to the previous owner or a financing source, for purchasing the business. This will limit your cash flow for a certain length of time.

2. **Possible Problems.** No business is without problems. Normally you

only want the "Good" problems, but in buying a business that is not always the case. Later in this chapter, we will discuss some due diligence questions that should help you reduce the unknown problems. However, it will not take away all the problems in a business.

3. **Ownership Transfer Issues.** Different issues pop up after all the documents have been signed. Selling a business is sometimes an emotional issue for the original owner, which makes it hard for them to let the new owner take control. In  addition, it is difficult to document all of the assets in the sale of a business. For this reason, it is important to work with an advisor/attorney that has experience in buying and selling businesses. They can help you identify the most important items that you will need to put in the agreements.

4. **Purchase Financing may be difficult to find.** Most of the decision to lend on a purchase of a business will be on the historical financials of that business. If the business is not doing well with the current owner, you will have to prove what you will do differently to improve the sales of the business.

5. **Difficult to find the RIGHT Opportunity.** Sometimes you want to open a retail dress shop, but finding the one that will work can be difficult. This becomes increasingly difficult if you as the new owner want to install significant changes. Customers and employees are used to the "way things were".

6. **Unknown issues** with the business or the previous owner. One issue

may be the pay history of the previous owner to the suppliers. Suppliers can not run an efficient business when their customers do not pay on time. If an owner has a history of late payments, it may reflect on your relationship with the supplier. One issue that is very important if you are purchasing property is the unknown environmental issue. You as a new owner can be held responsible for environmental clean up if you do not have adequate protection in the documents from buying the business.

ADVANTAGES TO STARTING A BUSINESS FROM SCRATCH

1. **Your own thing.** One of the great joys in life is the fulfillment of a dream especially if the dream is that of having one's own business. How often does one have this childhood dream of having a business of their own and actually seeing fulfillment of the dream during their adulthood? Or, if having one's own business is not a childhood dream, how often does one work for someone else and feel he or she is not appreciated?

Regardless of why one wants to go into their own business the end result is that it satisfies the dream of "doing one's own thing." When this relates to one's own business, it is usually done with enjoyment and the desire to be successful.

2. **Enthusiastic exuberance.** Have you ever seen a child with a new toy? Can you describe the reaction on the child's face? If you can, imagine your own feelings and reaction, when you open the doors to your new business for the first time. You have boundless energy. Your chest swells with pride. Your feelings are one of excitement, anticipation and satisfaction. It is a culmination and fulfillment of one's dreams and aspiration. All of this leads to what one calls "enthusiastic

exuberance." Such a feeling is much stronger when starting a business from scratch rather then purchasing an existing business.

3. New kid on the block. There is nothing like something that is new. Whether it be an automobile, new dress or suit of clothes, piece of jewelry, or for kids, a new bicycle, pair of skates or a sound system. They all attract the attention of friends and neighbors. Likewise, the same can be said about a new business especially if it the "new kid on the block." If it is a retail store or offering a potential consumer service, everyone who may possibly be a prospect or customer of the new kid wants to see what the premises look like, what products and services are offered and who are the owners.

Should the new business offer products and services that one has an interest now, or, in the future, then curiosity will prevail. One will want to see what products are being offered? What does the establishment look like? Who are the owners and employees? How are items priced? Even if it is a business that may not offer merchandise that one has an interest, the curiosity factor still prevails.

Take for example a restaurant that features an ethnic or nationality type food. Most people do not have a taste for every type of ethnic food whether it is Chinese, Indian, Mexican, French, Italian, New England early American, or Cajun style. Yet, most people are curious enough to see how is the restaurant decorated? What is on the menu?

4. Location. One major advantage of starting a business from scratch is the opportunity to choose where to locate the business. The only restriction is availability, zoning and cost. Aside from these, one has the opportunity to study the market and market conditions, and determine where their customers are concentrated.

When starting a business from scratch, you can select a location where you feel you can maximize sales and profits. A site or location can be chosen where there will be no restraints with regards to parking, hours of operation, traffic flow, and access.

5. New surroundings-leasehold improvements. Whether one opens their business in a new building or leases space which formerly housed a

business, the owner has the opportunity to do all phases of the interior decorating to their wishes. One is not strapped with past facility restrictions. Like the "new kid on the block" one can have the lease hold improvements which best suits their clientele and in the new business owner's opinion best meets their needs and likes.

6. All new inventory. When one purchases a business, the entire existing inventory normally is included. If it is a manufacturing firm, the raw materials, goods in process and finished goods make up the inventory. If it is a retail or wholesale establishment, then the inventory includes all of the items available for resale. Or, if it is a service company, then the inventory is made up of the parts and supplies used for resale.

One disadvantage to purchasing a business is the fact that a portion of the inventory is outdated, damaged or obsolete. For example, should one purchase a gift store, most likely twenty five per cent (25%) is outdated. When one opens a new gift store, all of the inventory is current and will include all current and new giftware items hitting the market. This is especially true for a business in which the seasons of the year are of major importance.

Examples of seasonal businesses include gift stores, lawn and garden centers, and clothing stores such as women, men's and children's ware.

7. **New suppliers, co-op advertising and assistance.** As with a new inventory, starting a business "from scratch" enables the owner to work with new suppliers. Continuing to work with existing suppliers, may present several wonderful opportunities. For example, suppliers often like to present special incentives to their new customer such as introductory discounts, cooperative advertising dollars for grand opening advertisements, free goods included in first time orders, special assistance whether it be technical, marketing or service.

8. **New image and advertising.** Opening a new business presents marvelous opportunities to the owner to present oneself as the exciting "new kid on the block." How often does one see a grand opening newspaper advertisement full of special discounts, free merchandise, door prizes, free drawings and free factory personnel assistance and say: "gee, I am anxious to see this new store or. . . .try this new restaurant?" In addition, one can paint an entirely new image, possibly one in which high prospect and customer appeal will prevail.

9. **Publicity opportunities.** Just like the advantage of "new image and advertising" has, the opportunity for "publicity" abounds. Unlike advertising, publicity usually comes with no cost. Instead, it relies heavily on the news worthiness of the subject. With a new business, there are endless publicity subjects such as the:

-A unique name for the business
-The business itself-what it does-Who it is!
-Uniqueness of the product lines
-Who is the owner-Experience-Known in the community

72
2005 Copyright of the American Institute of Small Business

-Why the business-Fill an existing void

-New location-Servicing the community

-Grand opening specials-Sales-Give-always

-Meet factory representatives

10. New equipment and supplies. The word "new" appears in almost every area of this "Advantages Of Starting a Business From Scratch" section of the chapter. As in new inventory, the business will have new equipment and supplies. This is so very important especially if it be a manufacturing firm where production machinery is so vital. Here one does not have to worry about breakdowns or repairs since most new equipment is covered by a warranty. The same is true for a retail or service business where computers, office equipment and delivery vehicles are used.

11. Training employees to your mold. There is an old saying which says: "You can lead a horse to water, but you can't make it drink." This usually applies to employees who have worked under one set of conditions for a long period of time. Thus, when a new business opens its doors for the very first time, the owner has the opportunity to set forth the working conditions and business policies that the business will operate under.

This may include such areas as working hours, dress code, return policies, credit policies, gift wrapping, and all of the many employee fringe benefits including sick leave, insurance, bonus and commission schedules, over-time, and vacation and holiday time.

12. **Fresh banking arrangements.** The opportunity for a new business owner to work with suppliers for the very first time yields several potential benefits. The same opportunities exist to the new business owner relative to his or her "banker" relationship. One of the principal sources of income to any bank are the business loans that they make. A new business start-up affords the bank several interesting opportunities which, when turned  about, offer several advantages to the borrower.

First every banker is looking for new business opportunities, which have the potential for future growth. A $25,000 loan today may turn out to be a $250,000 loan tomorrow. For the business owner, having one's banker on one's side can yield many benefits. These include:

-Opening a line of credit
-Credit reference to suppliers and vendors
-New business prospect and customer referrals
-Potential source for business advice

13. **Financing opportunities.** Depending upon the nature of a new business, the starting of one may present the owner with a number of financing opportunities not necessarily available to the purchaser of an existing business. For example, if the business is in high technology whether it is in computers, bio or medical technology, electronics, or filling an important business need where none currently exists, non-traditional financiers are ready at hand to provide capital.

These include venture capitalists, silent partners, and private investors who are unlike banks, do not rely upon collateral to make a loan. Often the loan is available without interest and without a payback requirement.

14. **No bad history.** A business that "starts from scratch" comes into the market place without any history: good or bad! The latter is particularly important since it does not open with so called bad baggage or be looked upon unfavorably due to past actions. For example, some businesses which are purchased and opened under new ownership may be strapped with having had faulty products, bad service or treated its customers rudely.

It is often difficult to remove this stain or past bad image. On the other hand, a new business starts with a clean slate in all aspects of the business be it products, customer service, customer relationships, employees, location and image.

15. **Knowing your competition.** No one should ever go into a business without first knowing one's competition. It has often been said that if one starts a new business, then in order to guarantee its success is to at least be equal to what competition does, if not exceeding what it does. When purchasing a business, one often relies upon the seller to have all of the intimate knowledge of competition.

Who it is? How it operates? What product lines does it carry? What is their pricing policy? What are their hours? Who are their key employees? What makes them successful? What are they missing that would make them more

75

successful?

However, the owner or owners may not be that knowledgeable. When one starts a business, a business plan not only should be prepared, but **MUST** be prepared. One of the most important parts of any business plan is to know everything there is to know about competition such as the answers to the questions mentioned above. Knowing your competition is like having an insurance policy.

One would not think about purchasing a home without having adequate insurance. Likewise, one should not start a new business without knowing one's competition.

16. Filling market wants and needs. One never starts a new business unless he or she has a strong feeling as to what consumers want in products and services. This is especially true if starting a business from the ground floor. That is opening the doors for the very first time. Unlike purchasing a business in which the buyer may be strapped with outdated merchandise or not offering the most up-to-date services, the owner of a new business has

obviously studied consumer wants and needs. This is usually the first prerequisites in starting a new business.

Consumer needs and wants vary within each community and from one community to another. History has shown that new businesses generally do not fail as a result of not filling consumer needs and wants. Rather, from under financing and poor management.

DISADVANTAGES OF STARTING A BUSINESS FROM SCRATCH

Every business scenario has its advantages and its disadvantages. Starting a business is no exception. The following are some of the disadvantages of starting a business from scratch:

1. **Financing.** Finding money for a non-existent business is much more difficult than finding money for a currently running business. This is true even if the business was not making money. Financing sources understand the market better with company history.

2. **Uncertain Idea.** Even if you are creating a duplicate of another business, but in a different area, the idea is still unproven. Nobody really knows for certain if a business is going to "make it". In this case the formula has not been proven.

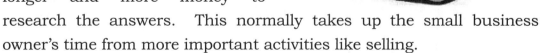

3. **Most Difficult for Inexperienced Entrepreneur.** New businesses have lots of decisions that need to be made. With an inexperienced entrepreneur, the decisions take longer and more money to research the answers. This normally takes up the small business owner's time from more important activities like selling.

In this Chapter you have learned:

1. *When starting or buying a business you need good advisors to reduce the disadvantages associated with each scenario.*
2. *Buying a business has many advantages that can help you get up and running faster, including:*
    a. *Name recognition and company logos*
    b. *Customer base*
    c. *Employees*
    d. *Location familiarity*
    e. *Business Policies*
3. *On the other hand, buying a business has disadvantages including:*
    a. *Ownership transfer issues*
    b. *Difficult finding purchase financing*
    c. *Unknown issues from previous owner*
4. *When starting a business from scratch, the new owner has control of all the different aspects of the new business, from choosing the building, the inventory, and the image of the new company.*
5. *Starting a business from scratch may give you more control, it will also take up more time. Disadvantages also include difficultly in finding financing and the uncertainty of the future of the business.*

Chapter 4

Home Based Businesses

Working at Home

Sometimes it's necessary, sometimes it's a choice. Working out of the home has become the established way of making a living for millions and millions of Americans. For some it is the practical answer to the problem of where to work between outside jobs or when the budget is too tight to afford rental office space. For others, and these are in the majority, the home office offers the best way to spend the working day.

A Growing Trend

According to a recent study, almost one third of all American workers would prefer to work at home. Today 43.2 million Americans (just about one-third of the work force) are working at least part of the time from a home office. These figures include both home-based business people (more that 13 million of them) and "telecommuters," or corporate employees who work out of their homes and keep in touch with the office by telephone, computer and fax machine.

Compare that with only a few years ago, when only 21 percent of the work force was working from home. Federal government figures indicate a growing trend. With an average of 4.2 million people starting up home businesses each year, it is now expected that the home-worker population will increase by roughly 15 percent a year, to eventually reach 56 million.

Like anything else, there are plusses and minuses on both sides and that's what we'll be discussing in this chapter. Whatever else they are doing, the home-based professionals are changing the way Americans are looking at work and the workplace.

THE HOME BASED BUSINESS VS. THE TRADITIONAL BUSINESS

The latest force for the growth of home based businesses came in the early 1990s as America went through a new kind of recession. Unlike other business slowdowns, in which "blue collar" workers were most affected, this recession touched middle and upper management as well. Tens of thousands of "white collar" people were put out of work.

Since many companies in a particular industry were likewise affected, there weren't enough jobs available to take up the slack for management people. This was something totally new for people born after World War II and it was a shock.

Only two choices were left for "white collar" workers: moving to a new industry, which meant changing careers, or setting up their own business. At the same time, the computer, the fax and other electronics, started to make home-based business a very attractive alternative. The growth of these businesses continues at a rapid pace.

What Goes Around Comes Around

Home based businesses have been on the American scene ever since the Pilgrims landed at Plymouth Rock. As recently as the beginning of the century most people worked out of their homes, which were usually farms or ranches. They raised their own food, made what they needed at home, repaired the machines they used at home and took care of their finances on their own.

Today, home-based businesses are making a major comeback. But this time they tend to be efficient, well-run businesses such as consulting firms, advertising services, publishing companies, bed and breakfast inns, photography, free-lance writing businesses and event-planning services, to mention just a few.

It's a Business Trend to Be Taken Seriously

For some people working at home is definitely no substitute for working in a large office. They consider it a halfhearted, dead-end, lonely attempt to make ends meet while they look and hope for a "real" job to come along.

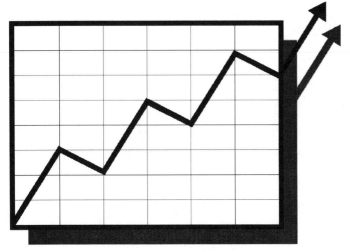

The truth of the matter is that plenty of energetic men and women have discovered that they can make as good a living as they had in a corporate job and even increase their take home pay as a self-employed person. As an extra benefit, they avoid costly commuting time, energy consuming office politics, sometimes unreasonable bosses, and gain more time with the family.

The constantly rising cost of housing forces many people to live far way from their jobs. Two hour commutes each way has become acceptable for many people. Now, it has become obvious that many jobs, usually done in an office, can be performed just as well at home - anywhere a telephone line can reach. Many of these same jobs can be done by individuals or small businesses. Even large companies have encouraged employees to go "out on their own" and operate right out of their homes.

According to the National Center for Policy Analysis, 70 percent of home-based businesses are run by women, in part because of the expanding number of mothers who prefer to stay at home to raise their children while having a career.

Retirees form another large group of likely home office workers. The downsizing of American business has forced many employees to take early retirement from companies that are anxious to cut their payrolls. Then there are large numbers of people in their fifties and early sixties, retired before their time, who aren't satisfied to sit back and watch the world roll by. They have the energy and drive to run their own companies. And, the logical and most economical place to work is in their own homes.

ADVANTAGES OF A HOME BASED BUSINESS

There are a great number of advantages of having a home based business. The list is as varied as the number of people who work at home. Some are:

1. **TIME SAVINGS:** Getting to work is never a problem - neither rain, nor snow, nor dark of night, can keep a home office worker from getting the job done. It's no problem to arrive at the office early and stay late. You can turn on the radio, or even the TV, listen to music while you work, without any complaints.

2. **WORK WITHIN YOUR OWN TIME FRAME:** Do you want to get up and work at midnight, or start to work at 7:00 in the evening? You can come and go as you please. This is the kind of time shifting you can enjoy easily when you run your business out of your own home.

3. **COST SAVINGS:** This is one of the biggest single factors why people set up home based businesses, rather then operating out of a conventional office. There are many fiscal savings. Rent is just the beginning. Typical office space can run from $10 per square foot all the way up to $30 depending upon the location. And retail space, in a shopping mall, can begin at $30 per square foot. But in addition to rent savings there are several others:

utilities, parking (a costly factor for many people locating in a downtown building), restaurant lunches, car expenses or train, bus or subway costs.

4. **TAX SAVINGS:** A home based business offers distinct tax advantages. You can deduct a portion of your mortgage, including interest on the mortgage at tax time. Your home office can be located in your basement, den, study, garage or a spare bedroom. Or, it could include a number of these spaces in your home. But you must use the space just for your business. One important note: KEEP TRACK OF ALL YOUR EXPENSES AND SAVE YOUR RECEIPTS FOR TAX PURPOSES.

5. **DECORATING AND MAINTENANCE:** Many people who rent office space  discover that the landlord will not handle redecoration or fix-up costs. They are confronted with "lease hold improvements," added expenses at their new location. By operating out of one's home numerous costly maintenance expenses can be avoided.

6. **SET YOUR OWN DRESS CODE:** Want to wear Blue Jeans to work? Is it a hot day and you want to wear shorts? Too early to change out of your PJ's? If your answer is YES, then put your formal business outfits in mothballs, except for client meeting attire. If, on the other hand you want to wear a tux or a ball  gown to your home office you won't be out of place.

DISADVANTAGES OF HAVING A HOME BASED BUSINESS

For as many advantages there are to having a Home Office Business, there are an equal number of disadvantages. These include:

1. **<u>A BUSINESS AWAY FROM HOME</u>:** It is truly a business place, all business with no home interruptions. Distractions from the significant other, the children, the personal telephone calls and visits from neighbors stay safely at home.

2. **<u>A HOME AWAY FROM HOME</u>:** Everyone needs diversity. This is true for all members of a family. Many people cannot be with their families 24 hours a day. It has nothing to do with love and caring but simply that some people need their own space for some part of the day. So, for some, a home office could introduce troublesome interpersonal pressures that don't arise when business is separated from personal life.

3. **<u>BUSINESS PEOPLE NEED BUSINESS PEOPLE</u>:** Operating a business out of a standard business setting provides the opportunity to come in daily contact with other business people. In friendly discussions and "brain storming." this contact can often lead to valuable ideas, suggestions and support for one's business.

4. **<u>CREATING THE BUSINESS IMAGE</u>:** Having a standard business setting location conveys the message that you are serious factor in the market at a permanent business location. It never hurts to show customers, clients and suppliers that yours is a successful enterprise. There is a certain prestige reflected on a businessperson who presents a prosperous appearance.

5. **<u>LACK OF ACCESSIBILITY</u>:** Having your business in a conventional business location usually means you will probably be close to the local office supply store and other suppliers. It means you will have ample parking for customers and any employees.

Further, it you have a business that is dependent on pick-up and deliveries by UPS, Federal Express, U.S. Mail and suppliers, then operating out of your home can be a cause for concern since your home may not always be accessible.

6. **FAMILY AND NEIGHBOR HARMONY:** Having a home-based business can lead to problems not only with one's own family but with neighbors and friends. Frequently family members feel their own sense of  privacy is destroyed. Or the wife and children simply may be upset at having a business mixed in with their lives. Likewise, for neighbors, a home based business may bring forth feelings of envy, jealousy, sense that their neighborhood is being converted to a commercial area, thus affecting their real estate values, or they may feel their own privacy is being invaded.

HOME OFFICE BASICS

All your life, your home has been a place to - well, come home to. As a student, you got up, ate breakfast, and went to class. You did your work and then came home. When you went into the work force, you followed pretty much the same routine. When it comes to working at home, you don't usually associate your living room or spare bedroom with a workplace.

What it takes is very simple and not too expensive. First, you need a suitable workspace that is comfortable, well lit and with plenty of room for equipment and files.

According to your needs you may have to start with, or will be satisfied with, a small corner of a room and a typewriter on a folding card table. But the possibilities for today's home-based office can match anything you can think of in layout, design and technology. There are furniture, lighting, and fabric designs intended specially for offices that must make the most of every inch of space. The newest developments in home-office furniture have an impact on both your personal comfort and professional image. Setting up your office right means investing in the right equipment from copiers to telephones, fax machines to computers.

Margaret expects to retire in only a few years from her job with a major food corporation. She has gotten an early start with a party catering service that runs right out of her own kitchen.

Wesley, a Certified Public Accountant who took early retirement keeps quite busy with his tax and financial advisory business. Interestingly enough his business is such that most of his work takes place in his clients' offices, so the subject of Wesley's office space rarely comes up.

Setting Up for Business

It's important to choose the right office location within the home, but it's equally important to design the right setup for the business functions you will have to perform.

If you will be selling by mail you'll need space to store, package and wrap items for shipping. When choosing the area for your office notice the sunlight patterns. Morning sunlight hitting your computer screen can make work impossible. Incidentally, standard bulb light fixtures are generally preferred for room lighting and halogen desk lamps for task lighting.

Keeping Comfortable and Efficient

If possible, it is best to work in a room with a door and to establish firm rules about visiting. It's especially important to have it understood that you cannot drop work and run out to perform an errand during business hours. Remember, even if your work space is merely a card table in a corner of a recreation room it's your office and must be treated as such if you're to get your work done and keep your business growing.

An important consideration is having a well-designed desk, chair, and filing system. It's worth taking a fair amount of time with these choices because they can make a real difference in your day-to-day business effectiveness. You've heard about all those painful joint and nerve conditions that office workers can suffer from. Well, you'll be working longer hours than the average office worker but still in roughly the same situation.

Furnish for Comfort and Convenience

Your office chair should be chosen for long term support, so it should offer height and back adjustments. The more prongs on chair's base the more

stable it will be, especially if you like to wheel between desk and file cabinets. It's also a good idea, if you have a rug, to get a plastic rug protector or a remnant to cover any parts of your office that will get extra wear.

If possible, position your desk in a space that has natural light. Add soft overhead bulbs and strong task lighting, (halogen is warm and inexpensive). If you're using a computer, situate your monitor to reduce the kind of eye strain, which glare from windows or other reflective surfaces may cause.

If you have enough room, consider horizontal file cabinets. They hold legal-size file folders and allow for easier access than vertical cabinets. And make sure you position the cabinets so you can reach vital information without racing across the room.

Handling Business Visitors

You may need a waiting area. You may want a completely private place for meetings with customers. If, for example, you're setting up a crafts business you'll need a studio where you can attractively display your output.

If you want customers to come to your home, you'll have to design your office and workspaces to accommodate them while not disturbing the normal operations of your house. The best way to do this is to spend some time observing the activities of the other family members. Where do the children usually play? How does your husband or wife conduct his or her activities during the day? When and how do members of the family come and go, through which rooms? Listen for the noise tendencies in the house and outside. You can't get much done over the telephone if there are constant noises coming from the street or from children at play.

If you don't want business visitors coming into your home on a regular basis or at certain times, there are a few options you can try: Rent a conference room or office space just for the time you need it. These professional suites are offered by office buildings or leasing services. You'll find them listed in the Yellow Pages.

Another idea is to join a club which has facilities for meetings and entertaining clients or potential clients.

Conduct business as much as possible by fax, telephone or mail. Use a courier service to pick up and deliver materials. Today people expect to work at a distance easily and conveniently. You could work by telephone, and send documents by fax to a client for months without knowing that he works out of his home office.

Tell the World

Working out of your home doesn't mean working at a disadvantage. Although as a home-based business you'll be competing against larger and better established firms, you will still be known and valued by the quality of the work you do, and by the face you present to your public. You can be just as impressive as your bigger competition in some important ways.

Choose a company name that conveys what you do with strength and distinction. For example, United Consumers Club, a consumer buying club has a name that tells exactly what their business is and indicates they offer a special consumer benefit. In Denver, The Secreteam company's clever name invites interest in their word processing, transcribing, desktop publishing and other office support services.

In Sonoma California, The Screen Machine is a mobile service business specializing in making and repairing window screens. A good name is a good start for any business.

Incidentally, all of these companies are run out of their owners' homes.

After you settle on a name you'll want to project a stylish look through your company logo and the look and feel of your business cards, stationery and business brochures. It's important that these should all look attractive and professional because they are, in many cases, the first impression  customers get of your organization and abilities. It's worthwhile to get in touch with an artist or graphic designer (there are plenty who work out of their homes too!) and get a first class set of images for your company.

Where Do Nice Guys Finish?

Take the case of Al Riggins, a representative for an industrial computer software firm, who decided he didn't need a large office. His selling was mostly through personal contact, over the phone, or in his clients' or prospects' offices. He set aside part of a guest room for his work, installed separate business phone lines, and bought a fax machine and a computer.

In the beginning things went fine. Al would get out of bed - an hour later than when he had gone to his office. For several hours, he made phone contacts, starting with his East coast clients and working across the country. Then he would do his computer work, preparing estimates, proposals and billing.

But eventually a problem arose. Al's friends, neighbors, and even former co-workers started dropping in for visits. Being friendly, Al at first welcomed the sociability. But soon, the time Al had set aside for calling and preparing projects began to be displaced by social phone calls and unexpected visitors.

At first Al accepted the phone calls and visits as welcome breaks in his work day. He soon realized that something would have to change. The sad fact is that Al was such a nice, friendly guy he was unable to make the necessary changes. A few months later he was back in an office but he still hoped to realize his dream of working out of his home.

What could Al have done? He could have stopped the interruptions at the beginning. Unfortunately Al was new at the home office business and didn't see the problem coming. In his old job he was used to having a buffer, in the form of a secretary, who constantly screened calls and visitors. It was now up to Al to be strict with social callers and that was a skill he had to learn.

A Home Office is Not a Prison

Al's example is only one of the downsides of working at home. Emotional problems are among the most critical because they concern how you handle working alone, how you get yourself to work against deadlines, or how you resist the urge to constantly overwork.

One of the biggest blocks to people who must be self-starters is lack of concentration. Working at home demands independence and self-discipline, two qualities that may not be quite as important when you are working for a salary in an office. But when you are on your own, no two ways about it, you've got to have them.

Get Out of the House

Working at home doesn't mean never leaving home base. When a prominent television script writer, who usually works at home, has a major project, he takes off to a cabin, far from Los Angeles and his family, in order to write without distractions.

Only a short time ago I received an agitated phone call from another friend who had quit his job and started working full time at home. After cruising through the first three months, suddenly he was feeling solitary and shakily upset. Worst of all, he wasn't able to manage his time and get his work done on schedule.

"There are many days,@ he told me, Awhen I find myself working into the early hours. Next morning I come right downstairs to my office, and get right back to work. But some days, I may not even leave the house. I can spend the whole day working in my robe. I start to feel isolated and uncomfortable. I don't want to go back to an office job, but I'm having difficulty managing by myself.@

There was nothing unusual about my friend's experiences. When the office is only footsteps away, it's always too easy to slip into the office to get some details out of the way before breakfast, and get lost in the serious need to complete some jobs.

What frequently happens is that you never Ahave the need or opportunity@ to get out of the office. In that way, some people turn their house into a jail, a lonely place, away from outside friendships and contacts that mean so much in a normal life.

This is the kind of problem that often arises for self-employed people who must take on the tasks that were handled by others in their previous offices. Suddenly they become their company's secretary, cashier, marketing expert and salesperson. They do whatever needs to be done, because they have to, at least until they grow large enough to afford to hire help.

The Secret is Organization

There are ways for even the busiest self-employed people to cut down the time they spend isolated in the office, at home. Here are a few suggestions to make more time to enjoy all the good things in life you're working so hard to achieve:

Keep a careful record of your projects. Note down the time it takes to complete each of your activities. Then, after a week or two, look over the list. Consider - did you waste time on "busy work" - unimportant tasks you could have done without? Were all your phone calls necessary? Are you setting up barriers for yourself by spending time on one new business idea after another - without completing projects already scheduled? Eliminate such time-wasting activities, and you'll shorten your work day.

If you feel the pressure of too much work and you can see your way clear to hiring a full or part-time assistant. High school students, women who want to work while their children are in school, and retirees often are interested in part time work for very little money. They either want to gain job skills or keep busy. Even an inexpensive helper will reduce your work load, and help you to maintain a more business-like attitude.

The Challenge is Isolation

There are various ways home workers can challenge feelings of solitude and loneliness, if they occur. Here are a few suggestions:

 N Resolve to have business lunches or even dinners at least a few times a week. Contact your competitors. You will not only get out of the house, you will also be building a system of contacts with whom you can share common interests.

N Join trade and professional organizations. Their meetings, seminars, and dinners are ideal places to meet, greet, be seen and pick up the latest business news. In a slightly different way and just for relaxation join a club that involves a hobby; woodworking, for instance, or photography. In one of these groups, away from usual problems, it will be easier to relax. You may even find a new interest that could lead you into a profitable business some day.

❖ Take courses at your local university or trade school. Business connected or just interesting, it's always enjoyable to learn things and meet new people.

❖ Arrange business calls to take you out of the house fairly frequently. Even if it takes a little more effort, it's always a good idea to go out and visit with your clients or prospects face to face.

❖ Make good use of the time you spend away from work. Keep up your social contacts and go out and meet with new people. Consider scheduling free time for yourself during the day. Make sure you stick to the timetable by making appointments to meet others for lunch, tennis, golf, even walking. You might want to get a dog, so that you'll have the perfect excuse to take a daily walk. There are plenty of dog walkers in every community. Anything that will get you out of the house and preferably in contact with other people is good.

While you may feel uneasy about the interruption to your day at first, eventually you'll find that you will accomplish more when you take a break than you do when you work nonstop to exhaustion from morning till night. And, remember the old adage - haste makes waste. Take the time to do the job right the first time.

Licenses, Permits, Taxes and Zoning Regulations

Before you start to work in your home office there are a few items that you had better look into. First, you should check out what your community requires concerning licenses, permits and zoning regulations for the business you're planning. In most cases regulations will offer no problems, and those that do will be easy to take care of.

Some Yellow Pages telephone books have a special section under Agovernment offices@ devoted to small business. It may not be immediately clear which agency can answer your questions. Try one that sounds logical and if it doesn't have the information you need, the people there can direct you to an office that will help.

Check In To Any Special Taxes.

Contact your city or town hall or the appropriate regulatory agency for information about any occupational license you may need. For example, if you intend to make or distribute food you may need approval from the local health department. Don't ignore this kind of requirement. You don't want to grow to success and suddenly find that the city can close you down because of a trivial technicality.

Such businesses as child-care services may also require special licensing. Find out before you jump in.

If there is a sales tax to be collected, make sure you contact the proper authorities to determine what your responsibilities are. Too many small businesses have been hit years after they started with tax bills they didn't know they owed.

Zoning

Zoning regulations may be a little trickier. They tend to concentrate on the impact of particular activities. They are often called Anuisance laws@ by the business people who have to abide by them. But you must realize that they are designed to protect neighborhoods from annoying noise, traffic, odors, and other things that would tend to bother people where they live.

In some places, especially rural or far suburban areas, there's usually nothing to worry about. In more heavily populated areas, however, there are often special conditions in the zoning laws concerning home occupations. A great deal depends on the nature of your home-based business, the neighborhood you live in, and local and state ordinances.

Keep Your Community Happy

If there is any chance that your business activities are going to disturb your community, or violate the zoning requirements, you may be looking for trouble from the neighbors and from the municipality. If large trucks will be delivering merchandise to your garage, or if the business will attract large numbers of cars to regularly park on your street, you will probably be hearing from your neighbors, the police or city hall. The options will then be to straighten out the situation, move the business or leave the neighborhood.

It is really up to you to determine what regulations apply to your business. It is unlikely that you will need any zoning approval if you are just operating a simple office from one of your spare rooms. But if you go one step further, like setting up a small assembly line to make fishing lures, you should still make sure that you are not violating any local zoning regulations. Obviously, using common sense will keep you out of trouble.

Another area that should be checked out is signage. There may be all kinds of limits on the signs you can put up on your property. Use good judgment and check out the laws that apply.

There Are Still Some Silly Laws on the Books

Don't be surprised if the laws in your locality are outdated. It's a common experience. Not long ago, within the city limits of one of our major cities, it was illegal to use electrical equipment in a home occupation. That meant no calculators, no typewriters, no computers. After complaints from small business people the city council changed the ordinances to be more helpful to home work. If you run up against similar old-fashioned barriers to your business, it's possible for you or, better still, a group of like-minded people to activate zoning changes in your city.

Zoning boards are made up of your neighbors and local business people, and it is likely they are unaware of problems caused by outdated zoning ordinances. If you are frustrated by your city's zoning code, get to know these people, attend some meetings, and propose that the laws be changed.

The Personal Computer Revolution

Computers to the Rescue

The growth of home-based-business could not have happened so fast, inexpensively or efficiently without the introduction of low-cost micro computers. The economical computer has made it possible to do so many business tasks at home, so much better and faster than ever before.

Personal computers have made it possible for one man or woman to do the work of two or three people. Specialized software is like having a consultant at your side. Fax machines and modems can keep you in constant and substantial contact with your clients and suppliers. There are very few things a standard office can offer that you can't match at home, these days, with comparatively inexpensive business equipment. You can even buy a personal water cooler if that will help you over the psychological hump.

Manufacturers have recognized the value of the home-based business market; which happens to be about $20 billion a year! So naturally each manufacturer is going to do everything it can to make their line the most attractive to home office buyers. Each year, the newest equipment is becoming more compact and offers more and more helpful features. Just as important, prices keep falling so that a fully equipped computer can be

thousands of dollars cheaper than it was just a few years ago; and fax machines, hundreds less.

How the Telephone Has Become Your Partner

If any one ingredient in the office mix has made the home office as effective as it is today, it has got to be the telephone. The fax and computer modem are directly dependent on the telephone network that reaches into almost every home and every business in the world.

The basic value of your telephone is enhanced by such moderately priced services as call waiting, 800 numbers, and call forwarding. You can use all these special services to make it easier for your customers to do business with you. One wonderful telephone innovation is "Voice Mail." Here you can administer your home office as if it is a "multi-employee" facility. You can receive your messages away from your office and leave specific messages for people you are expecting to call.

The answering machine and telephone company answering services enable a one-person operation to survive without missing important calls. And the star of them all is the cellular telephone, which makes it possible to call and receive telephone calls almost anywhere. Home office or main office, if you are available and willing to answer the phone any time during or after the business day, you've got a leg up on the competition.

The Financial Picture

Independent Contractors

Home office workers are usually paid as independent contractors. This means that you are considered a kind of company of your own and are financially entirely responsible for yourself.

Self-Employment Tax

There are benefits and disadvantages in being an independent contractor. The most important requirement, as far as the government is concerned, is that you'll be responsible for your own taxes, especially the ASelf-Employment Tax@ which is really your Social Security tax.

Business Expense Deductions

A major financial benefit from Uncle Sam are the business expenses deductions you'll be entitled to under tax law. But, to get the most value at tax time, you will need to keep a record of every business expense item right from the start. You can get more detailed information on what these deductions are call the IRS for their detailed list of business deductions allowed. Remember, there can be changes in the list from year to year.

The Home Office Deduction Benefit

The Home Office Deduction is the most valuable because it generally offers most home workers the most substantial way to reduce their federal taxes. In order to claim this deduction, you must show that your home work space is used regularly and exclusively as your principal place of business.

Home office expenses are deductible mostly based on the percentage of square footage of your home that you use as a workspace. If your home is 1,000 square feet and you use 200 square feet exclusively for workspace you can normally deduct 20% of your total mortgage or rent payments on your tax return.

But, be careful: if you use your workspace for any other purpose than work, you cannot deduct any of these expenses. For example, working on the kitchen table is a bad idea, as far as tax deductions go, unless you really don't have any choice.

The last time we looked, there were some 23 possible tax deductions for a home office. To make sure you don't miss any, get a copy of IRS Publication 587, ABusiness Use of the Home.@ It is available free by phone or from an IRS office and is updated annually, so if you don't use the latest year's publication you may be missing a valuable deduction.

Some Handy Home Office Deduction Guidelines

Here are a few explanations that should help clear up questions you may have about the home office deduction on your federal income tax return. **Before applying these deductions, be sure to check with an accountant for recent tax changes.**

1. The term "home office deduction" does not apply to all expenses you accumulate while running a business from your home. The term applies only to a portion of your normal household costs for things like electricity, heating, air conditioning, water, real estate taxes, mortgage interest and depreciation on the business portion of your home.

2. If you are the only owner of your business, you should use Schedule C to record all income and expenses related to that business. You figure the net profit or loss from the business on Schedule C, then transfer the figure to Form 1040. But you must also include a copy of Schedule C with your tax return.

3. Direct costs of doing business such as advertising expense, cost of office supplies (paper, ribbons, diskettes, etc.), professional fees (for instance legal services), transportation and business-related dues for example, are fully deductible business expenses whether or not you choose to take the home office deduction. Check with the IRS or an accountant to be sure you are getting all the deductions you are entitled to.

4. The percentage of household maintenance costs you may deduct is based on the percentage of your home used for business. If you use 10 percent of your home for business you may deduct up to 10% of allowable household expenses. The amount you can declare for depreciation is determined by both the percent of space used for business and your "basis" (original cost plus improvements, minus value of the land your house sits on).

5. The amount you take as a home office deduction may not exceed your income from the business. But, if direct business expenses exceed your income from the business you can declare a business loss on Schedule C and subtract that loss from any other income you report on Schedule 1040.

6. Basic telephone line charges (the fee you pay to have the phone in the house) are not deductible unless you have a separate business phone. You can, however, deduct long distance charges connected with your business even if you have only one phone line in the house, but you must keep records to make clear the reasons for such charges.

7. If you use a computer more than 50% of the time in your home business you can deduct a percentage of your computer costs equal to the percentage of time you use the computer for business. In other words if you use the computer 75% of the time for business, and you have spent $5,000 on computer equipment during the year, you can deduct $3,750 (75% of that particular expense.) The deduction cannot exceed your income from the business, and is limited to a $10,000 maximum.

To prove the business use of a computer that is not used exclusively for business, you must keep an accurate log showing how often the computer was utilized for business and how often for personal use.

Are You Ready to Work Home Alone – SELF QUIZ

If there are still any doubts in your mind as to whether you would be happy and successful working out of your home, we've created some questions that might help you decide. These are all intended to help you look into your own attitudes to determine if your personality and outlook fit you to be a home-based worker.

1. **If you work in an office, are you an early morning or an after 5 o'clock person? In other words do you tend to get more done when no one else is in the office?**

If you work better when you are alone you should be able to work at home effectively and enjoyably.

2. **How well do you concentrate on the task at hand? Are you easily distracted from important jobs to less important things?**

It's always important to recognize which tasks are the real bread and butter of your livelihood and to stick to them no matter what. As an individual, on your own, it's up to you to keep at the important jobs until they are finished and not be distracted to less important tasks.

3. **Do you currently set and achieve goals you set for yourself?**

Just like you will have to set up a schedule to make sure everything gets done, you will succeed in business if you can set some milestones to which

---

to work towards. As the saying goes: The shortest distance between two points is a straight line. If you don't know where you are going, you may never get there. Setting goals is very important to succeeding in small business.

4. Do you get impatient and feel overwhelmed when your desk is loaded with a pile of jobs to do?

Working at home can be a comfortable, satisfying experience, but it won't often offer the possibility of concentrating on one job at a time. If you have become accustomed to having an efficient secretary to keep your work in order, that's a luxury you can probably forget. When you work out of a home office, you have to be ready to accept a pretty mixed-up schedule.

5. If you have a young family, are you able to block out the sounds of television and children playing while you concentrate on the work at hand? Do you really believe your home with all its distractions can serve as a place of business?

It's critical to keep your home-based business on a serious foundation. Concentration on the job despite distractions is extremely important. One suggestion would be to create a place or folder or drawer where you can keep all your work stuff together. When you sit with the folder or at the desk you will only perform work related tasks, no others. If you can, try not to use the same space for "living" as you do for "working".

6. Do you need someone else to bounce your ideas off of before you are sure that you're right?

Everyone needs self confidence, and that's especially true of people who work at home. It's always good to have others you can consult with, friends or business associates, but there will always be plenty of quick decisions you'll have to make strictly on your own.

7. Are you capable of self criticism? Can you view your actions open-mindedly and honestly?

Too many people aren't able to look at their situations impartially. That's why there are so many helping professions. But, in a business situation, where judgments must be made daily you have to be able to rely on yourself to make good decisions on a regular basis. In running a home-based business, the more you can rely on yourself, the more likely you will be successful.

8. Can you "punch off the clock" at the end of the day?

It is not good for your business or personal life to "live" your business. You must be able to concentrate on family or personal time when it is appropriate. Many people who start businesses at home do not make enough time for family and therefore it causes problems within the family structure. You may need more hours to get the business off the ground, but remember to balance both personal and business lives.

9. Are you able to place a time limit on telephone calls from friends or salespeople during the business day?

It's all too easy to get sidetracked from your main business by social calls and people trying to sell you things; from mutual funds to new siding for your home. Some callers can be entertaining and you haven't taken a vow of silence. But when you should be able to quickly say that you don't have time to talk or you are not interested in what's being sold and don't want to waste the salesperson's time. It isn't necessary to hurt others' feelings but if you can't turn off these distractions you're at a disadvantage in running your business.

10. Can you work on a wide variety of different tasks during the day?

There are some people who can juggle a dozen jobs at once. If you are one of these, and you feel confident of being able to handle numerous details on multiple tasks when the problem arises, as it no doubt will, you will probably make a great home-office worker.

11. Are you able to learn about a variety of tasks, even though it isn't what you like to do?

Being in business for yourself means that many times you have to manage a task that you wouldn't normally do. For example, you may need to be in charge of your own bookkeeping, taxes, insurance and other important tasks. You need to be able to find the answers you need to make sure you

are in compliance with government agencies and that your books are in order.

Even though you may miss the extra benefits that a corporate job offers - such as health care, insurance, paid vacations and sick days, you do get the chance to increase your income. Employers earn a profit on their workers and that's where the money comes from to pay for all those corporate extras. So, in fact, when you get to keep it all (less taxes of course) you can afford to pay for many corporate goodies for yourself.

A Major Change

Working at home changes the standards. You're up in the morning and at work after a very short walk to your office. There's no boss to tell you what to do, except that small voice inside your head that says, Aget going, get earning.@ There are no dress codes - you can wear anything you want. In your home office it's just you, the phone, the fax and your computer.

At the start you may just need a small corner of a room and a computer on a card table. However, as your business grows, you will have to invest in equipment - from computers to copiers to telephones and fax machines that will help you maintain a professional operation without more paid help.

Unpaid Help

If you're used to working in a corporate office environment you'll have to learn how to handle your own communications; and scheduling. However, there are plenty of computer programs that can do a pretty good job of helping manage your record keeping and communications.

Personal computers have made it possible for one man or woman to do the work of two or three people. Specialized software is available that's like having an expert and a secretary at your side. Electronic communications can now keep you in regular contact with your clients and suppliers and cellular telephones keep you available whenever needed. There are very few things a standard office can offer that you can't match at home these days with relatively inexpensive business equipment. In fact many stores, these days, offer long term, interest free payment programs for the electronic equipment you'll need.

It's All Up To You

There can be times when working at home can feel lonely. However, there are some things you can do to avoid feeling isolated. Have business lunches or even dinners at least a few times a week. Join trade and professional organizations. Arrange business calls to take you out of the house fairly often.

As far as taxes and regulations are concerned, it's up to you to determine which apply to your operation. Failure to satisfy governmental agencies could result in penalties, a business stoppage, even the annoyance of having to move.

Working at home demands independence and self-discipline - two qualities that may not be quite as important when you are working for a salary in an office. But when you are on your own, no two ways about it, you've got to have them.

WORKING WITH YOUR SPOUSE

Many people dream of spending more time with their spouse and then decide that a business together would be a perfect fit. Although this may seem like a good idea in the beginning it is important to manage each person's expectations. Here are some suggestions for success when starting a business with your spouse:

Identify Role & Responsibilities

In any partnership, it is necessary to divide the duties up between each partner. Who will be responsible for the accounting, sales, marketing, customer service, and order fulfillment? Many people chose to separate tasks by functionality where one person handles all the customer contact, sales, marketing and customer services while the other partner handles the "back office" jobs, including accounting, taxes, invoicing, inventory and fulfillment. In identifying what role each spouse should play, look at each other's strengths and weaknesses.

Define a Process to Resolve Disagreements

While good communication is mandatory for any partnership to work well, it is also important to be able to communicate issues within the business. Normally married couples have learned to discuss different views in parenting and living together, now you need a process to discuss business matters. Couples who have difficulty compromising on simple issues, such as deciding what fax machine to buy, will have a lot of trouble determining future direction of the company. One way to deal with on-going issues is to have a set time to meet and discuss issues. For example, every Friday afternoon you can meet together and get all the open issues out in the open. Resolutions can be determined and the company can continue to move forward. When Fred DeLuca from Subway started his first sandwich shop, he and his partner met every Monday night to discuss everything that was going "right" and everything that needed attention. In doing this on a continuing basis, both partners were always informed. It worked well then and continues to work well for the company now.

Discuss Child-Care Needs

Even though you will both be home full-time, you still need to discuss child-care. If you have small children, there may be too many distractions to have both the business and the children at home. As a couple, you must make a decision as to what the kids will do when you are conducting business. If they are too small to understand that they can not talk to you when you are on the phone, it may be best to place them in a place outside your home to make sure you can get you business up and running smoothly.

Room for Everyone To Work

Make sure both of you have enough adequate room to perform your work functions. If one person is selling to customers on the phone and the other person is shipping products out, there may need to be two rooms for your home office. If space is tight, shipping may be able to be handled in the kitchen or garage, while the sales calls may need to be made in the second bedroom or den. Be sure to understand the needs of each partner. One may need silence and privacy and one may need large open spaces.

Agree on How to Get Out

Any good business plan or partnership agreement contemplates the option for one person to get out of the business. Talk about exit strategies with your partner. Each of you will have different expectations about the business. One of the biggest reasons for failure of a partnership is a life changing event with one of the partners, including death of family member, divorce, financial difficulty or other life changing event. One spouse may want to leave the business to pursue a life-long dream or to focus on raising children. If you talk about these sensitive issues in the beginning of your home-based business, you can plan for them much more easily.

PROTECTING YOURSELF FROM THE HOME BUSINESS "SCAM"

While there are many legitimate home based businesses, it is important to be wary of some before you invest your time and money. The Better Business Bureau receives more questions about home based business opportunities than any other type of business. As a matter of fact, the BBB received more than 450,000 inquiries in 2001.

Here is a list of things to remember when looking at a home based business opportunity.

1. Evaluate your skills and abilities. Does the business opportunity match your skills and work desires? If you have been a salesperson for many years will you be happy working at home on the computer without human interaction everyday?

2. Does the market want the product? Will you be working with something that you and your contacts will be excited about?

3. Normally legitimate businesses will wait for you to seek them out. They are interested in the kind of representative that you will make of their company. Typically they will not spam your email account or contact you through direct mail. Some will advertise in magazines like Entrepreneur or Inc or be found in books with good credentials. Look also for information on their websites.

4. Research them online. Look for information on their history and the experience of other people that have worked with them.

5. Be wary of deals that look too good to be true. Many have large promises that can not be fulfilled.

6. Be cautious if you feel pressured to make a decision quickly. Legitimate companies will help you work through your questions and respond to you accordingly.

7. Contact the Better Business Bureau to see there has been any complaints against the company.

8. Check out the training and support that they give to the other operators. Does it match with the support you need to run a successful company?

9. You should not have to "pay" for your job. One of the most common scam techniques will ask you to pay up front for services.

10. Is the company listed in the telephone directory? Watch for companies that only list a Post Office Box address. Check these online

with www.switchboard.com.

11. Visit the headquarters, if you can. Check out the financial strength of the company.

Choosing a business opportunity is an investment. You wouldn't necessarily put money into a company that you didn't think would pay you back, would you? You need to use the same caution in looking and investing in a business opportunity.

Ongoing Help for Home Workers

Associations and Agencies

Following are some of the organizations that can be helpful to you as you pursue your career in your home office. For further help there are also plenty of books with good ideas on being able to work more effectively.

American Home Business Association
4505 South Wasatch Blvd, #140
Salt Lake City, UT 84124
800-664-2422
www.homebusiness.com

American Home Business Association is a national association offering essential and innovative benefits and services dedicated to supporting the needs of home business, small business and entrepreneurs.

Home Based Working Moms
PO Box 500164
Austin, TX 78750
512-266-0900
hbwm@hbwm.com

The goal of Home Based Working Moms is to help moms create lifestyles that enable them more freedom and flexibility to truly enjoy their family and their life.

International Franchise Association (IFA)
1350 New York Avenue NW, Suite 900
Washington, DC 20005
(202) 628-8000
www.franchise.org

The IFA has a membership of 700 businesses that offer franchise opportunities (less than a third of 2,600 plus that do so).

Call or write for information on selecting and investigating a franchise. The ASell Franchise Opportunities Guide,@ which lists thousands of franchises, is $21. Call (800) 543-1038.

Small Office Home Office America
PO Box 941
Hurst, TX 76053-0941
www.soho.org

SOHO America exists to provide you with a virtual community where you can interact with other small-office/home-office professionals—people like you—who are facing the day-to-day challenges, the risks and rewards, of running a SOHO business. With your participation, we will build an interactive community—a global small town—where our citizens can exchange ideas and network with their peers. Here at SOHO Online, you will find the knowledge, resources and inspiration you need to succeed.

In this chapter you have learned:

1. *The home office offers many benefits and can provide a satisfying experience.*
2. *You are the boss; in business for yourself and by yourself.*
3. *The home office offers just about the best opportunity for getting started in your own business with the smallest amount of capital and the lowest overhead.*

Chapter 5

Franchising a Business

How to be in business for yourself, not by yourself.

The business pages of newspapers are full of success stories. All about people who got an idea, got financial backing and started their own enterprises. It's an old story, yet always new and fascinating, especially to people who have decided it's time to stop working for a boss and start working for themselves, taking a chance for independence.

Take caution not to overlook the other stories farther down the page announcing business failures, i.e. bankruptcies. These people devoted money and effort to create businesses but, for one reason or another, couldn't make a go of it. The news articles hardly ever tell you the real reasons businesses flop--inexperience, lack of knowledge of the market they put themselves in, and lack of understanding basic merchandising principles. It's a sad story, but one you don't have to repeat. There is a way to get the training and continuing guidance that can remove many of the uncertainties of starting and operating a business.

In this chapter you will learn:

1. *What is franchising?*
2. *What are the different types of franchises?*
3. *How a franchise works.*
4. *Why companies franchise?*
5. *How to rate a franchise before you buy.*
6. *What to expect from your franchisor?*
7. *Where do you go for help with franchise questions?*

Take the example of John and Mary Samples, a two-income family in their 40s. John was a draftsman, had a pretty good job and had been with his company for fifteen years. Mary was a librarian, worked for the city and had excellent job security. They had two children and an average income. About ten years ago they got the itch, they wanted to start an enterprise of their own.

Neither of these people had the kind of background giving them any specialized know-how for a venture that would provide them a better income or a better life than they already had.

John and Mary had a dream; they talked for years about owning a restaurant. They went to the library and took out a stack of books on small business in general, and restaurants in particular. They discovered a lot of things they never expected pertaining to the pitfalls of running a restaurant. They became aware that restaurant operation was risky--too complicated to give people with their background a good chance at success. It appeared John and Mary were going to have to look for something that would be more in keeping with their experience.

However, Mary had responded to a magazine ad for a restaurant franchise opportunity. The information they received described a complete franchise program for opening and operating a McDonald's restaurant. It promised continuous direction and support from people who were experts in the field. With that kind of help, it looked more like the opportunity the Samples had been searching for. It answered their questions pertaining to  running a business they had never been in and how to make a go of it. Best of all, they discovered the company had a franchise available in their hometown.

They did some research, checked with franchisees and a banker and a lawyer. After a great deal of soul searching they decided to take the plunge. So they invested in their McDonald's franchise, and with the help of some very capable food industry specialists and a lot of hard work, they now have a highly successful restaurant. John and Mary found a business of their own and they had a partner who had as much interest in their success as they did. It turned out to be a winning combination.

Or take the case of Mark Silverstone, a man in his mid-fifties, whose job had been terminated when his employer of 25 years sold the company. Mark and his wife, Emily, decided that it was time they considered a business of their own. They looked into a number of opportunities, but didn't find anything right away that fit in with their experience, money situation or interests.

Then one day they heard about a printing franchise that was available. Mark had always been an amateur photographer and Emily had an interest in the graphic arts. It sounded like a possibility. They contacted the Minuteman Press company and discovered that the franchise agreement being offered included help in finding a location, outfitting the store, advertising, getting supplies and helping the franchisee establish and operate a print shop.

Without any experience in the printing trade, the Silverstone's would have had a hard time making a success of the business. Through the franchise agreement they had all the help they needed to launch and maintain a successful instant print operation. After two years, they're now considering opening a second franchise location.

These are only two examples of the way some people, who have wanted to establish small businesses, have taken advantage of the franchising idea. Franchises enabled the Sample's and the Silverstone's to set up ventures that wouldn't have made sense for them any other way. It's the course many people have used to get valuable professional help in avoiding the countless traps that are always present in starting and running a business.

This chapter is devoted to explaining the concept of franchising, how it works, what it can do for you, what you should look for in establishing a franchising relationship, how to get financing and where you can find and check out good franchising opportunities.

FRANCHISING--A BIG BUSINESS

There are franchise opportunities in almost every industry: fast foods, motels, automobiles and parts, maid service, business services, dry cleaning, home repair, health clubs, industrial supplies, building products, schools, vending operations -- the list is growing every year. Franchising is a business method used by companies that are active in more than 60 different types of business enterprises.

The idea of franchising businesses is not new but its growth in recent years has been outstanding. Government statistics show a tremendous increase in activity in every segment of the franchise economy.

According to a report of the House Government Operations Committee, "The concept of modern franchising, particularly in its evolution since the late 1960s, has opened a remarkable door of opportunity for many of our country's small businessmen and women."

The Commerce Department calls franchising a, "significant part of the U. S. economy", and reports that franchising, "continues to prove its validity as a marketing method adaptable to an ever-widening array of industries and professions while providing immediate identity and recognition for prospective entrepreneurs joining the system."

FRANCHISING TODAY

In 2000, analysts estimate sales of goods and services through franchise companies and their franchisees were $1 trillion in annual U. S. retail sales from 320,000 franchised small businesses in 75 industries. Analysts also estimate that franchising employs more than 18 million people.

The leading association in the field, the International Franchise Association (IFA), was founded by Dunkin Donuts entrepreneur William Rosenberg and other franchise pioneers. And they're only part of the growing franchising universe.

On an average, a new franchise outlet opens in the United States once every 8 minutes around the clock.

The **Top 10 Franchise Industries** from the IFA:
1. Fast Food
2. Retail
3. Service
4. Automotive
5. Restaurants
6. Maintenance
7. Building & Construction
8. Retail – Food
9. Business Services
10. Lodging

Top 10 Franchises for 2004 from Entrepreneur Magazine:
1) Subway – has grown to over 20,000 locations globally
2) Curves for Women – over 7,000 clubs
3) Quizno's Franchise Co. – 3,000 sandwich restaurants
4) 7-Eleven Inc. – 3,300 stores
5) Jackson Hewitt Tax Service – 4,900 tax preparation offices
6) UPS Store – 3,679 old Mail Boxes Etc. franchise
7) McDonald's – 30,000+ restaurants in 119 countries
8) Jani-King – 10,000+ owners in commercial cleaning
9) Dunkin' Donuts – 5,836 doughnut shops
10) Baskin-Robbins USA – 5,105 ice cream shops

The **most interesting** industries include:

- Check Cashing/Financial Services
- Internet Services
- Dating Services
- Home Inspection/Radon & Leak Detection
- Bio-Environmental Services

WHAT IS FRANCHISING?

A franchise or a franchising operation is a legal agreement between the owner (franchisor) of a trademark, service mark, trade name, or advertising symbol and an individual or group (franchisee) wishing to use the trademark, etc in a business. The franchise controls the relationship for conducting business between the two parties.

As a franchisee you use a franchisor's name, special supplies and method of running the business. You pay for the opportunity and operate the way the franchisor tells you. It's your business, but the franchisor controls what you do. The basis of the franchise is an agreement which spells out both the rights and the obligations of you and your franchisor.

The franchisor owns all the trademarks, business methods and supplies that it allows others to use under their contract. The difference between a franchisor and a corporation operating a chain of stores is that the chain store has store managers who are company employees, whereas the franchise operation is owned and managed by self-employed business people.

The franchisor offers the use of a trade name, a store design, standardized operating methods and a protected territory. In addition the franchisor generally accepts the responsibility of keeping a continuing interest in the business of the franchisee.

The franchisor will usually help in such areas as site location, management training, financing, marketing, promotion, and record keeping. The franchisee, in return, agrees to operate under the conditions specified by the franchisor and pays a royalty fee.

For the help and services provided, the franchisee is usually expected to make a capital investment in the business and to pay fees and royalties to the franchisor. In some cases the franchisee agrees to buy all of his products from the franchisor.

A Practical Partnership

The appeal of franchising for the independent business man or woman is that it is a practical and economic means of fulfilling the franchisee's desire for independence with a minimum of risk and investment and maximum opportunities for success through the use of a proven product or service and a proven marketing method. Franchising is a way to be in business for yourself, not by yourself.

A franchising company depends upon the successful operation of franchise outlets to stay in business and build its profits. It needs individuals who are determined to succeed, are willing to learn the business, and have the energy for hard work. A good franchisor can supply the other basics for successful operation of the business.

KINDS OF FRANCHISES

There are two types of franchise systems:

1. **Product or trade name franchising** is the sales relationship between a supplier and dealer in which the dealer has been given some of the identity of the supplier. Automobile dealerships, gasoline service stations and soft drink bottlers are some examples. As you would guess, they require large amounts of financial investment, frequently in the millions of dollars.

2. The field we're most interested in is called **business format franchising** because it deals with opportunities which are within the reach of millions of Americans. Some business format franchise opportunities require investments as small as a few thousand dollars,

and there are many proven franchise businesses that can be started with an initial capital outlay of less than $100,000. Business format franchising accounts for more than 90 percent of the franchise operations in business today.

Business format franchising involves a continuing relationship between the franchisor and its franchisees. That relationship generally involves:

- A product or service
- A trademark
- A marketing system
- Location search and assistance in selecting a business site
- Lease negotiation
- Store design, store development aid and equipment purchasing
- Signage
- Financial assistance in the establishment of the business
- Operating manuals and procedures for standardized procedures and operations
- Initial employee and management training, and continuing management counseling training programs
- Centralized purchasing with the benefit of cost savings
- Advertising and merchandising support.
- Advertising counsel and assistance.
- Access to other franchisees for help or ideas.
- Ongoing assistance and guidance from the franchisor.

The greatest attraction of franchising is that it is one opportunity no one has to miss. Even with its impressive growth over the past decade, franchising is a young system of marketing. Thousands of great opportunities still exist for new franchisees.

HOW A FRANCHISE WORKS

In addition to the original idea for the business, the franchisor provides the identity and in many cases, the product which may have taken years and a good deal of money to establish. The franchisor offers a refined and tested operating system developed through years of experience of headquarters specialists and earlier franchisees.

The franchisee is an independent business owner who pays the franchisor for the right to put this recipe for success to use. As a franchisee you provide all or nearly all the working capital to establish and develop the outlet. There is a continuous financial relationship, usually including a fee paid in advance, plus a continuing royalty based on an established percentage of gross revenues.

Ideally, when you purchase a franchise, you are also purchasing a pre-packaged business. Although you own every part of it, you have a partner, your franchisor, who can insist or sometimes merely suggest how you run your business.

As you start searching for the exact franchise business that would meet your requirements, you will notice the large differences among them; the differences in quality of image, polish and approach. Some franchisors will seem aggressive, organized and professional. Others will seem thorough, plodding and simple. Still others may come across as slick, rigid and too anxious to close the deal.

It's important to keep in mind that your franchise decision has three sides: rational, emotional and financial. The following list can help you organize your thoughts, keep the franchise search logical and help you keep from making a costly mistake.

A Respected Identity

The most important thing a franchisor has to offer is a good name in the industry. The worth of a franchise identity is also the result of the recognition, reputation and goodwill of the franchise organization. People who invest in franchises are looking for a successful image. When you take on a franchise, your franchisor's character, in effect, becomes your identity.

The day you open up for business you cease being just an individual and become someone with something special to offer the public; you'll suddenly become Mr. Burger King...Ms. Nutri/System...or Mr. and Mrs. Dollar Rental.

A Successful Operating System

When you buy a franchise, you are purchasing more than just a trade name; you are also counting on a proven formula for success. So, one of the most important elements of franchising is the simplicity with which the organization's systems and procedures can be transferred to a franchisee.

Some franchisors will offer you a complete "turn-key" outlet; when you are finished with franchise school, you receive the keys to a business in which everything has been set up for a ready-to-run operation. More commonly, a franchisor will provide you with blueprints, manuals, specifications, and training; then it's your responsibility to use your own drive to get the business established.

The franchisor's "how-to" bible is the franchise operating manual. The manual covers everything from accounting procedures to employee supervision. It also spells out standards and policies that all franchisees are expected to follow.

The manual is lent to you for the term of the franchise agreement. When the agreement is ended, you must return the complete manual to the franchisor. This requirement is intended to maintain the condition of secrecy about the franchise system and the know-how it takes to run it. After all, if the formula wasn't a valuable and special secret, why would you pay good money to purchase it?

At the same time, there will be questions that come up as you learn the business and even at times when new situations arise. That's when you'll need continuing help from the franchisee.

Here's what one franchisee has to say:

For Kay Lange, a former data processing consultant, McMaid (a maid service franchise) proved to be the right decision, bringing her more than $750,000 in annual sales. McMaid appealed to Lange because of its training and franchise services. "Ongoing service support is as important as training. The home office has helped me with everything from bulk purchases of equipment and supplies, to a marketing program. Help is just a phone call away."

THE FINANCIAL RELATIONSHIP

How does the franchisor receive payment for the franchisee's use of its identity and operating system? It collects a fee from the franchisee. The most usual franchise fee arrangement consists of three parts:

- The initial payment due on signing of the franchise agreement.
- A continuous royalty, usually charged on the gross revenues of the outlet.
- Royalty or contribution to a co-operative advertising fund.

Usually, a new or small franchise will charge a comparatively small fee. On the other hand, the larger the franchise organization, the more you can expect to pay for the privilege of joining.

WHY DO COMPANIES FRANCHISE?

Franchising provides many benefits to commercial organizations. It allows a company to hold on to its own capital and to establish a distribution system in the shortest possible time. It takes a large amount of money and a long while to develop a major distribution system. Using franchises will save time and money for the franchisor. The franchisee finances part of the system through his or her initial franchise fee. At the same time it is easier and faster to sign up independent men and women who will have a financial interest in the success of the business. Also, franchising cuts marketing costs and reduces fixed overhead expenses like personnel administration for the franchisor.

WHY DO PEOPLE BUY FRANCHISES?

For the new entrepreneur, a franchise often makes it easier to go into business because it cuts down on the amount of capital required and provides a sense of security through the experience and help offered by the franchisor. Buying a franchise allows entrepreneurs to JUMP START their businesses. They can get set up more quickly and not have to spend time figuring out business policies. Franchising is one good way for small business operators to avoid problems that can ruin a business.

Everyone who goes into business for him or herself is going after financial independence and security. Those people who are attracted by the franchise idea expect more from life than the day in day out grind of wage-earning. They have a high level of ambition and a firm belief that the rewards outweigh the risks.

Another important reason for buying a franchise is the desire to be a winner. We all have the ambition for a positive self-image and a good reputation. Franchisees enjoy the identity of success and, through their national tie-in, the industry importance that goes with the business. Many people buy franchises in the hope that some of their franchisor's successful image will rub off on their small business.

The franchisee is like a middle range executive; not a chief operating officer, but more like a top manager who is qualified to issue orders of his own and relies on the broad objectives and general guidance of a superior.

Even if money may not be the number one consideration in the minds of all franchise owners, it's still high on the list. The franchisee is in the game for financial growth and finally, riches.

WHAT YOU GET WITH A FRANCHISE

The most powerful reason to buy a franchise is to obtain training and guidance from an experienced insider. Franchisees are more likely than other entrepreneurs to recognize their own limitations. They know it takes a broad

range of understanding and skills to develop a successful business. After all, who can lay claim to being an effective chief executive and industry expert, as well as a master advertising director, skilled financial officer and experienced personnel director?

Franchise buyers seek know-how and support in the broader aspects of running a business, especially advertising, accounting and industry practices. Franchising provides a head start in the serious business of starting and running a business.

Lastly, people decide to buy franchises because they perceive the business to be an asset of lasting value. They believe the franchise has more permanence than other businesses, perhaps because a franchise agreement has a defined long term. Most independent businesses are lucky to survive five years. In contrast, the average franchise agreement has a term of ten years, and is almost always renewable.

Tom Fulner "just wanted to make a living" when he bought a PIP Printing franchise in 1972. Today, he owns 15 PIP stores in Indianapolis and Nashville with annual sales of more than $4 million.

"My advice to someone starting out in franchising is to go with a good franchise company. Check their financial strength. Talk with at least 10 franchisees to see if they are satisfied. That way you can balance the highs and the lows. And once you sign on, utilize the information and system the company provides to minimize your mistakes. There's no sense reinventing the wheel."

"As a franchisee you get certain services for your franchise fee and royalties - equipment, supplies, research and development, legal advice, operations help, training. You'd be crazy not to take advantage of it."

"When I first started out I used to come in an hour or an hour and a half before everyone else in the morning. It was hard to stay away. I was doing what I like to do. I wouldn't have been there, if I didn't want to do it."

"Being a franchisee is a hedge against failure, but it's the individual that makes it go. Take care of the customer. Don't be afraid to work, and don't milk your company. Reinvest in the business. Constantly upgrade equipment and personnel."*

WHAT KIND OF FRANCHISES ARE THERE?

Food

By far the most popular franchise category is restaurants, especially fast food operations. The number of fast food commercials shown on television will give you an idea of the way competition is expanding. In response fast food outlets and restaurants have been changing the way they do business. A greater emphasis is being placed on customer satisfaction. New or increased services, such as expanded menus, delivery or take-out offerings are becoming more popular.

Convenience Stores

By combining features of grocery stores, restaurants and gas stations, convenience stores answer customer demands for convenience. As two income families continue to increase the workforce, one-stop shopping convenience and the longer business hours of such stores answer the needs of a growing portion of the population.

General Merchandise

The franchised sale of non-food items such as auto parts, draperies, picture frames and a host of others are also affected by the changing life styles of a growing population.

Diet and Services

Everybody knows about Weight Watchers, but there are numerous other franchisors who offer affordable, popular opportunities in this active market. Diet franchises are looking at a potential diet base of almost 40 million people according to the National Center for Health Statistics.

The three most numerous diet services are Diet Center, Nutri/System and Jenny Craig - one of the fastest growing franchise companies in the United States.

Fitness Services

With the population aging and more and more people trying to lose weight, individuals are looking for fast, efficient and easy ways to get a fitness workout. Fitness franchises are rapidly expanding across the country as well as across the world.

Business Services

A variety of business franchises including accounting services and tax preparation services have experienced growing success in recent years.

Real Estate Services

Real Estate Services include franchises like real estate agents (Coldwell Banker, Century 21) or other real estate services like home estimators or mortgage brokers.

Employment Services

There has been an upswing in demand for temporary employees and for middle-and-upper-management personnel. Employment service franchises include businesses that look for jobs for individuals or look for individuals for companies.

Printing/Photocopying Services

This has been a high-growth area in franchising for several years, and the growth trend is expected to continue. Franchises in this area include businesses such as Minuteman Press, Mr. Print, Insty Prints and Sir Speedy.

Automobile/Truck Rental Services

Franchises in this are include businesses such as Rent-A-Wreck or U-Save Auto Rental.

Construction/Home Improvement Services

Franchised services that include carpet cleaning, sewer and drain cleaning and lawn care are becoming more popular. Within this franchising area, maid service franchises have shown exceptional potential for growth.

Laundry/Dry Cleaning Services

Although the new textiles and improved home laundry equipment have lowered the demand for laundry and dry cleaning services these establishments continue to thrive. Much of this growth can be traced to expanded service offerings, such as drapery cleaning and alteration services.

Educational Services

This sector includes many different types of specialized franchises. A leader is daycare/early education centers that answer the need of an increasing number of working mothers. The growth trend also includes pre-school and school age educational services that reflect the need felt by many parents for teaching children earlier in life. Tutoring centers are also becoming more and more popular.

Hair Care Services

Both the revenues and the number of hair care franchises have increased by approximately 28 percent. The success of hair care franchises can be traced to the lower prices and quick service they offer.

Leisure and Travel

As with other franchises, rising disposable income, greater leisure time especially for retired individuals, and an increase in the number of single member households is normally responsible for this growth.

Automotive

The expansion of this sector is related to a reduction in the number of gas/service stations. Services including car washes, muffler and transmission shops, general car care centers and retail tire outlets are becoming increasingly popular.

THE VALUE OF EXPERIENCE

Investment in a franchise gains for the new business owner access to important specialized information, developed and organized by people who have already been successful in the business. The franchisor is a source of detailed working information that a new franchisee would find difficult to acquire without spending thousands of dollars and years of effort to acquire.

Franchising sets up a common economic interest between the franchisor and the franchisee, who share risk as well as profit. The franchisor has a built-in interest in helping its franchisee partner.

FUTURE TRENDS

The outlook for franchising depends in large part on the way economic conditions develop as well as continuing acceptance by manufacturers, retailers, service firms and the public, on which you depend for success.

In recent years, business format franchising has profited by rising incomes and the major entry of women into the labor force. These trends are expected to continue for the immediate future, and the growth in franchising can be expected to remain strong.

Restaurants are expected to remain a leader in the franchise movement. Continued growth also is expected especially for security systems services, automotive maintenance and repair, video equipment and rental stores, travel agencies, home furnishings stores, maid services and home repair services.

In general, franchising has established itself as a marketing idea that offers advantages to both franchisor and franchisee. Prospects seem favorable because an increasing number of firms are finding franchising to be an easy and relatively inexpensive way to expand, and franchisees benefit from their access to the financial and managerial resources of a larger firm. Another consideration is that as a franchisee it's often easier to get loans that are needed to get a business started and keep it running.

IS FRANCHISING RIGHT FOR YOU?

Now that you know what a franchise is all about, the big questions are; is franchising right for you, are you right for franchising? Despite all the tempting true success stories about franchising performance in creating successful small business owners; a franchise is not the ideal method of entrepreneurship for everybody.

Before you spend your money to make the big move, it's especially important to spend some serious thought and time on self-analysis.

Think about it, do the reasons for considering franchising outweigh the advantages of simply making a go of it on your own? You might well come to the conclusion that your personality, abilities and skills place you among the twenty percent of independent business owners who succeed on their own without becoming a franchise owner.

Consider that in a number of ways, the franchisee is not his or her own boss. The franchisor's main interest is to maintain the special conditions and the uniformity of the franchised service he is selling, and to insure that the operations of each outlet will reflect successfully on the organization as a whole.

The franchisor wants to protect and build its good will. So the franchisor generally insists on a large degree of continuing control over the operations of franchisees and requires them to meet the franchisor's special standards. In some cases, franchisees are required to conduct every part of their operation strictly by the book, following every instruction in the franchisor's manual. Desirable or not, to your way of thinking, most franchisees are prepared to follow the franchisor's directions all the way.

What all this means is that the owner of a franchised business must give up some options and freedom of action in business decisions that would be open to the owner of a non-franchised business. When you buy a franchise, you will have to sacrifice some part of your business freedom. The big question is, can you live with the requirements and restrictions of a franchise agreement?

With all of this, as a franchisee, you are still an independent business owner, with the final responsibility for your business' success or failure. Are you willing to accept all the limits to your independence in return for all the benefits you'll receive from a successful franchisor?

FACTORS TO CONSIDER

As you think about whether or not to become a franchisee, you are faced with the necessity of taking on not one, but three types of responsibilities:

1. **Financial**

   The first, of course, is the financial obligation to pay the initial fee, proceed with the cost of building and running the business, and giving up a share of the gross revenues.

2. **Logical**

   You must be prepared to accept the responsibilities of starting, developing and managing a business with your franchisor. You must be prepared to accept the long hours, the extra effort, the operational headaches, and the burdens of a heavy paper work load.

   You must be willing to accept the standards, restrictions, requirements and operating guidelines of your franchisor. You must be prepared to sacrifice some measure of freedom in exchange for the franchisor's ready-to-go business format.

3. **Emotional**

   The emotional commitment is just as important as the financial.

Entrepreneurs often have a genuine love/hate relationship with their businesses. It always starts with love. They are enthusiastic about the industry they're in; the product, the image and identity the business provides for them. Eventually that love may turn to hate when the franchisee realizes the relationship is not working out exactly as planned, and may even turn sour.

As a prospective franchisee, you need to analyze your emotional investment in the business. Think of yourself in the franchise environment. How do you feel about spending a great many of your waking hours there? Will you be proud to call yourself the owner of the business? Does it stimulate pride, enthusiasm, self-esteem? How do you feel about the franchisor and his staff? Do they inspire loyalty, motivation, confidence? Will you feel comfortable working with your franchisor for the entire term of the agreement?

ARE YOU READY TO MAKE THE COMMITMENTS?

Here are some questions you should be asking yourself before you make any serious moves into franchising.

Financial Questions
- ☑ With everything you've learned about franchising and the particular franchisor, does the business seem worth the investment?

- ☑ Considering that most franchisors devote the entire initial fee they collect from a franchisee to setting up the business, do you think the amount they're charging is fair?

- ☑ How do you really feel about paying the franchise royalty every month from your gross revenues?

- ☑ After deducting your royalty payments, will you still be able to earn a decent profit?

- ☑ Can you handle the investment? Do you need partners?

☑ Can you obtain financing?

Logical Questions

☑ What does the franchisor offer that you can't do or accomplish by yourself?

☑ Will the value of the business increase over the years?

☑ Does the franchisor have a solid track record?

☑ Are the franchisor's other franchisees satisfied with their investments?

☑ Would you like to own one location or many?

Emotional Questions

☑ If you had your choice of any business to enter, would this particular franchise be your number one choice?

☑ If you buy the franchise, will you be proud to be its owner?

☑ Do you have a special interest or hobby related to the business? Does this franchise require specialized knowledge that you can only get from experience?

☑ Are you excited about belonging to this field?

☑ Can you see yourself working in this business for many years?

HOW TO RATE A FRANCHISE BEFORE YOU BUY

Once you've decided that a franchise is the best way for you to go, it's time to answer the question that will determine your success or failure in business and may likely have a critical influence on your life for years to come. How can you can tell whether a franchise is worth buying? Since there are thousands of franchises available, there is certainly no quick or easy way to make a decision.

The first thing to decide is the category of business you'll be most interested in, and then to get the necessary information for five to ten franchises in that category.

Most franchisors will send you a package of brochures that contain the information you will need to make an initial decision on which franchises you want to seriously consider. Much of the business data you need for this first step is available from a representative of the franchise through the Uniform Franchise Offering Circular, or UFOC.

Here are some of the factors you'll definitely want to keep in mind:

Background
Consider the history of the franchise; how it was started, who are the people who began it, who have operated it and what kind of results have they experienced in the past. Obtain additional facts and statistics about the particular industry that include the franchise you're interested in. Your local library can probably supply a great deal of the materials for the information you'll need.

People in your area, who are acquainted with a particular business, can provide another good source. Professional organizations, universities and the local chapter of the American Association of Retired Persons are also good likely sources of background information.

Demand for the Product
In any business you need to determine if there is demand in your community

for the type of product or service the franchise has to offer. In some instances, the demand is there, but there are too many other businesses supplying that service. Another business in that industry will take away from all the rest. Is the demand seasonal? Is the demand increasing or decreasing? Is it a fad or does it encourage repeat customers?

Competition

What is the level of competition for your product or service in your community? What are the restrictions for the franchisor to put in another store across the street from yours? Are the competitors well known, with better name recognition? Do they offer similar goods and services at lower prices?

Business Background

Length of experience is one good indicator of the kind of success that can be expected. Consider how many years a company has been in business. How many years has the company been offering franchises? For example, McDonald's has been in business and offering franchises since 1955. No commercial enterprise can stay in business unless it is profitable, so if it has passed the test of time, it's a pretty good bet that it knows how to weather the ups and downs of business conditions.

Look carefully at the franchisor's financial condition. Examine financial documents especially for indications of the company's solidity and credit worthiness.   Sometimes franchisors go out of business.   Do you need the franchisor to be successful?   Will you have access to suppliers?

Number of Franchises

Obviously the more outlets a franchisor has the more acceptance its business program has gained with entrepreneurs and the public. The total size of the business is another indication of how likely it is to be an ongoing operation with the greatest expectation of success.

Minimum Franchise Fee

As always, financial considerations are critical. If you can afford the price of admission, a more expensive franchise fee is less likely to be a consideration. If your funds are limited, for all practical purposes, you will have to limit your choices to those franchises that will accept a lower entry fee.

Minimum Capital Requirements

The franchise fee is one thing, the next most important financial consideration is the minimum capital required. This item includes your estimated or the franchisor's required minimum amount of cash and financing needed to begin the franchise operation. For the small investor the less expensive an operation is the more realistic prospect it becomes.

Company-Owned Stores

Many franchisors also have company-owned franchises. Certainly the fewer of these there are, the better from the franchisee's point of view. If a franchisor's profits are coming mostly from actual franchise operations, it will tend to pay more attention to its franchisees.

Growth Patterns

Consider how many franchises the company has opened in past years. Notice if the trend is up, or if the franchisor has reduced the number of franchises it has. Naturally, older firms may show a pattern of fewer new franchises as they mature, while newer companies may show greater activity shortly after they enter the market.

Total Royalty Fees

This item includes all monthly royalties and payments, advertising royalties and any other payment required from the franchisee by the franchising firm. To get a true picture of the value offered, it will be necessary to compare total royalties to the kind and quantity of services offered.

Financing Provided

Some franchisors will supply financial assistance to the franchisee to pay the initial and ongoing costs of conducting the business. Although an attractive extra, financial assistance should not be considered as a major decision factor; or a substitute for very careful, thorough investigation into all the facts in your choice of any franchise. It is simply another element that can be put into the mix.

How to Get Information

Contact both the national and local Better Business Bureaus. They may be able to give you an informed outsider's look at the company's financial and consumer relations experience.

Call or visit local current and past owners of the kind of franchises that you're interested in. Ask them what they think of the franchise company, its operations and the kind of help the franchisor has given them. Another good idea is to call or write some franchisees in other parts of the country. They may be experiencing better or worse economic situations in their areas and could give you an idea of how the particular business reacts to changed economic conditions.

Talk with your banker. He or she should have access to solid facts that will give you another view of the franchise's economic situation. Your banker may have inside details on the franchises you are considering and a good idea of the problems or opportunities you will have in gaining financing for your franchise venture.

Talk with an accountant. Have him or her check over the pro forma figures provided by the franchisor. These can include projected profit and loss statements, balance sheets, cash flow statements and projections for your location based on a similar demographic location. Have your accountant determine if they make financial sense.

Finally, talk with your lawyer and get a professional analysis of the franchise and the terms you are being offered. It is very important that your lawyer go over the franchise contract with extreme care. Remember, an agreement is just that; a bargain between two or more parties, and it can be changed or modified.

A contract that satisfies the needs of both parties at the beginning of the relationship can spare you grief and financial problems in the future, when it could be too late to change the arrangement.

Most important, avoid financial commitments before the agreement is completely worked out. Some franchisors may push for decisions before you have all the facts by offering special considerations. Avoid these situations at all costs, the final cost may be too high.

WHAT TO EXPECT FROM YOUR FRANCHISOR

CO-OP ADVERTISING

Your franchise must be promoted before, during, and after opening. You must sell yourself and your business however and wherever you can. It is rare for even the best product or service to succeed within a reasonable length of time without an active and intelligent advertising and promotion program.

Besides the initial fee and monthly royalty, most franchisors also require franchisees to pay a monthly ad royalty, usually a small percentage of their gross income, into a co-op fund. Monies gathered in an advertising fund are pooled to finance national and regional advertising campaigns for the benefit of all franchisees.

The franchisor benefits from increased promotion of the trade name and business, which in turn increases the value of your franchise and the amount of royalty dollars you will contribute.

Not all franchisors have a co-op advertising fund. Many franchise systems have no central advertising program but require franchisees to manage and pay for their own advertising. The problem with this arrangement is that it can lead to a loss of control over the franchise image you paid for. Helter skelter promotions by various franchisees can lead to lowering the value of the franchise for all franchisees.

NETWORK WITH OTHER FRANCHISEES

Being a part of a franchise system has some incredible benefits. One benefit is the access to other people that are running the same business as you, but in different areas of the country. Really good franchise companies are setting up methods for franchisees to communicate with each other. Some suggestions to look for are Intranet site, protected chat rooms, email addresses, and on-going conference calls and communications. These methods help all franchisee exchange data and ideas to each other.

SITE SELECTION HELP

The best franchise companies have established systems that can help you find a good location and acquire it on the best available terms. Actually, working with a franchisee in site selection, helping in the construction of a store or fixing up a storefront, are such important activities in the business mix that franchisors have become more active in these areas over the years.

A favorable site for one type of business will not necessarily be good for another. Each different business requires certain qualities that you will be seeking in a good location: a quality site for a Jiffy Lube shop will definitely be wrong for a Karmelkorn Shoppe or a Mr. Donut. Each business appeals to particular kinds of individuals with different tastes, needs and habits.

Many franchise companies have developed exact and scientifically selected requirements for locations in which experience shows their particular franchise operations will do best. Some companies have staffs that include marketing specialists who study census, population distribution and trend information about the best potential areas for franchises. This is valuable information for any entrepreneur who wants to have every possible advantage on his or her side.

The franchisor may have real-estate specialists who constantly seek out and update lists of available sites - vacant land, shopping centers under construction, empty storefronts, and so on, within the targeted areas. In some cases, a franchisor may already have made arrangements for ready-to-rent or purchase locations within your territory.

Some franchisors help negotiate the purchase or lease of your land or building. They may help arrange for a contractor to build the facility or, with an owner/developer, to lease it to you. If you are locating in an existing center or mall, the franchise company may lease a storefront and sublet it to you on as good or better terms than you could obtain for yourself.

If you have to build a structure, the franchisor may even provide plans that are already approved by local government agencies. In the case of most fast-food and some other franchises you will be required to build a store according to their set plans; put up required signage, and install the required equipment in a certain way.

Then again, there are franchisors who don't do any of these things. In that case you will have the whole burden of doing market research, finding a suitable location, leasing or buying the space, laying out the interior, fixing up the exterior, even buying a new structure. So, it's important to determine what the franchisor will do to help you find the best location and then make sure these steps are put into the agreement in writing.

TRAINING

Most men and women who buy franchises have no experience in the business they're entering. That's natural because a majority of the people who buy franchises are changing careers. But, in order to succeed, new franchisees must learn a great deal about what's involved in their new career before opening for business.

The best way to do this is to make the most out of the franchisor's training program.

The franchisor may offer training at a headquarters "college". These are usually well planned to provide the background you need to get the business off to a good start and to use all the know-how the franchisor has to offer. Formal training sessions are one of the most helpful supports a franchisor can provide to a franchisee and you should take advantage of as much as you can get.

But you should take one step more - get training at an actual store or franchise location. As part of your franchise arrangement, or if necessary, on your own seek out the opportunity to work for a week or two in a functioning store. Make hamburgers, clean carpets, sell mufflers, sweep floors - learn whatever you can that a seasoned operator knows is needed to make that franchise work.

Added to your classroom training, in-the-field practical experience will give you a first hand understanding of what you have to do to make your new business work.

Some franchisors will send a field representative to help train you and your new employees before the grand opening. If your franchisor doesn't offer this service you're on your own, so it's important to find out early how much on-site training is included in the franchise package and where you can locate the help you'll need.

Most franchisors offer some type of on-going training, even if it's only newsletters or regularly scheduled seminars. You'll want to find out about where your franchisor stands on such valuable services as advanced training on accounting and computer systems, new products and supplying a steady stream of marketing ideas.

It's a good idea to check with existing franchisees to find out just how effective the franchisor's training program is. If it looks like you won't be getting all the training support you'll need, the best source of help again is other franchisees who have faced the problem before you. They're usually very willing to help new people in the business and have often set up franchisee committees to provide mutual support.

OPERATING PRACTICES

The operations manual and the franchise contract will require you to meet the company's standards of quality and uniformity of appearance in these areas among others:

- ❖ Product, equipment, fixtures and furniture
- ❖ Number, quality, quantity, type, size and shape of products
- ❖ Product availability
- ❖ Advertising and marketing controls
- ❖ Internal security
- ❖ Auditing procedures
- ❖ Employee conduct

Several court decisions have held that a franchisor cannot require you to buy products or services only from them. Most however, can and do, enforce quality standards and specifications. Violations of these can lead to the termination of your contract. There have been cases in which franchisees have been found in breach of contract for such seemingly minor violations as having smudges on a men's room mirror. Franchisors can get very picky when they think you might be tampering with their image and business. That's why franchisors maintain staffs of company inspectors.

The contract may also dictate the days and business hours you must be open; set any sales quota and penalties for not meeting them and explain any wholesale or discount purchasing plans available through the franchisor

ONGOING MANAGEMENT ASSISTANCE

Continuing help for franchisees can range anywhere from advice over the phone to having a company representative visit you whenever you feel the need for guidance and advice. In dealing with some franchisors you may have to pay an hourly rate or flat fee every time you ask the company to help you solve a problem.

One franchisee may be so unsure of himself/herself that he demands a helping hand every time something doesn't go according to the manual. Others may be so confident of their own abilities that they feel no need to ever see the field rep and want no help or interference at all.

Here's how one outstanding franchisor, Midas Muffler supports its franchisees:

A field force of division and district representatives meet on a regular basis with franchisees.

Midas' real-estate, marketing, advertising and sales promotion executives work directly with all franchisees.

There is an open-door policy by which franchisees can go right to the top and get in direct touch with the president of the company.

The company goes to the dealers and asks their advice before any new programs are put into effect. Midas understands that the franchisees must believe in and support new programs to make them work.

The franchisor encourages its franchisees to expand. To support such a move Midas provides high quality market research.

Midas has a policy of giving current franchisees first crack at expanding and opening new outlets in their area.

That's how one first-class franchisor deals with its franchisees, builds a happy family of franchisors and a highly successful business.

INGREDIENTS OF A WINNING FRANCHISE

Now that we've covered some of the main points of how you should go about choosing a franchise it's time to close in on more specific considerations. By this point in the process you should have a pretty firm idea of just what kind of business you want to get into and some initial information on several franchise operations.

Here is a checklist that can help you establish the finalists in your search:

IDENTITY

One of the primary reasons for purchasing a franchise is the right to use the trade name. The more name recognition, the less you will have to spend in educating customers on the services you provide. How well known is the trade name? If it's already a household name like Kentucky Fried Chicken, or Baskin-Robbins, you know their identity is well established. If you're considering a newer company, is the trade name memorable or unique enough to catch the interest of the buying public?

Some new franchisors might purposely choose a trade name that sounds like an already successful business. That may cause legal problems in the future. Another question might be, is the name so similar to another business name or trade mark that it might cause confusion to potential customers?

Will you be comfortable with the identity that's built into the business? Does the image fit in with your feelings of suitability for a venture that will represent you to the community?

OPERATING SYSTEM

This is especially important if you're going into a field of business with which you have no previous experience. Does the franchisor offer a training program? If so how long is it? What topics does it cover?

Will the franchisor help you select a site for the business?

Does the franchisor provide an operating manual? If so, does it cover these important subjects?

- ❖ Opening for business
- ❖ Training - for yourself and employees
- ❖ Setting up books and records
- ❖ Accounting and reports
- ❖ Advertising and publicity
- ❖ Purchasing and inventory
- ❖ Marketing and sales
- ❖ Daily operating procedures
- ❖ Technical information

Does the franchisor provide ready-to-use signs, menus, fixtures, decorations, forms etc. If not, will he help you get them?

Can the franchisor help you purchase equipment, supplies or inventory at a discount? Are the prices really better than you can get for yourself?

FINANCIAL RELATIONSHIP

Is there an initial franchise fee?

Does the fee vary from one location to another? If so, what is the amount for the location or territory you have in mind?

Does the franchisor charge an ongoing franchise royalty? If so, what is the percentage?

Is the royalty set for the entire term of the franchise, or can it be raised or lowered in the future?

If the royalty is not set, what factors will the franchisor use to determine it?

Does the franchisor charge a co-op advertising royalty in addition to the basic franchise royalty?

Is the co-op advertising royalty set for the entire term of the franchise, or can it be raised or lowered in the future?

THINGS TO LOOK OUT FOR

We've spent most of this chapter discussing the benefits of operating a franchise operation - and there are plenty of them. There have been success stories enough to fill a raft of magazines and books. But, be warned; as in most things that look too good to be true, there are serious downside considerations as well.

As we've mentioned before, and it bears repeating, as a franchisee you are locked into a single company, and are required by contract to accept the company's rules, regulations and methods of doing business. There's always small print in the contract that defines your relationship to the franchise company for better or worse. In some ways a franchise relationship is like a marriage in which each side counts on the other party to provide help and support.

Sometimes this means that you, as an entrepreneur, are stuck in a situation where you cannot move quickly to meet your business' particular local needs - to take quick action against a competitor or meet changing financial or market conditions. As a franchisee you may have to wait for word from headquarters before you take steps to solve the problem.

Franchise fees are forever, or at least for the duration of the contract. When you sign that contract you are tied to a relationship that requires you to pay for the privilege of franchising and the advantages you get every month, every year.

Finally, if the franchise firm has business reverses, through no fault of yours, you have to live with the results of their actions. Everything they do reflects on you and your operation.

IT'S NOT ALL ROSES

Articles in business publications and franchisors who are anxious to sell you, indicate that buying a franchise is a guarantee of good fortune. Amazing success rates of 95 percent to 99 percent have been reported. Even the government seems to support these figures. Although franchising is the most foolproof way of getting a business going, there are still failures; nothing like the rate of failure for independent small businesses but enough to keep potential franchisees on their toes.

You know what they say about liars figuring and figures lying. The statistics don't tell you about the franchisee in Des Moines who invested $100,000 in a business and eventually had to sell it to someone else for $15,000 because that was all he could get. The business is still in operation and it's included in the success statistics - the $85,000 loss however, is not shown anywhere.

Franchisors are not very anxious to report failures within their system. Some buy back failed franchises either at the original cost or at a loss to the franchisee. Others attempt to sell their distressed operations. A few hope their failures will simply go away and still others carry a franchise on their records even though it's been closed for months. When a franchisor states they have 250 operating units, there may only be 200 actually open for business. Fifty have been closed and are up for sale.

One man, anxious to get in on the franchise bonanza was contacted by a company that offered him not only a franchise but three existing company-owned locations. To complete the deal he was required to pay, in addition to the royalty fees, for the buildings and the equipment.

It wasn't until after he had signed the contracts and had been in business for months that he discovered the restaurants he had purchased were sold by the owners because they had not made a profit in over three years – while they were being operated by the franchisor. What's more he found that the used equipment he had purchased could have been bought new, on the open market, for less. It can not be emphasized too much - as in any venture, it is best to beware of who you are doing business with.

By and large franchising is the safest form of independent business ownership, but you should never think franchising is a sure thing. You can't give a franchisor a check and automatically expect instant success. Consider franchising with the same thorough eye you would any other investment.

If you look on a franchise as a guardian angel that won't let you fail, no matter what, you are unlikely to succeed for two reasons: A good franchisor who gets the idea that you're not likely to work hard at make it a success probably won't let you buy in.

Second, even the best franchise in the business cannot prevent lack of ability from causing failure. A franchisor may finally help to save an unsuccessful operation to preserve the franchisor's reputation and keep a store open, but you still carry the burden of success or failure. At worst you could lose your franchise and your investment – and your store may go on to another franchisee that could make a success of it without you.

In this chapter you have learned:
1. *Franchising is a form of business partnership with a franchisor.*
2. *Franchises come in many different forms and industries.*
3. *Franchising has serious commitments, just like any other small business.*
4. *As a franchisee there are certain things you should expect from your franchisor.*
5. *Choosing a franchise takes as much research and time (may be more) as starting your own small business. Each opportunity its own positive and negative issues.*

Chapter 6

Forming a Company

What you need to know about your business and the law

This chapter is by no means meant to give any legal advice. Be sure to always contact a competent attorney for all legal questions. Business people are often overwhelmed by all the decisions that have to be made in so many unfamiliar areas of business operation. Even the simplest one-person operation eventually comes up against the need for informed, intelligent help. An individual's judgment, personal experience and the advice from counselors and professional consultants, especially lawyers.

One thing is certain; sooner or later, the day will come when a lawyer will be needed; to help set up the structure of the business, to legally protect your ideas, prepare contracts or defend against legal actions.

Chances are, at the beginning, you will be dealing with a small one or two person law firm. The good news is that computer technology has made it possible for he smallest firms to put out the same quality product as any large firm. A small firm, at its best, offers flexibility and closer one-on-one contact with clients at a cost more small businesses can afford.

You have plenty of choices. There are a lot of lawyers out there – over one million in the United States, and it is expected to increase over the next few years.

This chapter is not intended to replace your lawyer. Don't mistake it for that. But you will find that after you have read and understood this chapter you will be more confident about talking to a lawyer and asking the right questions or raising the right objections if some of his or her explanations seem like Greek to you. As an independent business person, you should know there is no mystery in our legal and fiscal system. You can make it work for you.

In this chapter you will learn:

1. *How to make an intelligent choice in picking the right form of business (sole proprietorship, partnership, corporation or limited liability company); how to evaluate different forms of organizing your business.*
2. *How to come up with a successful name for your business; and how to protect it.*
3. *How to act responsibly as an employer.*
4. *What to watch out for when you think buying a business is better than building one.*
5. *What to watch out for when you have to deal with corporate landlords.*
6. *How to choose a lawyer.*
7. *How to maintain a solid working relationship with your lawyer.*

SELECTING AN APPROPRIATE FORM FOR YOUR BUSINESS

General Considerations

Making a choice as to the legal form of your business involves choosing to protect your personal assets and, in most cases, enhance your personal wealth by selecting tax efficient methods of withdrawing capital from an enterprise. A choice has to be made though. The absence of choice is, in and of itself, a choice to conduct your business as a sole proprietor or partnership (if you are in business with someone else who ignores the decision). As you will see, sole proprietorship and partnership forms are not particularly efficient from an asset protection view. Unless you are judgment proof, you expose your personal assets to liability. While there are some opportunities to efficiently enhance your wealth as a sole proprietor or partnership, they are normally outweighed by the tremendous exposure to liability.

Before we go into the details, let's look at the most basic questions to ask before you start:

- To what extent are you personally able and your family willing to be responsible for business debts and losses?
- Are you judgment proof or do you have assets that exceed your state's asset exemption laws?
- How much profit do you expect to make –the more profitable the more issues there are with the withdrawing the profits with tax efficiency?
- Will you be employing family members?
- Are you in a profession where liability can't be shielded?
- How likely is someone to assert a claim?
- How important is the ability to deduct your health insurance or other fringe benefits?

Sole Proprietorship

The oldest and simplest form of business entity is called "sole proprietorship". Under this framework no other owners or partners are involved. At any time you can transfer funds into or out of the business from your personal assets. It is all yours, the good and the bad. In legal terms, you and the business are identical.

Setting up legally is very simple; you start conducting business in your own name. If you want to conduct business under something other than your own name, usually it's a matter of getting a DBA ("doing business as") or similar form from the state. The advantages and disadvantages are considerable. A sole proprietorship involves the least amount of bureaucratic red tape; it is the least expensive arrangement to set up your business initially and needs the least amount of paperwork to get started. Its simplicity and convenience make this the usual form for the small business at inception. Sometimes you also need (or may want) to file an assumed name and to obtain a license. Both of these formalities are very easy to take care of.

Other advantages to a sole proprietorship are:

1. First and foremost, you alone are the boss. You make the decisions. No one is second guessing you or vetoing your decisions.
2. In a sole proprietorship, you have the opportunity to reflect your personality in the business. You can mold it in any manner you wish.
3. Filing federal and state income tax returns, bookkeeping, and accounting can be quite simple. No fancy accounting is necessary. You simply keep track of your expenses and deduct them from your sales to determine your profit and/or loss. All one needs for filing with your Federal Tax return is an IRS Schedule "C".
4. In the event that you may want to close down the company, it is a relatively easy thing to do with no partners or shareholders to be concerned about.
5. You have the opportunity to set up a simple retirement arrangement such as a Simple IRA or a Keogh Plan.
6. You can pay your immediate family wages with paying a FICA or other wage withholding obligations. This can amount to a 15.3% benefit.

7. You can initiate a Medical Expense Reimbursement Plan, employ your spouse and deduct expenses.
8. Sole proprietors who employ their spouse and the spouse elects family coverage can also deduct health insurance.

However, if you are planning to expand, the sole proprietorship can lead to problems. The biggest disadvantage is that you also have unlimited personal liability. Since there is no firm separation between your business and your personal assets, business liabilities are completely yours. Creditors can take your personal assets, including the equity in your house which exceeds your state's homestead exemption, as well as non-exempt equity in your car. Creditors can garnish or levy upon your car or bank account if the company's funds are inadequate to pay them and if they have a judgment. Since you, as the owner, are personally subject to unlimited liability for the company's obligations, you will probably want to use sole proprietorship only if you intend to operate very conservatively.

Sometimes even the most conservative person can get into trouble, consider the following:

Your planning was good, the advice you got was excellent. You start your retail business by shelling out about $25,000 for leasing space, ordering supplies and merchandise, and so on. Before you really get started there happens to be an economic down turn in the economy and people (your prospective customers) stop spending disposable income. There has not been any substantial business income to pay the bills. Now you are personally stuck. Your creditors want cash, no returns. You have to sell to a liquidator (if you can find one) at a substantial loss. Beyond your business, you may lose your personal bank account, your car, maybe your home!

Another equally scary scenario: Your employee engages in inappropriate conduct leading another employee to claim sexual harassment. The victim sues for lost wages. You are not adequately insured (many business policies now exclude sexual harassment coverage unless specifically included).

And there are more specific disadvantages. The income of a sole proprietorship is taxed when it is earned and it is all considered wages, even if you have a substantial investment in the business. Wages are subject to 15.3% self-employment tax. This is generally the case, even if the income is really a return on investment from the assets you placed into service. You also get taxed, even if you do not withdraw the profits from the business. There are no retained earnings for a sole proprietorship. If your income increases you become a candidate for a higher tax bracket. If you need to withdraw money to satisfy the tax payments, those earnings will not be available to the business for expansion.

Also, as a sole proprietor, you don't qualify for tax advantages which corporations get when you offer fringe benefits, such as insurance programs and some medical reimbursement plans.

General Partnership

Formerly, a very popular method of operating a business, especially service based professional organizations, has now been largely replaced with the limited liability company and limited liability partnership.

Perhaps the single best feature of a partnership is the ability to distribute partnership assets (as with a sole proprietorship) to the owner without creating tax consequences. For example, if the partnership acquires an interest in a condominium in Florida, rents that condominium over the course of 20 years and then decides to make personal use of the condominium in retirement, unlike a corporation, the distribution results in no tax consequences.

Most states have adopted what is called the Uniform Partnership Act ("UPA"). It defines a partnership as "an association of two or more persons to carry on as co-owners a business for profit". <u>No legal contract between the partners is required since the UPA will supplement the disputed terms of the relationship.</u> Needless to say, you would be wise to have one anyway. You and your partner(s) can define your relationship just about any way you wish. The partnership agreement stipulates how much capital is contributed by each partner, what duties each will perform and how the profits will be distributed.

In a partnership each partner "acts as the agent" of all the other partners. Each one can "bind the partnership". This means no matter whether Jill, your childhood friend and business partner, signs a $500 or a $500,000 contract on behalf of the partnership, each partner has unlimited liability for the company's obligations. It does not matter whether or not you had given prior consent. Again, as with a sole proprietorship, you have personal liability exposure. This time though, the exposure is magnified by your partner's conduct. On the other hand, no one can join the partnership without the permission of all the other partners.

Partnerships don't have to be 50-50 deals. For instance, you may have ten slices of the cake and leave just two or three for your companion. Or, if you are bold, you may even consider your mother-in-law as a third partner.

An important consideration in a partnership is that each partner is entitled to full information, regardless of subject, about the affairs that concern the partnership. The partners are bound by a "fiduciary" relationship. Each partner owes the other the highest possible duty of good faith, loyalty and fairness. The notion of "conflict of interest" becomes quite important: Your partner Jill could not run a competing business as a sole proprietor without your consent.

In many respects, a partnership is not much different from a sole proprietorship. Your personal assets are in jeopardy, in addition to any assets of the partnership. Also, death has a critical impact. Legally, a partnership dissolves upon the death or withdrawal of any partner; thus, its duration is uncertain. As far as taxes are concerned, a partnership cannot take advantage of planning flexibility and fringe benefits offered by a C corporation. It does not pay any income taxes. But don't jump to premature conclusions: Profits or losses have to be reported, along with information that determines each partner's share. Now each partner is taxed on his or her share (along with income from other sources), whether or not the money was actually distributed during the year. Payroll withholding taxes are owed on the partner's share of profits.

Because of the risks involved, partnerships now are rare between natural persons. There are far more efficient methods of operating a business than in a partnership. You should exert your energies on finding the appropriate entity to form rather than operating as a partnership.

Limited Partnership

Under this type of agreement, the **limited** partners share in the partnership's liabilities only up to the amount of their investment in the limited partnership. There must be one "general" partner and at least one "limited" partner. The general partner is exposed to all the liabilities of the limited partnership. In contrast, a limited partner is more like a stockholder. The limited partner does not have unlimited personal liability. Limited partners are only responsible for the amount of money they paid into the business. Normally the limited partners do not participate in day-to-day activities of the business. If a limited partner participates in the day-to-day activities, he or she may lose the limited liability status they enjoy. The death or withdrawal of a limited partner has little impact on the survival of the partnership as a legal entity.

While this may sound like a perfect solution for your business ambitions, there is a catch. A limited partner faces no restriction if she wants to sell her partnership interest to somebody else. No consent by the other partners is typically necessary. Since limited partnerships can accommodate many interests, objectives, different characters and personal backgrounds, state legislatures keep a special eye on this form of business. If you are selling stock to a limited partner, you may have to file special forms with the Securities and Exchange Commission. Be sure to consult a lawyer before deciding on this type of business structure to make sure you are in compliance with regulations.

Limited Liability Partnership

The Limited Liability Partnership is a blend between a General Partnership and a Limited Partnership. It has the unique advantage of limited liabilities to the business just as in a corporation. It permits that same tax status as a partnership at both the state and federal levels.

For example, in the past, the partners of a general partnership have automatically been responsible for the total liabilities of the enterprise, regardless of the extent of involvement by each of the partners. The Limited Liability Partnership does what the name says; it operates in much the same way as a corporation-like shield against liability.

However, in order to obtain such protection, the partnership must include in its name the phrase "Limited Liability Partnership" or the abbreviation "LLP". And in most states, the "LLP" must register each year with the appropriate State department office in order to maintain this status.

The other major advantage of the "LLP" is that it still permits the enterprise to file state and federal partnership tax returns. Each state has its own registration procedures including an annual filing fee.

Limited Liability Company

The limited liability company (LLC) is an unusual mix that combines the structure and attributes of partnerships and corporations. In its simplest sense, it is like a partnership in which all of the partners have limited liability. Limited liability companies are, generally, regarded by the federal government as a partnership for tax purposes.[1] For the purposes of liability exposure, Limited liability companies are treated as the equivalent of corporations by state law.

The creation of the limited liability company business form has its origins with enhancing domestic oil exploration opportunities. Investors sought to

---

[1] With the onset of "check the box" regulations, a limited liability company can choose to be taxed as an S corporation, a partnership or even a traditional corporation.

create a business form that had the limited liability features of a corporation with the tax features of a partnership. For example, the assets of the company can be distributed to the owners without the tax consequence, even if the assets have appreciated in value. Other countries had created business forms similar to the current limited liability company's, i.e. Panamanian limitadas. An oil exploration investment group approached the state Legislature for Wyoming (after being unsuccessful in Alaska) and successfully passed a limited liability statute in 1977. More than 10 years later, in 1988, the Internal Revenue Service issued an interpretation which allowed limited liability company's two have partnership tax classification despite the presence of limited liability. In 1990, Colorado in Kansas each passed limited liability company statute's authorizing the creation of a limited liability company. By 1994, 48 states have adopted the limited liability company form.

There is much less complexity, tax and organizational baggage in the limited liability company organization. In short, the LLC is an efficient and flexible form of business that allows its members many worthwhile benefits plus partnership federal income tax treatment. There are some differences in the way various states operate their LLCs but there has been a movement to make this more uniform. Information about your state's LLC requirements can be obtained from the state authority that oversees corporate affairs.

The Corporation

When the term corporation is used, you may think of IBM or Shell Oil. A corporation is in many ways the ideal business form even if your business is tiny in comparison to the ones above. Think of a corporation as an artificial person with a separate existence for legal, tax and economic purposes. In a corporation, investors have limited liability; they can lose no more than they initially invested in the company. A corporation allows you to control the financial risks of owning a company.

There will be no nightmares involving your house, car or personal bank account. Even if some of your employees have made costly mistakes, have been careless or negligent, there is no need for total panic. Along the same lines, if your company receives a loan from a bank, but cannot repay the loan for some reason, the bank must take the loss on your loan. Yet those instances would be rare. Most banks will require you to co-sign or guarantee with your personal assets, which puts your assets at risk. Even though you own all the stock of the corporation and you may be its only employee, you and the corporation are separate for legal, financial and tax purposes.

The liability granted to investors within the corporate form applies only to conventional business debts. If the corporation goes bankrupt, creditors cannot recover their bills out of personal assets of the stockholders. But the liability is limited in that it does not cover criminal or improper actions. The corporate form does not automatically protect the management of the company from lawsuits directed against them personally.

A corporation is not difficult to set up. Do-it-yourself kits and books are available. The cost of incorporating is much lower than most people think. For non-complex corporations that have few shareholders, many of the forms are available from your Secretary of State offices. It is likely that you can set up a corporation for less than $1,000. If your corporation is complex, consult with a lawyer for direction and the proper forms.

There are certain differences between a public and a closed (closely held) corporation. We will focus on the Closed corporation. This is an enterprise that you own either by yourself or with a few other people. We base our arguments and reasoning on the assumption that all the owners of the corporation are involved in the day-to-day management and that no stock is sold to the general public.

The most important feature of a corporation is that it is a legally separate entity from the individuals who own and operate it.

Legally, a corporation has a definite, eternal existence. This means that even if the owner dies, the business does not. It does not matter who owns the stock. And, it is very easy to transfer ownership. If this is done within your family, you might want to include in your will that your shares (which may actually account for 100%) will be taken over by your spouse, child or whomever you have in mind. If later on this becomes a burden for the heir, he or she can give away or sell the shares of stock.

Previously, establishing a corporation required six people -- three incorporators and three directors. Today most states have changed their legislation to allow for only one incorporator and one director.

It has become easier to run a closely held corporation. Formalities have been substantially reduced. While it is normally a prudent practice to institute bylaws to govern the operation of a corporation and require shareholders two entry into a subscription agreement evidencing their investment intent, in many states, shareholders meetings and boards of director meetings can be by unanimous written consent instead of holding formal, expensive, time-consuming meetings. They can also be held by phone.

As for corporate taxes, the corporation must pay income taxes on its earnings. In addition, when you withdraw some or all of those earnings as dividends, you must include them in your individual tax return and pay taxes a second time for the same item. But this in itself is no reason to avoid corporation status. With a little thinking and a little advice from your lawyer or accountant, the double-tax issue can be minimized or completely eliminated.

You may want to consider having a corporation adopt a preemptive right for shareholders. Preemptive rights allow shareholders to acquire a fraction of the unissued shares, or a right to purchase unissued shares, before the corporation may offer them to somebody else. It is intended to provide original shareholders the opportunity to preserve their control. Another important right to consider is cumulative voting. Cumulative voting allows minority shareholders to determine one or more of the members of the burden of director pursuant to a formula which allows them to cumulative votes. This ensures that they have representation of the Board of Director level. Most states allow cumulative voting for directors.

"S" Corporation (Formerly Subchapter S")

Most small businesses can opt to be treated as an "S" corporation. This is a straight-forward and inexpensive procedure, requiring only one form (Form 2553) to be filed with the Internal Revenue Service. It must be signed by all stockholders. Other requirements are that you must opt for the "S" designation within the first 75 days of any tax year or within the first 75 days of business operations. Your company can only issue one class of stock. For instance, you cannot make a distinction between voting stock and nonvoting stock. If somebody has the right to control 40% of the corporation, they must generally own 40% stock. Another requirement is that there can be no more than 75 stockholders. The shareholders also have to be natural persons (the breathing individual), resident aliens or a qualified subchapter S subsidiary or trust.

So when it's "your" corporation, you can get away with only one signature. Being the owner of such a corporation means being free of any corporate income taxes! The corporation serves basically as a vehicle for establishing income (or losses). It only files an information return and the income or loss becomes part of your personal tax return.

By going "S", you kill more than one bird with one stone. You enjoy immunity from unlimited personal liability and you avoid double taxation. Furthermore, you are able to determine what your reasonable salary is and make distinctions between the income which is subject to the ordinary income tax and wage withholding tax of 15.3% versus that which is subject only to ordinary income tax.

What's the catch? There are cases when shareholders/owners may actually want to have their corporate income taxed separately. This is especially the case during growth periods, when it is to the advantage of the corporation to retain some of its earnings for expansion purposes. If it does take this route of financing, the benefits or savings result from the fact that the tax rate on corporate earnings is lower than the tax rate on individual earnings. Had the owner declared the corporate profits on his personal tax form, not only would he have been taxed at a higher rate he would not have the advantage of using the money for personal purposes. You probably will not be able to claim your health care costs as tax exempt, if any of it.

Stockholders working for their company are considered employees. As an employee, you are eligible for insurance programs and similar fringe benefits. For the corporation, these fringe benefits turn into tax-deductible expenses of doing business. Thus the financial effect for you should be clear: The company writes off those costs as expenses before paying taxes.

As you probably see by now, this issue can be a rather complex one, especially when you are determined to use the sharpest pencils to maximize your profits. That's another way of saying, "Have a very good lawyer and accountant help you."

How to Incorporate

Setting up and operating a corporation requires special arrangements to assure that your business will be recognized as a corporation under the laws of the state or states in which you operate.

1. Apply to your state corporation authority (often the Secretary of State's office) for a corporate charter.
2. File articles of incorporation with the state. This operation varies from state to state. Some states have a reasonable simple fill-in-the-blanks form, so you can choose to seek a corporate charter yourself. If the procedure is complex in your state, you may need

the services of a lawyer.

3. Even if you do not use an attorney to file the necessary papers with the state, you should have an attorney review your stockholder agreement – unless you are the only stockholder.

4. The choice of name for your corporation may present problems. Your state authority will not grant a charter to your corporation if your intended name duplicates, or is close to, the name of another corporation chartered in your state. However, once you have submitted an acceptable name, the protection will be on your side.

5. File the annual registration forms with the corporation authority.

6. If you are going to operate in several states, you need to register in each state as a "foreign corporation".

7. Pay the necessary fee to the state or states, whether they are called registration, franchise or some other name for the fees.

8. Make sure the state of states has the correct name and addresses of directors, officers and in particular, the registered agent (may be you).

A business operating as an S corporation not only has to fulfill state laws, but it must also satisfy the IRS requirements.

SELECTING THE RIGHT NAME FOR YOUR BUSINESS ... AND PROTECTING IT

General Considerations

The proper name for your business is important as you want to leave this important "first impression".

Depending on your type of business, its name should convey some essential attributes: reliability, aggressiveness, creativity, prudence, or whatever your special image is. Always remember that the name not only has to look right, it has to sound right, too. So if you do come up with a catchy name, say it out loud repeatedly or let somebody else do this. Listen to it carefully. Do a little survey among your friends and acquaintances. This way you will catch double meanings and connotations you might have missed before. Marketing research experts would call this little exercise "administering a convenience pre-test".

If your last name is Jean, you probably won't christen your child "Blue". Similarly, if your last name is Smell or Smellie, you won't name your fast food restaurant "Smellieburger". If confidentiality or reliability are main aspects of your business, you should not use light, high-pitched sounds resulting from combinations of the vocal i -- as in "Didi". Choose low-pitched, solid sounds by combining the vocals a, o, u. Think of these companies: Allstate, State Farm, Target, Walmart, and Bank of America.

Legally speaking, you can be most creative and clever with your name selection. You can live out your fantasies, so to speak. There are only a few guidelines to observe. If you go corporate, this must be evident in the name. Most state laws will require that you include the terms "Corporation", "Company", "Incorporated", "Limited" or their abbreviations, "Corp.", "Co.", "Ltd." or "Inc". On the other hand, there is a way out, if you insist. Many states allow corporations to file assumed names. In those cases you would properly register your incorporated business by using one of the terms referred to above, while at the same time filing an assumed name for everyday, public usage.

Some terms are mandatory, yet others are prohibited or restricted. If you don't have legitimate, obvious reasons, it may be difficult to include such terms as "insurance", "trust", "medical", "national", or "bank" in your application. Also, be aware of names and phrases already in use. Most states will reject a name that too closely resembles one already on file. Not only that, the original owner of the name can take you to court.

A name search is quite tedious, particularly on a national level. Those instances would require legal assistance. If you handle your company like you have handled your children, that's fine. That is, you may actually have the name before the "birth" or incorporation. Most states let you reserve a potential corporate name for about three months. If you discover that somebody else was less prudent than you and operates a business under a name almost identical to the one you have on file -- take prompt action. Do this by phone call, letter, lawsuit -- whatever is needed to stop the practice. A judge will issue a court order; and if you show losses, you will most likely receive damage compensation.

Why and When to File

If you do not incorporate your business and use your full legal name to identify your business, there are no special filing requirements. Ralph R. Randall's Realty as a business name would not require filing procedures if Mr. Randall is the owner of the business. In contrast, "Triple R Realty" would have to be registered, as would "Randall Realty". The reason for this rather stringent regulation is to provide better information on the identity of the business owner or owners' -- not only for the customers, but for business partners (creditors) as well. The important thing to remember is that as soon as you want to use only a part of your legal personal name, i.e. the last name, as your business name, it's technically treated as an adoption of an assumed name and filing procedures apply.

Officially, this filing serves identification purposes only. It does not provide official protection against other persons filing the same name. It's the responsibility of the entrepreneur to take legal action if a duplication of names occurs. However, most states will notify the original filer of later filings that seem to constitute a problem.

On the other hand, there may be instances where your unregistered full legal name is duplicated because someone else (a corporation, for example) claims it as an assumed name. Although the authorities would most likely not prevent this (because they don't have you on their records), you do have certain rights in such a case because it's your name and you have had it longer. It's considered a matter of common law and would largely depend on an individual ruling by a judge.

There is another interesting aspect to the name game: You cannot "sneak in" on a corporate name hoping that the name you intend to file for your sole proprietorship business will be confused by many customers with the name of your famous competitor.

For example, if your name happens to be John Target and you wanted to name your gift store "Target's Store", you would be in a heap of trouble. The same would be true for names like "The Hallmark Card Shop", "Windy's Hamburgers", "Gen'ral Motors".

An assumed name must be "free of conflict". This means it is already turned down when it comes close to those of corporations. This, of course, is a matter of judgment. Therefore, you should check with the appropriate state offices before you go through the preliminary filing motions. You may also want to consider registering your name through the United States Patent and Trademark Office.

How to File an Assumed Name

The actual filing procedures may vary slightly from state to state. The following account is based on Minnesota law and should give you an idea of what is involved:

Get a "Certificate of Assumed Name" form from the Office of the Secretary of State. Complete it; and sign it and send it to the appropriate government office for certification. Have the approved Certificate published in two successive issues of a newspaper qualified to publish legal notices in the county serving as the principal place of the business. The ad must appear in the legal notice section, not as a display or classified ad. The notice must contain the same information that is provided on the Certificate.

After the paper has printed the information shown on the front of the Certificate, it will send you an affidavit stating that the Certificate was printed for the specified time. Make sure this affidavit bears an original signature and has a copy of the actual publication attached to it. All in all, your total cost for the application fee and the newspaper filing may reach about $100. If you try to get by without filing, you risk a fine and you make it impossible for your business to initiate lawsuits and other legal proceedings. As a general rule, your filing, if there are no changes, remains valid for 10 years. You will be notified six months prior to expiration.

What You Should Know About Copyrights, Trademarks And Patents

Many businesses have been built on the legal protection of ideas. There is enough difference among copyrights, trademarks and patents that you should be familiar with the basics of what they are, how they guard property rights and how you can use them. Copyrights, trademarks and patents can be searched at: http://www.uspto.gov/ebc/indexebc.html

Copyrights

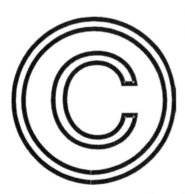

A copyright protects the original effort you put into the development of a literary, musical, artistic or other creative work. Copyrights cover various forms of expression such as books, films, computer programs, data bases, semiconductor chips, works of art, promotional brochures, product drawings, architectural plans and advertising copy.

The creators ("authors") and other rights holders of a copyright have the exclusive right to duplicate, sell, license, display, publicly perform and distribute all or part of a copyrighted work.

An idea, in and of itself, cannot be copyrighted. A copyright is created only when a person utilizes an original idea in an actual form of expression.

Registration with the United States Copyright Office is not necessary to establish an author's rights. Registration does, however, afford you certain clear legal advantages if you want to stop someone from copying your work or protecting it from unfair usage.

The term of a copyright (with some exceptions) is the life of the author(s) plus 50 years--instead of the previous term of 28 years (renewable for another 28)--measured usually from the date of first publication.

Trademarks

A trademark is a word or words, name, symbol, label, device, or picture attached to a manufacturer's or merchant's product to identify it and distinguish it from similar products. Its most common form is the brand name. A trademark is different from a copyright in that the protection is in the trademark symbol that distinguishes the product, not in the product itself.

A trademark comes into being as soon as and for as long as it is used - and if the legal requirements of proper trademark usage are observed. Registering trademarks does help protect them but only if they are strictly defended.

Trademarks that are not properly protected may become generic terms and available to all manufacturers. That's how Xerox almost went from being a trademark to a generic term for dry copying. That's how the term aspirin moved into the public domain.

> Some examples of other trademarks are:
> Intel, *The Computer Inside*
> IBM, *Solutions for a Small Planet*
> Pfizer, *We're Part of the Cure*
> Sherwin Williams, *We Cover the World*
> Lincoln, *What a Luxury Car Should Be*
> Ford, *Have You Driven a Ford Lately?*

A service mark is the same as a trademark except that it identifies and distinguishes the source of a service rather than a product. Normally, a trademark for goods appears on the product or on its packaging, while a service mark appears in advertising for the services.

For current copyright and trade mark information and registration contact the United States Patent and Trademark Office at (800) 786-9199 or on the World Wide Web at www.uspto.gov.

Patents

A U.S. patent gives its owner(s) the right to keep others from making, using, and selling the owner's invention in the United States for 17 years (14 years for design patents). Patents are not renewable, but a new and useful improvement of something already patented, as well as a new use of an old device, may be the subject of new patents.

Patents are granted only to the true inventor. Like a copyright, a patent cannot be obtained on just an idea or suggestion. Patents are issued only after a complete application is filed in the Patent Office, an official search of the prior process, machine, or composition of matter has been conducted, and the Patent Office is satisfied that all the claims are allowable. A patent may not be obtained if the invention was in public use or on sale in the United States for more than one year prior to the filing of the patent application.

Because a U.S. patent does not confer rights abroad, application must be made anywhere protection is sought.

EMPLOYER -- EMPLOYEE RELATIONSHIPS

Your Responsibilities as an Employer

Since you can not do everything yourself in a growing business, you may need to hire people to produce the work. You may believe that you are hiring independent contractors and then later find out that the law really considers them to be employees. Whether or not a person is an employee is not determined by the contract but by the totality of the circumstances.

Factors that are considered when determining whether a person is considered an employee versus an independent contractor include (a) the ability to instruct employee about where, when and how they are to work; (b) requiring that the services are to be performed by a particular person; (c) participating and requiring that the person undergo specific types and forms of training, attend specific meetings or require detailed reports; (d) determining or regulating the hours of performance; (e) furnishing the equipment for the person to perform services; (f) the services performed by the individual are exclusive to employer or are generally available to the public.

When you hire an employee, in most states the relationship that is created is an "employment at will." This means that the employer can discharge the employee, or the employee can quit, for any lawful reason. While this is the general rule, employers can sometimes accidentally offer an employment contract which modifies the "employment at will" relationship. Care should be given with respect to the language of advertisements, language of preprinted employment applications in the contents of the employment policies and procedure manual.

Employees can make or break a business. Therefore, you should be familiar with the basic requirements that ensure good relations and compliance with federal and state regulations. Your legal responsibility as an employer should center around five basic requirements:

1. Maintaining adequate records (pertaining to compensation/taxes, injuries and illnesses).

2. Complying with Human Rights Standards (observing anti discrimination procedures).

3. Complying with Occupational Safety and Health (OSHA) Standards -- assuring safe and healthful working conditions.

4. Creating an environment that does not allow for harassment. Owners need to make sure there is a process for addressing harassment complaints and that it is available to all employees. If employees do not feel there is no channel for complaints, it is as good as not having a policy and you as the employer are at fault.

5. Administering accurate benefits information including, medical, dental, 401K, life insurance, workers compensation, disability and pension.

Each of these issues represents a major subject of federal and state legislation. Don't under estimate the importance of state legislation. Often it is stricter than federal legislation and it puts additional obligations on you and your business.

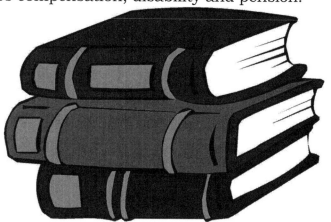

Beyond the five highlights above, you should be familiar with the many requirements involving employee and in some cases their families. Detailed information is available through appropriate federal and state agencies. You may also want to check with your local Chamber of Commerce if you want to understand the scope of voluntary action practiced by your competition. In particular, you should be aware of the following subjects and distinctions:

- Difference between salaries and wages. There are rules when an employee can be salaried verses hourly.

- Persons exempted from minimum wage/maximum hours requirements.

- Definition of overtime and its compensation.

- Definition of contract or temporary employees.

- Child Labor Laws (employment of minors) (Generally, minor refers to any person under the age of 18) notwithstanding certain exemptions (employing family members) the minimum age for hiring is age 16. The list of prohibited occupations for minors is a major aspect of the various child labor laws.

These are some of the most significant labor laws in effect now:

- The Civil Rights Act of 1964
  (applicable for any employer of 15 or more persons).
- The Age Discrimination in Employment Act
  (applicable for employees between ages 40 and 70).
- The Rehabilitation Act of 1973
  (applicable to any employer receiving federal financial assistance and/or federal contracts of $2,500 or more).
- Occupational Safety and Health (OSHA) Standards.
- The Federal Unemployment Tax Act
  (unemployment compensation regulation).
- Workers Compensation Laws
  (covering financial benefits for employees with work-related disabilities, illnesses or fatalities)
- Income Tax Laws
  (regulating computation and withholding procedures)
- Social Security Tax Laws
  (regulating computation and withholding procedures. In addition to the salary and benefits you pay them, you are required to pay FICA on their income, which can be as high as 7.65%.)
- The 1991 Civil Rights Act
  (provides compensatory and punitive damages for intentional discrimination)
- Civil Rights Act of 1866
- Equal Employment Opportunities Act of 1972
- Equal Pay Act of 1963
- Title I of the American with Disabilities Act of 1990

In addition to labor laws the following policies should also be mentioned:

- ERISA
- Grievance procedures and processes
- Fair Labor Standards Act

A 1993 Supreme Court ruling of major importance to large and small businesses made it easier for workers to win lawsuits claiming they were sexually harassed on the job. It established that victims of harassment need only show offensive conduct created an environment that, "a reasonable person would find hostile or abusive."

A Fair Work Place

It's up to you to strike a proper balance between your interests and those of your employees. As long as you don't discriminate, nobody interferes with your hiring and firing procedures. Make sure you know the legal definition of discrimination as provided by the various laws listed earlier. It virtually covers all minority groups, not only racial minorities.

At the same time, don't operate in a vacuum. You may have competitors who treat their employees better, show better interpersonal skills, offer better salaries. Then there are the unwritten social laws of ethics, etiquettes and other norms and conventions an employee might successfully appeal to when problems or litigation become imminent.

References

One of the basic rights an employee has upon leaving (voluntarily or forced) is certification of employment. You don't have to write flowery letters of reference or recommendation (especially when there is no justification), but you should provide basic data (length of employment, position occupied). Also, you have to provide essential information such as tax withholding (income and social security) certificates.

Employees' Insurance and Benefits

You might be concerned about the topic of "employees' insurance". It's not as complicated as it may appear, especially if you can stick with the minimum requirements. "Insurance" in this context is a somewhat vague term. Often, it constitutes the areas of social security, unemployment, workers compensation, and health and life insurance.

Social security is a federal matter. Unemployment compensation is regulated by both federal and state governments. You will have to check on the appropriate regulations for each.

Workers compensation, for the most part, is regulated on the state level; and you should check with the appropriate state agencies. In some states, for example, it's up to the individual employer to make arrangements with insurance companies. A group insurance policy may be obtained from any private company that is authorized by the state to provide such coverage. Also, there is a state compensation insurance fund employers may join. Making the right choice between those options would require extensive analysis and the cooperation of many specialists, such as your accountant, lawyer and various insurance agents.

Providing health care and life insurance is a strictly voluntary matter. For competitive reasons, however, you might need to offer at least some coverage. In fact, many employers do so. Since this is the domain of private insurance companies, it takes more than a few pages or hours of work to come up with sensible answers. Rates and conditions vary and numerous combinations between life and health coverage limits are available. Once you have opted to provide this type of insurance, many states stipulate certain standards be maintained.

A WORD ABOUT CONTRACTS

Most business transactions involve commitments to furnish goods, services or real property; these commitments are usually in the form of contracts - an agreement that is enforceable by law. Modern business could not exist without such understandings.

Use of the contract in business affairs ensures, to some extent, the performance of an agreement, since a party that breaks a contract may be sued in court for the damages caused by the breach. Sometimes, however, a party that breaks a contract may be persuaded to make an out-of-court settlement, thus saving the expense of legal proceedings.

Consideration

A contract is the results of a bargain. This implies that each party to the contract gives up something, or promises to, in exchange for something given up or promised by the other party. This is called consideration. For example, in the sale of an automobile, the consideration on one side is the promise to pay $15,000; and on the other, the promise to deliver a car. With rare exceptions, a promise by one party, without some form of consideration being offered by the other party, does not result in a contract, regardless of the sincerity of the promise.

Written or Oral

It is commonly accepted that an enforceable contract must be in writing. This is usually not correct. Most oral contracts *are* enforceable, but written contracts are easier to prove.

Some types of contracts *must* be in writing, for example, contracts for the purchase or sale of any interest in real property, contracts to pay debts of others, and contracts that require more than a year to perform. Contracts for the sale of personal property, that is, movable property, as distinguished from land, at a price above a specified sum set by law in your state, must be in writing.

As usual, be cautious of any document you put your signature on. Although only a few types of contract must be in writing, the terms of a written contract ordinarily may not be contradicted in court by oral testimony. The written items are what you must abide by.

THE LEASE

References on Lessor

While it may be desirable to own your own home, it might be to your disadvantage to own the building or space for your business. The major reason for a brand new entrepreneur to lease rather than to own property is that he does not tie up capital which he could otherwise use in the production process. Also, with a lease it's much easier to move into a new location if the business is successful and has to be expanded.

But before you rush into any lease agreement, check out your prospective landlord first -- the same way you would check out a lawyer. As a small business entrepreneur, you may have to deal with a landlord who is not a real person, but a rather huge property management firm or investors' association, represented by a manager, director or lawyer. In other words, you most likely will never have access to the owner or the many owners of the space you want to rent or lease.

Such a situation establishes a power balance that rarely tilts in favor of you as a tenant. Quite a few companies interpret their responsibilities and duties liberally. They may not provide enough parking space, may not furnish all the services and utilities they are supposed to; may not repair the air conditioning or heating systems; may be casual on window cleaning and snow removal, and much more.

To find out what company you can trust, which one has a good or at least fair reputation, check for references with the Better Business Bureau and the Chamber of Commerce. And, of course, don't forget to talk to the tenants in the complex or mall you would like to move into.

Once you have made such a pre-selection, your actual bargaining position will be relatively weak. In most cases you will be presented with a printed contract, prepared by the company's lawyers. Obviously, the terms will favor the lessor. Yet if he does have some vacancies or is relatively new in the market, you may have some leverage on a few key clauses. Concentrate on the ones you consider most crucial to your business. When possible, let your lawyer do the talking for you.

Characteristics of an Ideal Lease

The following summary of an ideal lease (from a tenant's point of view) should help you to better identify those provisions that are in your best interest -- try to come as close as possible with your actual lease.

1. The facilities you are leasing are in excellent condition. That is, almost new and well maintained. They provide just the type of space you need.

2. Your contract lists clearly all the common areas that you are entitled to use, such as number of parking spaces, driveways, loading docks, hallways, elevators, storage and waste space.

3. Your contract is based on fixed, flat amount rental payments.

4. No security deposits are required.

5. The rent is at least equal to, if not lower than, comparable space in a similar location.

6. You have a short-term lease (up to two years) with the option to renew, without clauses that stipulate periodic rent increase.

7. The lessor does not object to alterations you consider necessary. He allows you to remove any improvements upon your leaving.

8. The lessor is responsible for maintenance, repairs, utilities, taxes and insurance.

9. You can use the space for any (lawful) purpose.

10. You can sublet or assign the lease to someone else without prior permission.

11. There are minimal or no restrictions on your promotional activities.

12. The lessor won't accommodate direct competitors of yours, at least not the ones that are economically   stronger than you.

13. There is a contingency clause allowing you to cancel the lease (if the premises are substantially damaged by fire or other events, or if your business is less successful than you initially anticipated).

Remember, these are only guidelines. You will have to consider what is most important to your business then hold the line on those things in your negotiations.

The Shopping Center Lease

If it takes a fight to obtain a favorable lease in general, it takes a battle to obtain a good shopping center lease. Only major stores or chains have the power to negotiate. On the other hand, you might want to give it a try, particularly in those cases where you can appeal to "common sense" and "fair play".

For example, imagine that you want to move into a specific shopping center because you anticipate that the national department store already there will generate millions of customers who have to pass your location. In this case you should shoot for a provision that allows you to terminate your obligations if the "big boys" cease their operation there. Similarly, in cases of new shopping centers, reach an agreement saying that you are not obligated to begin business or pay rent until the major tenants have opened their facilities.

In addition, you may want to have your opening coincide with the start of your best selling season. This way your income is high during the first weeks of your operations. If nothing else, this should give you a strong psychological boost.

If the center has not even been built, ask for a site plan to be part of your lease. You should make sure that the space and size of the location you initially selected cannot be changed or rearranged without your consent. Also, make sure that other changes that might be made will not interfere with visibility and/or access to your location.

Besides those points, one of the most crucial factors is the type of payments you have agreed on. Generally, there are four different methods or ways of paying rent:

1. **The flat rental payment:** Your monthly or yearly payment remains the same over the entire lease term.

2. **Periodic increases in payment:** The period is usually defined as one year. Under a three-year lease you might be expected to pay a total of $12,000 during the first year, $14,000 during the second year, and $17,000 during the third year. Make sure you understand, and agree to, the basis for increases.

3. **The net lease:** You pay not only the basic rent as stated in your contract, you also pay taxes, insurance, repairs, and so on. Obviously, under such an agreement you -- instead of the lessor -- bear the risk of (substantial) cost increases and of not knowing what the real cost and/or benefits of the lease are.

4. **The percentage lease:** This method is equally tricky in terms of financial planning and cost control. Generally, a percentage lease specifies a minimum amount the lessor is entitled to, regardless of how well you do in your business. This portion is called "base rent". In addition, you have to pay a percentage of your gross sales. If you are forced into such an agreement, you should see that the percentage clause takes effect only on sales over a certain (relatively high) amount. You should also see that there is a cap -- an upper limit -- on the amount that has to be paid under the percentage clause.

For example: The lessor might receive $12,000 a year as base rent. If your gross sales exceed $250,000 a year, he might be entitled to 3.5 percent of those sales, but to not more than a total rent of $20,000. To make things even more delicate, be cautious in defining your gross sales. In particular, you may want to have excluded: sales to employees; sales taxes; refundable deposits; charges for deliveries and installations, etc.

Improvements and Repairs

As you may have gathered from the preceding information, improvements, repairs and maintenance, may rarely be bargaining chips at your disposal. On the other hand, if you are indeed responsible for most of those items, you would want a lease that spells out your responsibilities in detail. You don't want to carry one ounce more than necessary. Therefore, your lease should address the following questions:

- What condition will the premises be in when you start your business?

- At what times and to what extent, if at all, will the lessor provide promotional support for your business?

- Must your improvements and the contractors you select for maintenance be approved by the landlord?

- Who takes care of the common areas (restrooms, sidewalks, etc.)?

- Who takes care of the structure and the exterior of the building?

- Who takes care of repairs and reconstruction due to weather, fire, earthquakes, riots, etc.?

- Can you recover your investments for improvements?

If you need consent and approval of the lessor for a number of items, he should be required to defend his decisions reasonably.

Options to Renew

An option to renew a lease is especially desirable if you are somewhat uncertain about your business. It works well in cases where you think, "If it doesn't work out for me to be my own boss, I can quit or sell out," or when you really anticipate a smashing success and you might have to move into bigger facilities earlier than originally scheduled. Under an option clause, you may extend your lease beyond the initial term; but you don't have to. Generally, such a lease will specify how far in advance you must declare your intentions (usually 90 days before expiration date). If your original lease covers three years, you might want to reserve rights for an additional three or four 3-year terms. Ninety days before each period you let the lessor know whether or not you want to stay, that is, whether or not you want to take advantage of your option. But beware! If you toy with the thought of covering several more years by renewal options, the other party will insist on periodically increasing the rent. An option is not an automatic tool to beat inflation.

Usually, rent adjustments are part of the option clause and thus spelled out in advance. This way, you have a sound basis for calculating your cost. However, if you are in a negotiating position on this item, you might want to provide that the rent will be increased only at the time of each renewal.

Stay clear of any provision that says "the rent will be renegotiated at the beginning of each renewal period", or something to that extent. Most often an appropriate, mutually satisfying agreement cannot be reached then. Matters wind up in court. There, the judge will listen to expert testimony to determine a "reasonable rent". Such a solution will be time consuming and costly, to say the least.

Disputes, or: Their Opinion Against Yours

Although a well designed lease agreement minimizes chances for serious disputes, you have to anticipate some problems. In recent years, fortunately, tenants' rights have increased substantially. So, as a tenant, it's likely you can get off the hook even if the language of your contract seems to indicate otherwise -- in particular, when "fair play" or "equal economic chances" are at issue. There have been cases where judges have found it appropriate for a retailer to withhold rent because the shopping mall owner had violated his contract by leasing space to competitors. Judges have also ruled in favor of tenants wherein mall operators had arbitrarily curtailed parking space in connection with expansion and construction projects. Naturally, each case is different; but good legal advice does pay off.

Another issue that frequently intimidates tenants is the uncompromising language or paragraph that apparently gives the lessor the right to enter your business premises and regain possession if you don't pay your rent on time or fail to comply with some provisions in your lease. In most states the lessor has absolutely no chance of evicting you before going to court first -- despite what the lease says. Thus, if stormy weather is indeed inevitable, you will have plenty of time to prepare your case, to get your facts. Court hearings don't happen the next day. On the other hand, don't forget basic principles. Give the Property Management Company at least a chance to rectify apparent problems through personal (verbal or written) communication. If you think a letter is necessary, deliver it in person or by certified mail. Do this in the early stages of the disagreement. Don't wait for weeks or months. If a frank discussion or an explicit letter (perhaps some give and take) don't get results, that's when to take legal action.

HIRING A LAWYER

How to Find the Right One

Small enterprise or large, every businessperson, sooner or later, needs professional legal help. Too often the necessity and the decision occur at the same time. Too often choosing the wrong lawyer makes the problem worse. Selecting a lawyer should not be a makeshift decision, culled out of the Yellow Pages.

The time to choose a lawyer is before not after trouble arrives. A major failure of many small businesses is the reluctance to use outside professional help. Some think they can't afford hired experts. Others think they're too small to need the expertise. But often an outside, impartial, trained and experienced viewpoint is just what's needed.

How do you know if the person you've retained is right or a totally wrong fit for your need? Even if you already have a lawyer or accountant handling your personal affairs, keeping him or her for your company's needs too may not be a good idea. What you want is someone fully familiar with business law. Lawyer referral services operated by local bar associations, for the most part, provide only a list of names of lawyers and law firms. If they did rank lawyers by qualifications -- they would pretty soon find themselves in hot water, for competitive reasons.

Go out and do some walking and talk to other people in your neighborhood who have run a small business for a while. Visit the shoe store, tailor, grocer or service station manager. Ask them who their present lawyer is and what they think of that person. Ask them about other lawyers that they have used and what made them change.

Then go a step further. Talk to your banker, accountant, insurance agent or broker as well. These professionals have frequent contacts with lawyers representing business clients. Whomever you ask -- friends, relatives, business associates or your former boss -- make sure you ask about lawyers experienced with business clients.

Modern legal practice is extremely specialized. If you set up an appointment and tell them the reason, most lawyers will be, or at least should be, happy to give you about half an hour at no charge for a personal interview. Ask especially: Do you have other clients like me? Are you experienced in the kind of work I'll be asking you to do?

Most important is that you feel comfortable in dealing with the lawyer you choose. Keep in mind that you are interviewing a person who could someday be responsible for the life and health of your company. If you get the sense that he or she will feel personally responsible for protecting your interests and makes you feel like a friend as well as client you may well be talking to the right person for your company.

Startup businesses generally have two choices: a small law firm, or a junior person in a large legal office. Either alternative can offer a good candidate. However, in either case, here's a tip: Legal services can be quite expensive. When you need a legal document, such as a contract or a patent application—avoid asking your attorney to write it. Look around for a similar kind of document, and draft what you need yourself by copying as much as you feel you need. Then show it to your attorney and ask him or her to suggest revisions. This saves a lot of time and reduces the amount you spend on fees. Also, it helps to ensure that your lawyer understands clearly what you want the document to accomplish.

It might be necessary to get a new lawyer when things don't go as smoothly as you had expected. As a general rule, you can change your lawyer as easily as you can change your physician.

Characteristics of a Lawyer

In particular, consider the following points:

1. Your lawyer should have appropriate experience. He or she should have had clients in your field or in closely related fields.

2. Make sure that your business lawyer is familiar with the tax implications associated with your business form. He or she should understand the differences.

3. Your lawyer should be proactive and not reactive. You want someone who, when you describe your business, is making suggestions on how to improve your liability protection or create tax savings.

4. You should be able to test a lawyer's knowledge base by seeking business advice. If a lawyer presents a good business solution to your issue, he or she probably has the skill sets to find ways to make opportunities work, rather than to shoot them down.

5. Effective legal counsel cannot be given without appropriate background and a dedicated lawyer should want to have background of the particulars of your company. One example: A business lawyer with an almost perfect track record of winning cases for her department store and corporate clients may be of little benefit to you because she has no ties to or understanding of the local Small Business Administration office, where some of your most basic legal questions could be answered without any cost to you. This is another way of saying, "Spend your law dollars wisely.

6. Psychological factors are always important. Empathy and compatibility of personalities between you and your lawyer are the backbone of the relationship. If the first meeting makes you feel uncomfortable for any reason you are well advised to say goodbye instead of "see you later".

7. Your lawyer should have time for you. Ask immediately if the lawyer or his assistants can commit to returning your calls within a certain number of hours. Clients should be able to expect a return call within one day. Can you think of anything more aggravating than having a lawsuit hanging over your head or knowing a competitor is taking unfair advantage of you while your lawyer is unavailable because he has too many other clients or you are last on the list

because you are the smallest client in his or her office.

5. Beware of those lawyers who give you 395 reasons why something can't be done. In the meantime, you could be losing customers and money, as well as your temper and good manners. You need a lawyer who is able to find a proper balance between prudence and practicality --someone who comes up with the right solution, and is willing and able to go to bat for you and your interests.

6. Last, but not least, the price has to be right. That is, skip the cheap ones as well as those with the golden doorknobs. Look for the ones who charge around $175 to $275 an hour. (In smaller cities and rural areas, rates should be much lower.)

About Fees and Bills

Once you have decided on a specific lawyer and you are about ready to give him/her the first assignment, make sure you understand how charges are made for various services. If your lawyer is among those who forgets or is hesitant to spell out the financial rules of the game in detail, ask for them explicitly. Don't be bashful. It is perfectly legitimate for you to know what's going on and at what stage of the process you might strain your financial resources. Ask for a written retainer, a cost estimate for services. You can get a good feeling about what will be out-of-pocket expenses and estimated cost for services. During a legal issue, ask for updates on costs incurred, so that when you are finished you don't get slapped with a bill that you didn't expect.

Remember that everything is negotiable, even lawyers pricing.

Usually lawyers have three basic ways of charging:

1. Hourly charges, depending on where the lawyer practices and on his/her skills and experience.

2.   A flat fee for a specific assignment. Done on this basis, the drawing up of a real estate purchase agreement or contract currently goes for about $400, a simple will for about $600, and incorporating procedures for roughly $1,000. With a flat fee arrangement, you are protected and know exactly how much money to set aside regardless of how much time the lawyer actually spends on the job.

3.   When the stakes are really high, a lawyer may propose a contingency fee. This is a percentage, quite often a considerable one, of the amount a lawyer obtains for you in a negotiated settlement or through a trial. At first glance you might not like this option too well, in particular when the percentage exceeds 30 percent and you anticipate winning close to a million dollars or so. But think twice. Often law is not an airtight, predictable science. If the wind shifts and your lawyer does not recover anything, this means your fee is zero under such an arrangement.

Independent from any basic fee arrangement agreed upon, lawyers usually expect reimbursement for out-of-pocket expenses. These would include mileage, parking, long distance phone calls, postage, transcripts of testimony, among others. Sometimes a case involves a combination of all of the three methods explained above or a very individual agreement will be necessary. This is usually the case in instances that represent a unique problem, one that has not been described in the law books or one that involves a large volume of evening or weekend work.

Even though you may have disregarded the lowest cost lawyer in the first place, do a little computing and figuring anyhow. Someone who charges a reasonable $150 an hour may not be a bargain if he needs two hours for a job that might be done elsewhere in one hour for $175.

By now you have probably realized: Legal fees are not engraved in stone. They

---

are negotiable and what really counts is the bottom line -- the amount you put on the check for your lawyer. In other words, the hourly fee is only a relative indicator of a lawyer's attractiveness. Before you make a contract, get the whole story as clearly as you can. One way to get a good deal, to get "high mileage" out of your legal expenses, is to guarantee a minimum number of hours of work during the year. This usually leads to a reduced hourly rate with a discount somewhere between 10 and 15 percent. This means a $200 an hour lawyer may be willing to settle for $180 or $170 an hour if you guarantee 150 or 200 hours of work.

If you do have to deal with large or prolonged cases, don't forget to ask your lawyer for progress reports, either at certain stages (after important letters have been received or sent off) or at certain times (twice a month, for example) of the case. As one part of these reports, look for statements by your lawyer in regard to expenses -- remaining or still anticipated. This, in turn, should help you decide whether to go ahead and intensify your efforts or to bring the case to an early conclusion.

A Word About Ethics or Moral Responsibilities

Law as a profession is, much like medicine, strictly regulated by professional organizations. One aspect of supervision is that lawyers have to operate within a rigid framework of ethical considerations. If they look the other way or attempt to cut corners, they are subject to disciplinary action and they could even lose their license to practice. Since the regulatory agencies (the bar associations) have to rely on incidents of problems or misconduct which are reported, a client has to air his or her complaints officially to get action. On the other hand, if some problems actually  develop, most can and will be taken care of by talking them over with your lawyer. The lawyer must keep secret and confidential all that you say in connection with your legal representation. The lawyer cannot disclose any of your information, be it in court or elsewhere, without your consent. Self-interest is no excuse for not giving you proper, unrestricted attention.

If your lawyer has personal business interests or connections that might prevent him from being objective, he must let you know this before he takes on the job. Then it's up to you to decide what to do -- stick with him or look for someone else.

The ethics of law also require that the lawyer is completely competent. This means that if it turns out that he has an insufficient background to do the job for which you hired him, he must either refer you to somebody else or seek the help of a colleague with appropriate experience.

Our legal system is highly competitive; some critics maintain that the real issue is not justice but winning a case. By the same token, our legal system provides that a lawyer must work vigorously for your interests. On the other hand, he or she is bound by basic rules of behavior. Your lawyer may not knowingly use perjured testimony or false evidence. (He may not knowingly make false statements of law or fact in court.) And, among many other stipulations, a lawyer is not allowed to encourage or support activities of the client which are evidently illegal or fraudulent. So, don't make unreasonable demands or expect wonders.

Your Legal Rights as a Client

The rights of a client have been clearly spelled out and officially documented. Among the most important are the following:

1.   Receiving clear answers to all questions.

2.   Having matters handled diligently and competently.

3.   Being kept informed of the status of a case.

4. Receiving prompt responses to phone calls and letters.

5. Being charged fees that are reasonable, i.e. fees that can be defended rationally.

6. Receiving itemized statement of services performed as well as receiving full explanations of billing practices.

7. Being treated courteously by the lawyer and his or her associates and employees. You don't have to accept being talked down to.

8. Having confidential legal conferences, free from unwarranted interruptions. That means you are entitled to object if the conference you paid for is constantly interfered with by unrelated phone calls or other disturbances.

If Problems Do Develop

Your lawyer is responsible for using reasonable care in representing you. If you feel such care is missing:

-   have a conference with your lawyer explaining how you see the issue.

-   follow up with a letter, repeating your main concerns.

-   if you don't reach a satisfactory agreement, consider pursuing your concern on higher levels.

-   if you think you have strong evidence of fraud, deceit or negligence, consider suing for malpractice.

-   if the problem appears to be more of an ethical nature, i.e. if he or she has violated good taste, manners and professional codes of conduct, you may initiate grievance procedures with the state bar association.

These suggestions should not leave you with the impression that most lawyers attempt to take unfair advantage of you and your hard-earned money. Just the opposite is true. As in any other personal relationship, most conflicts (real or apparent) can be resolved through a candid conversation.

In this chapter you have learned:

Business Forms
1. *Most entrepreneurs start out as sole proprietors, partners or by establishing a closed corporation.*
2. *Selecting the right form for your business requires close cooperation and coordination between you, your lawyer and your accountant.*
3. *The main disadvantage of a sole proprietorship as well as a partnership is that the owners face unlimited personal liability if the business goes belly-up, or if threatened by a substantial lawsuit.*
4. *The main advantages of forming a corporation are limited personal liability and flexibility in tax matters.*
5. *Incorporating has become rather easy in recent years, making it an ideal form of business even for small businesses. One caution: Government regulation calls for more paperwork when you incorporate.*

The Business Name
1. *As soon as you use anything but your full name for doing business, you are required to file an assumed name.*
2. *Filing an assumed name does not protect your name against usage by others.*
3. *The business name is an integral part of your overall image. Choose it wisely and do some pre-testing before you make a final decision.*
4. *In most states corporations are allowed to file assumed names, i.e. you can disguise that your business is in fact incorporated. That means, you actually have to file twice -- for the corporate name as opposed to your own, plus for the assumed name of the corporation.*

Chapter 7

Asking the Right Questions - Everything depends on it

> *In this chapter you will learn:*
>
> 1. *What is market research?*
> 2. *How can you use market research before you go into business?*
> 3. *What are the ways of conducting market research?*
> 4. *How do you prepare a questionnaire?*
> 5. *How do you interpret and use the results of the survey?*
> 6. *What are some sources of information for market research?*

Several years ago, two Japanese car manufacturers, Toyota and Datsun, decided to survey American car owners on both their likes and dislikes about the automobiles they were driving.

The American owners' major complaint was that their cars were not "energy efficient". In other words, they felt they were not getting as many miles to the gallon as they would have liked.

The Japanese quickly realized that if they introduced their energy efficient cars into the American market, the cars would sell.

At the time of this research, the energy crisis had tripled the price which consumers were paying at the pumps. The Japanese brought their energy efficient cars to America and took advantage of the tremendous sales demand for them. These two cars are still very popular with consumers.

Another company, a leading food producer of margarine, conducted its market research for a different reason. In 1981 and 1982, one of its leading products, a special blend of margarine, enjoyed a sixty percent market share.

Then in October 1982, two competitors entered the market and the company immediately noticed a sharp decline in market share. Sales continued to decline in early 1983. To find out what the problem was, they did a consumer market research survey. It showed that the two competitors introduced their margarine blend with much stronger packaging which had far greater eye appeal.

As a direct result of these findings, the margarine producer redesigned its packaging and immediately began to recover some of its lost market share.

In both these examples, market research helped two big corporations make important decisions about their products. You've seen hundreds of examples of market research at work including the current "taste tests" of soft drinks, beer, cake mixes and peanut butter.

All these manufacturers realize, as you do, that it is the public who ultimately decides the fate of their companies.

But market research is by no means limited to big business. Indeed, smaller companies usually have more to gain from finding out what consumers want.

For example, a local car wash business felt that they weren't getting enough mileage out of their advertising dollars. The owner was spending his advertising budget on newspaper, direct mailing, and yellow pages advertising. Although the business was profitable, the owner felt it could be doing better.

He decided to set aside an entire week to conduct a market research survey and during that time, he asked every one of his customers how they had heard about his car wash. Much to his surprise, he found that the majority of customers had either seen his sign outside the car wash or received one of his advertising flyers in the mail. Only 5% of his customers had come to the car wash as a result of seeing advertising in either the newspaper or the yellow pages.

Since the owner was spending 80% of his advertising dollars on newspaper advertising, he quickly switched his concentration of advertising to direct mail and built a larger sign outside his car wash. Not surprisingly, his business doubled over the next year.

Likewise, the owner of a small restaurant specializing in authentic Italian food, decided to conduct an informal survey on his business. His advertising campaign emphasized the restaurant as a good "American family" restaurant. The owner polled his customers and found that over 90% of them patronized the restaurant because of the excellent Italian food. When he switched his advertising campaign to highlight the good "Italian" food, his business tripled.

In both cases, a market research survey brought direct, positive results in the form of increased sales and profits. Such a survey can help you in the same way. Market research may not always tell you what you should do, but it should always tell you what you should not do.

WHAT IS MARKET RESEARCH?

Market Research is, very simply, a way to get particular information from certain consumers and available resources. The main purpose of market research is to provide data that will help a small business's marketing efforts be more effective. Market research is absolutely necessary when you are starting a business from scratch.

Market Research tells you about the market and its preferences, opinions, habits, trends and plans. It also tells where the market is, its geography, its demographics (statistical characteristics) and information about the psychology of the market and the marketplace. The information you get from such research can help you make very important decisions affecting your business.

It is essential for a small business to have accurate, current consumer

information. A small business owner does not usually have large amounts of money to gamble on making a wrong move or wrong decisions regarding his business. For example, when Nabisco decided to introduce Oreo Cookie ice cream to the public, they chose three cities in which to test market their product.

Whether or not the ice cream made it to the national market depended on the public reaction from those three cities. This method of testing the market is probably the best way to determine if there is a public demand for products and services.

Unfortunately, a small business simply cannot afford to make a large investment in something that might not work. Of course, you want your business to be a success; but how can that be guaranteed? Well, it can't be. But using a market research survey can reduce some of the risks which you'll take.

One of the greatest thrills for the entrepreneur is to learn something new about his market that gives him a competitive edge. Imagine what you will be able to do if you can discover an unmet need in the marketplace - why, you could be the only one with the missing product or service, which means you can have **ALL** of the market share.

So -- in the process of learning about your market through your research, you will be able to attach definite numbers to your plans and verify your marketing strategy. And, if you're lucky, you will even be able to uncover unfilled needs that you can take advantage of!

TYPES OF MARKET RESEARCH

Market research is very important to the success of a small company. There are generally two types of market research, primary and secondary.

Primary Market Research

Primary market research is conducted by yourself or someone in your company. This type of research will can be exploratory or specific. The goal of **exploratory** research is to get to the heart of a customer problem. Typically you will use open-ended questions with long detailed answers. These interviews are longer in nature with fewer participants and require a more skilled interviewer. **Specific** research is used with larger groups and is used to find specific solutions to problems identified in the exploratory research. These interviews are fairly structured and scripted. In conducting specific research you can use direct mail, telemarketing or personal interviews. Specific research is more costly to perform.

Secondary Market Research

Secondary market research is research and data that have been collected and assembled by other parties. Examples may be a database of names you purchased, city property records or other government agencies. Secondary market research saves time and money in collecting the data on your own because you don't have to find people and conduct the surveys. Secondary sources of market research are located in libraries, government agencies, commercial businesses (Dun & Bradstreet) or education locations like colleges, universities and technical colleges. Business collections in public libraries carry a wealth of information for market research. Ask you librarian today!

Market research can be done by anyone who is able to ask questions, is able to record the information, and takes the time to learn what it says. It can be done by you or someone you hire. And there are several ways you can accomplish this. If you are about to go into business, here are some things you might want to know about:

MARKET DEMAND

- How much of your product is currently being purchased?
- Who is buying what you want to sell (individuals, companies)?
- Where are they buying the product now (Internet, Walmart etc)
- When do they buy this type of product? Bicycles, for example, are sold during summer.
- Are the current customers satisfied with the quality, price and convenience?

COMPETITION

- Who are the competitors currently selling this product/service?
- What exact products or services do they sell?
- What type of quality do they offer?
- What is their pricing?
- How are products packaged?
- Where can customers get your competitor's product?

TRENDS

- What are the long-term trends that will affect my business?
- What do buyers want to see changed about the product?
- How are your target customers changing? Are they aging, eating better, spending more?
- Can you see other groups starting to use the product?

MARKETING STRATEGIES

- How to factors like aging, gender, family income, the economy, brand loyalty or lifestyle affect your business?
- How have prices for your product changed in the last year and 3 years?
- What is the main factor that determines the price you can charge for your product (quality, size, demand, convenience)?
- What are the benefits of my product?

If you are already in business, use the information you have before you go anywhere. You have a gold mine of information at your fingertips that is unavailable to the person not yet in business -- your own business records.

If you record your customers' addresses on sales receipts or credit applications, you will be able to get a sense of what your market area is. Where do your customers come from? Your customers' phone numbers will provide you with the same information -- just check with the phone company to find out the areas of your community to which the prefixes (the first three digits) are assigned. Take a local map and mark an star everywhere you have a customer; then look at where they are concentrated. Is there a pattern? If there is, you may be able to concentrate your advertising dollar.

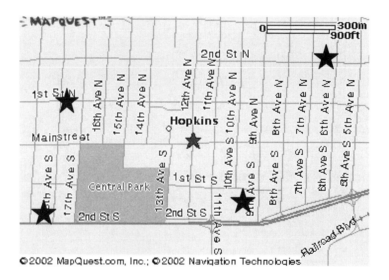

In some states, car license plate numbers are assigned by county. Send an employee out to your parking lot once in the morning, afternoon and evening to take a tally. In a couple of weeks, you will have a rough idea of how many of your customers live outside your county area.

After you are in business -- even for a short time -- your own employees will be an excellent source of information about customer characteristics and attitudes. Ask them to talk more with the customers they are serving over a one- or two-week period. What can they tell about their occupations, interests, and buying habits from some first-hand observation? You both may be surprised! Ask them to pay attention to what customers' request that you don't have in stock. Have them ask if they've tried anywhere else. Your employees will also know at what times of day you're the busiest, and what type of customers you're getting at those peak times.

If you are an established business, your market research will have a slightly different slant. Here are some examples:

- To whom is my advertising directed and is it reaching them?
- Is there a change in my customers' spending habits?
- Have my competitors made any recent changes?
- What services should I offer my customers?
- Should I be offering more than I offer now?
- What hours should I be open?
- What changes have taken place in the market?

These are just a few examples of the questions you might want to ask. Of course, you can easily alter the list to meet your individual needs.

How Do You Conduct Market Research?

Since Market Research is primarily the gathering of information about your market, there are any number of resources and places of information to help you. These include:

A. **The public library**. A trip to your public library is the best place to start. Come armed with a list of materials and head straight for the reference librarian. They're more than willing to help! Here are some of the resource materials available in your library.

1. **Magazines and reports**: Look in the Directory of Associations to find what trade associations there are for your type of business. This reference book will give the address and phone number of the association and a list of their publications. These association publications are a good source of information about all aspects of your business. Your library may have them or can find out how to get them for you.

2. **Sales and Marketing Management Magazine** publishes an annual "survey of buying power" issue. It is a source for a gold mine of information on every county in the U.S. and

cities over 10,000 in population. It provides the following information:

- Total population.

- Number of households: more crucial for many businesses than total population because products are bought to serve a household.

- Median cash income per household: tells you how affluent a city or county is compared to its neighbors.

- Population percentage breakdown by income: Income levels are broken down into a number of categories; for each income amount, tells you what percentage of households earn that much. Most businesses would rather have lots of households earning in the middle income range. This would mean there would be more customers. If there were a lot of poor people and a few rich ones, there would be fewer customers for your products, though the median cash income figure (above) might be the same.

- Total retail sales: how much is spent in retail stores by the customers?

- Total retail sales for each of these types of businesses: food, general merchandise, furniture and household appliances, automotive, and drug. (If you are in one of these businesses now, you can quickly find what percentage of the market you are capturing.)

B. **Any college in your area.**
Marketing departments of local universities and colleges will know where to find information that can help your business. If you are thinking of doing any survey research, they will be especially helpful -- and lots less expensive than professional market research firms. Call the business school or management department and ask for the person who coordinates the internship program or the outreach program. You will also profit from a visit to the college library.

C. **Vocational-Technical Institutes** (Vo-Tech schools) teach a wide variety of trade subjects. There are classes in running a supermarket, hardware store, landscaping, tree-trimming, home decorating and tailoring business. In addition, the individual instructors are a great source of information about the subjects they are teaching.

D. **Observation**. You can learn a great deal by simply observing what takes place in a shopping mall or individual store. You can count the number of people who pass by a certain store and watch their reactions. Do some people go in just to browse? You might even note the average length of time a customer spends in the store. Observation is one of the best methods of conducting market research. It provides quick and reliable information and is easy to do.

E. **Your Chamber of Commerce:** You probably are well acquainted with the activities of your local Chamber of Commerce. As part of their role as business boosters in your community, they collect information about the community and about local business. Chambers are often a good source for maps of the community.

Most of their services are free.

F. **Ask questions of potential consumers.** This is commonly known as conducting a survey. And because of the importance of asking the right questions we will concentrate heavily on this subject in the rest of the chapter.

G. **Wholesalers and Manufacturers.** This is a good source of information about a particular market, its customers and competition. Wholesalers, manufacturers and retailers generally know the trends in their business and will be pleased to help you. After all, when you go into business, you'll be buying from them!

H. **The Federal and State Government.** The U.S. Department of Commerce maintains field service offices throughout the country and each of these offices can provide you with pertinent information. The government also publishes reports on specific markets, industries and products, which may be of use to you. Likewise, you can obtain information from various state departments of commerce or business.

I. **Trade Associations**. The trade associations which serve a particular industry are wonderful sources of information about your industry and market.

J. **Business Publications.** Every industry has magazines, newsletters or pamphlets written exclusively for and about themselves. These can either be local or national.

K. **Media Representatives.** The advertising space salesmen who represent magazines, newspapers, radio stations and television stations are usually an excellent source of market information. Many of their companies maintain extensive research departments for this express purpose. And the information which they have is free.

L. **Competitors.** It is amazing what you can learn by going directly to your competition and asking for information, advice and help. If you feel uncomfortable about going to your direct competition, try contacting a business owner located 100 miles away or in the next state. Keep in mind, however, that information from a competitor, located even a short distance from you, may not necessarily apply to your business.

INTERNATIONAL MARKET RESEARCH

If you are looking at selling in the global economy, you need to expand your market research into the international arenas. Some specific resources for conducting international market research are:

Encyclopedia of Global Industries

This publication contains background information with trends and key statistics on 125 different business sectors.

Global Data Locator

By George Kurian

This book contains descriptions of the major international statistical publications with a listing of the tables found in them.

Guide to Country Information in International Governmental Organizations Publications

This guide will lead you to governmental sources of information on specific countries and topic areas. The book is organized by region and topic area.

International Business Information: How to Find It, How to Use It
By Ruth Pagel
The resource provides descriptive listings for sources of information that may be useful in researching company information, marketing data, industrial statistics or international transactions.

ASK THE RIGHT PEOPLE

If you can ask the right people the right questions, then interpret and apply the information to your best advantage, you'll be in Utopia. It's hard to find the "right" people, and it's difficult to formulate those perfect questions. But the time you invest at the front end will pay big rewards.

First, who are the "right" people? Naturally, they are the ones who are most like the people with whom you'll be doing business. At this point, you will have to do some "blue sky" thinking. If you know exactly what business you are going into, write down everything you know about the kinds of people who will buy from you. This could include factors such as:

Income level	Buying habits
Age	Special interests
Sex	Physical handicaps
Education	Own or rent a home
Location	Do-it-yourself type
Race	Eating habits
Religion	Spare time activities
Hobbies	Vacation activities
Skills	Age and type of car
Health	Household pets
Marital Status	Job and position
Number of children	Age of home

If you plan a business-to-business activity, develop a similar list from a business standpoint including:

Sales level	Titles of people you need to contact

# of employees	Duties
Geography	Buying power (authority to buy)
Industry	Specific needs
Category (doctors, lawyers, chiropractors)	
Qualifying criteria (what makes them a target)	
Charities supported	Company goals
Time frame for decisions	Dollar limits
Competitive products	Substitute products

When all the factors which apply to your potential customers are described completely, you have what is called a "customer profile":

CUSTOMER PROFILE

Income:	$30,000 to $55,000
Age:	21-35
Sex:	Male
Education:	Some College or graduated
Location:	10 mile radius
Hobbies:	Sports, especially hiking & biking
Health:	Excellent, very active
Married:	Yes

It could be a very specific profile, as it would be if you were selling chair lifts to handicapped homeowners. Or it could be a broad profile as it would be if you were opening a photography studio.

Your next step is to locate the right people to match your profile. A large number of possibilities exist. Do you stand on a street corner, watching for the most obvious match-ups? Do you stand near a store (that might offer the same product you plan to offer) and interview customers? Do you buy a mailing list that seems to match your profile then conduct a mail survey? Or -- if your profile is particularly tough -- do you first conduct a general survey, then try to extract a smaller group that matches your profile? You'll have to decide.

When you identify the group of people who most closely match your customer profile, these people become your "sample". They are a sample of the general public who are the type of people you will most likely do business with. If they are a truly representative sample, their number could be quite small. (National polling organizations, such as the Gallup Poll and the Harris Poll, use such a scientifically selected sample that they can reach conclusions from a tiny fraction of 1% of the total audience.) Just remember that the smaller your sample, the greater will be your margin of error. A sample that's too small, or poorly selected, can give you false information.

Surveys are an essential part of market research. As we've stated before, the object of a survey is to gather information from a group of individuals or businesses on a specific subject. There are basically four types of survey interviews:

1. Personal interview
2. Telephone interview
3. Mail interview
4. Focus groups or group interview

Personal Interview

This is the most popular questioning technique. It's the one which produces the most accurate and complete information. It is also the most costly and time consuming.

Using this method, you deal with people on a one-to-one basis. You conduct the interview yourself or hire someone to do it for you.

The participants in your survey can either be chosen randomly (i.e., on a downtown street corner) or specifically (i.e., in front of a particular store or every house on a block).

It is the most accurate method because you are talking directly to the people involved in the survey. In fact, you will probably find that some individuals will tell you more than you want to know on the subject.

It is the most costly because it involves a large amount of your time, especially if you, or people you hire, interview people in a number of different locations.

There are some very important advantages in using the personal interview survey. They include:

A You can ask your questions in great detail.
A You can show pictures and diagrams.
A You can ask follow-up questions.

One thing to keep in mind when conducting the survey is to aim for a good cross-section of the population. Or more specifically, look for people who are **most like** the customers you will serve. For example, if you are thinking of starting a cooking school, you might assume you need to interview only women. Wrong! There are plenty of boys and men who enjoy cooking and would like to start taking lessons. And, if they don't, they have wives, girlfriends, mothers and sisters who might have some very definite opinions on the subject.

The same is true if you're planning to open a sporting goods repair shop. Don't assume that all of your customers will be men. You might be omitting a very valuable group of people who could give you some necessary insights into your business.

Telephone Interview

The second, and perhaps the easiest, type of survey can be done by phone. You can conduct this type of interview from your home and do as many or as few as your schedule allows. One disadvantage is that it is much harder to choose a select group of people to interview using this system. Instead, you will probably have a very random sampling of people. Your questionnaire should be brief. People can become very impatient when they are kept on the phone for a long period of time. It's important to remember that every person you talk to is doing you a favor and they know it. Be considerate of their time schedules.

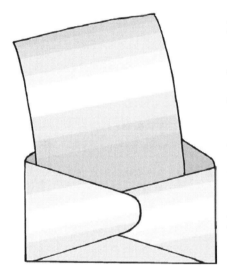

Mail Interview

This type of survey requires much more organization than the first two. You will need a select list of people and their mailing addresses to send out your questionnaire. You may find that a mailing list is available (at a cost of $20-$40 per thousand names) that enables you to reach just the right people. You must include postage or a reply envelope for the return mail.

It is ideal for reaching people living out-of-town or businessmen who are hard to reach by phone or in person.

The disadvantage is that you have no control over who will respond. The people to whom you send the questionnaire will see no advantage in helping you. Some will probably decide they do not wish to spend the time answering your questionnaire, some will immediately throw it away, and some will lose either the questionnaire or return envelope in the pile of mail on their desk. Those who do respond may scribble in unreadable answers, may answer some questions and not others, or may return the questionnaire **months** after you mail it to them. You will be lucky to get as high as a 5% return (that is 5 surveys returned for every 100 mailed out).

By comparison, the telephone survey should give you a 60% response; and the personal interview should give a response as high as 90%. With both of these, you will be better able to judge the accuracy of individual comments.

Focus Group or Group Interview

An interesting variation of the personal interview is the "focus group" or group interview. This technique enables you to get the reactions or opinions of several people at one time. It offers the advantages of a personal interview and adds the spontaneity and depth of a group.

Many companies use this technique when developing new products, new marketing strategies or new business procedures. It gives them quick feedback in a private atmosphere. Each member of the group has the opportunity to see, hear, taste or whatever is required, and offer opinions. Often one opinion or idea will spark another. And, if the group is encouraged to speak freely, a  highly productive brainstorming session develops.

You can organize your own focus group from among your friends, provided they are carefully chosen. Or you may find a local church, school or civic organization that may provide a group for a modest charge. Try to make sure, however, that the group bears some resemblance to that customer profile you developed.

To get maximum value from a group interview, here are a few rules to follow:

1. Use a strong leader. If that's not you, ask someone to take that important role. Every group needs a leader to keep steering in the right direction, to prevent someone else from dominating, and to ask the right questions.

2. Encourage the group to provide honest, accurate opinions and to express them openly.

3. Each individual, however negative he might be, represents a segment of your market. If he is silent or withdrawn, he must be encouraged to speak.

4. Do not feed opinions of your own or show your prejudices in any way to the group. This will lead to false feedback.

5. Use a blackboard or flip-chart to record opinions. The visual impact usually sparks helpful conversation.

6. Appoint someone to take notes for you.

7. Don't trust the results of one such group interview. Verify your findings through another group, or even a third one.

How to Design a Questionnaire

One of the keys to successful market research is to have a clear purpose in mind before you begin. This means you need to know which marketing questions will help you to conduct your business successfully. Having this purpose in mind will prevent you from wandering off the track into information that will not pay off for you. To determine the value of a question before you start your research, judge **how you would use the results.** Doing this exercise before you have the results usually will point out useless or inadequate questions. Make each of your questions worthwhile.

Since you have decided to go to the trouble and expense of conducting a market research survey, it's important that you develop questions which suit your needs. Basically, there are several rules to follow when designing a survey. They are:

1.	Keep your questions brief and clear. For example, asking: "When you purchase milk, what is the usual size you buy?" is much better than asking: "When you go to the store to make your grocery purchase and you stop in the dairy department after making other grocery purchases, when you select the milk you wish to purchase, what size or how large a purchase is it?" Vague questions lead to vague answers.

2.	Ask direct questions about your subject. In one survey conducted by a store manager, this question was asked:

	"What brought you here today?" The manager wanted to know **why** the customers had chosen to shop at his store. Unfortunately, some people misunderstood the question and put down such answers as "a car", "the bus", and "a friend brought me". The answers weren't wrong, but they didn't help the store manager find out what he wanted to know.

3.	Ask questions which can be answered easily, but remember to follow up most YES and NO questions with a "WHY" question or one that asks for more information.

4.	Ask questions which can be interpreted easily. You are going to be interviewing anywhere from 10 to 200 people and you need to get information from them that can help you make decisions about your business. When questions become too long and involved, so do the answers. And you will spend more time trying to figure out what people meant than is necessary.

5.   Make sure the questions are understandable to a wide range of people. You don't want to waste time explaining the same question again and again.

6.   Make sure your questions do not offend anyone. A recent merchandising survey done by a national magazine included the question: "Are you the head of the household?" The magazine was trying to find out if the person whom they were interviewing made the majority of the purchasing decisions. Many women (and men), however, found the question outdated and offensive. On a revised survey, the question was left out. Questions about family income, occupations and age should all be handled delicately, and included in your survey only if relevant.

7.   Be honest with the intent of the questionnaire. If you're thinking of opening a hardware store in the shopping mall, say that. Don't tell people that you're asking these questions to see how newspaper advertising affects the hardware business. It isn't fair to them and you could be cheating yourself as well. You may get a long speech on what's wrong with newspapers and advertising, and learn nothing about the potential customer's feelings about a hardware store in the shopping mall.

8.   Don't answer the questions for them. The reason you are interviewing consumers is to find out what they know, not what you know.

Recently, a computer company decided to do a survey on how their brand of computer was viewed by the public. They conducted the survey nationally, but cautioned the interviewers not to mention the name of the computer when asking various questions. Their reasoning was simple: If the results of the survey showed that a majority of people had not heard of their product, there was something wrong with their advertising campaign. The same is true for your questionnaires. Do not prompt people into saying something they don't mean.

9.   Give the person you are interviewing enough time to answer the questions. In point one we advised you to keep the questions brief. But this does not mean the answers have to be brief. The hardest obstacle you will encounter in doing a market research survey is getting someone to take the time to talk to you. Once they have agreed to do the survey, everything should go smoothly. So don't set a time limit of, say, 5 minutes per person, or you are going to miss out on some helpful comments. Don't cut someone off while they are responding. That isn't to say you should listen to the entire story of their last gall bladder operation or admire 17 pictures of grandchildren either. A good rule to follow is to treat the people interviewed the way you would like to be treated. Ask for their advice" and emphasize how much they are "helping" you.

10. Be sure you understand all the answers you receive. Don't be afraid to read back what was just said to make sure it's accurate.

11. Do not be alarmed or upset by any of the answers you receive. And if you are, don't show it. Don't argue about an answer to any of your questions. If the person says they've never heard of your product or service, they haven't. If they say they wouldn't want a health food restaurant in the shopping mall, take them at their word. Try to remember that you are doing this survey to find out what should be changed, and you need people to be as honest as possible.

12. Be courteous when asking people to participate in your survey. Some people simply will not have the time or the inclination to help you. Do not press them or act insulted when they refuse. In one case, a young woman told the interviewer she was in a hurry to get her shopping done. About an hour later, the same woman came back and said she had finished her shopping early and now had the time to fill out the

questionnaire. This probably won't happen often, but it doesn't cost you anything to be courteous to everyone you deal with.

A good way to double check your questions is to test them with another question: CAN THE ANSWER BE MEASURED? If the answers can't be counted or categorized in some way, be careful. Questions which ask for subjective answers should probably be changed.

It is a good idea to "test" your questionnaire on a few friends before you actually use it. That way, you can determine if your questions are clear and will give you the answers you need.

Questionnaire Examples

The following are four types of questionnaires which were designed by the owners of small businesses. In the first (the car wash survey mentioned earlier in the chapter), each customer was handed a clipboard and asked to fill out a questionnaire while their car was being washed.

This was not a random sampling because each person used was a customer of the Rose Car Wash. It was designed to be completed in the length of time it took to wash a car. And it was done over a week's time to reach the customers who washed their cars during the week as well as the weekend.

You'll note that the owner was primarily interested in how each customer had heard about his business. However, he also included questions on what he could do to improve his business such as changing the hours the car wash was open. As a result of his findings, he decided to keep his car wash open an additional 2 hours on Sunday.

The next survey, dealing with commercial warehouse space, was done by a businessman who was interested in building a warehouse. Before he made the commitment of time and money, however, he needed to know if there was a demand for such a service. He sent his survey to all business establishments within a two-mile radius of the proposed site.

He found that not only was there a demand, but several businesses wanted to reserve space before it was even built! He built a warehouse with space for 50,000 square feet of storage room, and before it was completed, 30,000 square feet had already been leased.

This same businessman developed the third questionnaire on warehouse space, but sent the survey to home and apartment dwellers. The results revealed that these people would represent a very small portion of his business. Therefore, he decided to emphasize business use in his advertising campaign.

The fourth questionnaire was designed by a man who wanted to know if there would be a demand for giftware from India and Pakistan in the small town where he lived. He found that the majority of people would be interested in such a store, particularly since there was nothing of that type in the surrounding area.

The last questionnaire was developed by a woman who was interested in opening a fabric store and offering sewing lessons. From the women she interviewed, she discovered that there was a real need for both a fabric store and sewing lessons. She opened the shop which did extremely well.

In each of these cases, the small business owners learned enough from a market research survey to make intelligent, responsible decisions. But what happens when the results of the survey aren't so positive? Does this mean you discard the idea and go into another business?

Not necessarily. To a certain extent you must use your own judgment. The market research survey should be used as a guide, not the final answer. If, for example, the survey on giftware from India and Pakistan had revealed that the majority of people were not interested in seeing a gift shop of this type in their town, you need to analyze why they responded that way.

It could be that the people were unfamiliar with this type of giftware. Maybe they assumed the items would be too expensive because they were imported. Whatever the case, the way they answered the questionnaire might not necessarily reflect the way they would react if the store were actually there.

In any case, the market research survey can give you some valuable information about your customers and potential business location. What you choose to do with the results is up to you.

ROSE CAR WASH SURVEY

We are interested in knowing what you think about our service. Accordingly, we have prepared a brief questionnaire which we would appreciate your answering while your car is being washed. Your candid criticisms, comments and suggestions are important to us.

Thank you, ROSE CAR WASH

1. Do you live/work in the area? (Circle one or both)

2. Why did you choose to come to ROSE CAR WASH today? (Circle all that apply.)
    Close to home
    Close to work
    Convenience
    Good Service
    Full Service Car Wash
    Other

3. How did you learn about us?
    (Circle one)
    Newspaper
    Mailing
    Drove by and stopped
    Recommended by someone
    Received coupon at work
    Other

4. How frequently do you have your car washed during the winter? (From November 1 to April 30) Please try to estimate.
    ____ times per month
    ____ Other

5. How frequently do you have your car washed during spring and summer? (May 1 to October 31)
    ____ times per month
    ____ Other

6. Which aspect of our car wash do you think needs improvement?

_____
_____
_____
_____

7. Our operating hours are from 8:30 a.m. to 6 p.m. weekdays and Saturdays and from 9 a.m. to 2 p.m. on Sunday. We are closed on legal holidays. What changes in our operating hours would be better for you?

Weekdays	Saturday	Sunday
Open 8 a.m.	Open 8 a.m.	Close 3 p.m.
Close 7 p.m.	Close 7 p.m.	Close 4 p.m.
Close 8 p.m.	Close 8 p.m.	Close 5 p.m.
Close 9 p.m.	Close 9 p.m.	No change
No change	No change	

8. Approximate age: Circle one
    Under 25   26-39   40-59   Over 60

Comments: (Favorable and Unfavorable)

_____
_____
_____

COMMERCIAL WAREHOUSE QUESTIONNAIRE

1.   Are you presently renting any commercial warehousing space?
        Yes _____   No _____

        If NO, go to question 2. If YES, continue with questions 1a to 1f.

1a.   Where do you presently rent your warehouse space (name and address):
        _____

1b.   How many times a month do you enter the warehouse or use it?
        _____

1c.   Is your warehouse space heated? ____ yes ____ no ____ don't know

1d.   Approximately how much warehouse space are you renting?
        _____ square feet

1e.   Do you think you will need additional space in the future?
        _____ Yes _____ No

1f.   Are there any changes or improvements you would like to see made in your
        present warehousing arrangements?
        _____ Yes _____ No _____ Don't Know
        If YES, what improvements would you like to see made?
        _____
        _____

2.   Are you planning on using any rented storage or warehouse space?
        _____ Yes _____ No _____ Don't Know
        If NO, end interview. If YES or DON'T KNOW, continue to questions 2a
        through 2d.

2a.   If you are planning to rent warehouse space or may rent such space, how long
        in terms of time would you be willing to travel to use your space?
        _____ minutes

2b.   What would be the approximate size of your storage space needs?
        _____ square feet

2c.   How much monthly rent would you be willing to pay?
        $_____ per square foot/month

2d.   Would you require heat for your rented warehouse space?
        _____ Yes _____ No _____ Don't Know

NAME:_____TITLE:_____

Business Name: _____
Business Address: _____

IMPORTED HANDMADE GIFTWARES QUESTIONNAIRE

1. Have you ever purchased or received as gifts any imported handmade giftware?

   Yes _____ No _____

2. Have you ever purchased or received as gifts any handmade giftware from India or Pakistan?

   Yes _____ No _____

   If Yes, what type of giftware?

   Wooden _____ Marble _____ Brass _____

   Copper _____ Cotton _____ Other _____

   Please specify:

3. Would you be interested in purchasing the above mentioned handmade gifts from Pakistan or India?

   Yes _____ No _____

   If Yes, would the item be used:
   a. In your home for you or your family's enjoyment _____
   b. As a gift _____
   c. Other _____ Please specify:

4. Do you know where to shop for such giftware?

   Yes _____ No _____

5. When buying foreign handmade giftware, what do you value the most? On a scale of 1 through 4, list in order according to preference beginning with number 1 as your most valued choice:

   Craftsmanship _____ Cost _____ Uniqueness _____

   Other _____ Please specify

FABRIC STORE QUESTIONNAIRE

1. Do you do home sewing? _____ Yes _____ No
    If NO, please answer questions to Part A.
    If YES, please answer questions to Part B.

A. Please check reasons for not doing home sewing.
    Lack of interest _____
    Lack of knowledge _____
    Poor availability of fabric selection _____
    Other

B. Check type of sewing you do.
    Children's wear _____
    Ladies wear _____
    Home decorating _____
    Other

    Which patterns do you use?

    _____ McCall's _____ Simplicity _____ Kwik Sew

    _____ Butterick _____ Vogue

    Check your age group
    10 - 18 _____
    19 - 29 _____
    30 & Over _____

    Where do you buy your material?

    In town _____ Out of town _____

    How far do you live from our town?

    In town _____ 10-15 miles _____ Out of town _____

    Do you think our town needs a fabric shop?

    Would you be interested in sewing classes? Yes_____ No _____

    What classes would interest you?

    Basic sewing _____   Lingerie   _____
    T-shirt   _____   Infant wear   _____
    Pants   _____   Men's wear   _____
    Tailoring   _____   Other   _____

Please note any suggestions or comments you might have.

Other Types of Market Research

There are other types of research you can do yourself that may be easier than a survey -- and more creative too!

You can learn a lot from **your competitors**. Pretend you're a customer and visit them at different times of the day. When you're back in your car, fill out a competitor analysis form. (See chapter on Site Location.) Your answers will give you lots to think about for improving your own operation.

Try a license plate analysis of your competitors. Where do they come from? How many of these people would find it more convenient to shop at your establishment?

Another great way to get information is to **make your advertising** dollar do double duty.

When you look into the advertising chapter, you will learn about tracking for advertising. What this means is that when you advertise, there are a number of ways for you to find out who responded to your ad.

For example, whenever you run a coupon in a publication, code it so that when your customer redeems it, you will know where it came from. For instance, code the coupon offer in the campus paper "A", and the ones in the neighborhood papers "B" and "C". Save all the coupons that are redeemed and when the offer is over, figure out which paper had more customer response. Or more important, figure the cost per inquiry for each publication. Also, when the coupons are redeemed, you can write the customers' phone numbers on the coupons (let them know you won't be calling them) and you can pinpoint the responses even better.

The same can be done with broadcast ads. Do

a "Tell 'em Joe sent you" ad for one radio station and a different one for the second station. Try rock, country, classical, or easy listening format stations. Keep track of which station sent in the most customers. Then check with the station to find out who their average listener is -- age, occupation, income, etc. -- you'll find out about your clientele for the same money you're using to boost sales.

Another group that really knows your territory is the **sales reps** and **wholesalers**. These hardworking men and women make it their business to know what is happening in your business community. Take one out for coffee and pick his or her brain.

One final word: Don't fall blindly in love with your research findings. There might have been flaws in your survey or the people you questioned. But if you ask the right people the right questions, you can use the results to draw up a blueprint for the future.

But don't stop there. You'll need more surveys later to tell you about the trends, preferences and attitudes of your customers.

In this chapter you have learned:

1. *If you are considering going into a small business, market research can be very valuable in helping you answer certain questions you may have.*
2. *If you are already in a small business, market research can be a valuable tool for you in solving problems.*
3. *Market research is a tool by which you can gather information from people like your future customers.*
4. *There are four basic methods you may use when conducting a market research survey: 1. personal interview; 2. telephone interview; 3. mail interview; and 4. focus group or group interview. Of these, the personal interview will give you the most accurate and complete information.*
5. *The design of your questionnaire is very important in getting the right information for your business. You have learned just what to include to make yours the most accurate for your individual needs.*

---

6. *There are many places in your community where you may gather information: libraries, vocational-technical schools, competitors, customers, potential customers, trade associations, publications and government agencies.*

RESOURCES OF INFORMATION

The listings in this Bibliography give reference resources of interest to persons needing information, statistics and maps for market analysis projects. All prices and availability of publications listed are subject to change. No slight is intended toward reference sources not included. AISB would appreciate receiving information about new publications in this field and about changes in the present listings for consideration when this Bibliography is revised.

Many of the publications listed, especially those issued by Government agencies, are available in most public and university libraries, field offices of the Small Business Administration and field office libraries of the Department of Commerce.

The publisher's name and address are given along with the title of the publications with a brief description. Most of these listings may be purchased or ordered by mail directly from the publisher. Contact the publisher or source for price information.

Government publications can be ordered from the Superintendent of Documents, U.S. Government Printing Office, Washington, D.C. 20402. When ordering, give the publication's title, series number if given, and the name of issuing agency. In many instances, there will be a charge for government publications. This cost or charge will be furnished upon request to the Superintendent of Documents, U.S. Government Printing Office.

The statistical and map reference materials listed in this Bibliography are useful in such market analysis tasks as allocation of sales effort by area; appraisal of market opportunity; control of sales performance, design of sales compensation and incentive plans; establishment of sales quotas and marketing goals; and planning of distribution facilities and methods.

Consult your local library for additional reference material or write to the American Institute of Small Business, 7515 Wayzata Boulevard, Suite 129, Minneapolis, MN 55426.

GOVERNMENT PUBLICATIONS

CENSUS CATALOG AND GUIDE
(Annual), U.S. Department of Commerce, Bureau of Census. Contains comprehensive Listings of Census Bureau publications and products. The catalog groups publications by subject areas that

correspond to censuses, such as "Business-Trade and Services." There are subject and title indexes, ordering information and a directory of sources for assistance. C3.163/3 Item 0138 ASI 2304-2 S/N 003-024-07009-0. Superintendent of Documents, U.S. Government Printing Office, Washington, DC 20402, or Customer Services, Data User Services Division, Bureau of the Census, Washington, DC 20233

GUIDE TO THE 2001 ECONOMIC CENSUSES AND RELATED STATISTICS (2001) U.S.

Department of Commerce, Bureau of Census. Contains general information of the economic censuses; description of each census with information on scope, methodology, and use; annotated listing of publications in each census with sample tables; information on related publications. C3253 EC92-R-2. Item 0131-H Data User Services Division, Bureau of the Census, Washington, DC 20233. Business information includes Census of Retail Trade for the United States, individual states, County Business Patterns for the country and individual states. Includes such references as:

Census of Retail Trade for the U.S. and each individual state as well as major retail centers in

standard metropolitan statistical areas.

Census of Service Industries consisting of approximately 53 reports such as:

! Capital Expenditures, Depreciable Assets, and Operating Expenses. Establishment and Firm Size. Hotels, Motels, and Other Lodging Places.
! Miscellaneous Subjects (Including Census of Transportation Establishment Statistics). Motion Picture Industry.

Census of Wholesale Trade for the United States and individual states. Information includes such topics as: Sales, firm size, and other subjects.

County Business Patterns includes information on employment, payrolls, number and employment size of establishments by detailed industry.

Census of Industry Reports include those on:
! Agriculture
! Construction Industries - Geographic Area and Industry Series Manufacturers - Geographic Area and Industry Series.
! Mineral Industries - Geographic Area and Industry Series

227

! Retail Trade - Geographic
Area Series
! Retail Trade - Major Retail
Centers
! Retail Trade - Merchandise
Line Sales.
! Service Industries -
Geographic Area
! Transportation - Truck
Inventory and Use Survey
! Wholesale Trade -
Geographic Area Series

Information on related publications.
C3253: EC92-R-2. Item 0131-H.
Data User Services Division, Bureau
of the Census, Washington, DC
20233

COUNTY AND CITY DATA BOOK,
1998 (12th edition) A total of 195
statistical items tabulated for the
U.S., its regions, and each county
and state; 190 items for each city;
and 161 items for 277 Standard
Metropolitan Statistical Areas.
Information is derived from latest
available censuses of population,
housing, governments, retail and
wholesale trade, and selected
services. Superintendent of
Documents, U.S. Government
Printing Office, Washington, DC
20402

**STATISTICAL ABSTRACT OF THE
UNITED STATES**, 1999 (119th

edition) The standard summary of
statistics on the social, political and
economic status of government and
business in the United States.
Designed to serve as a convenient
statistical source. Includes an
introductory text to each section,
appendices, and an index. Comes
with pocket-size supplement "USA
Statistics in Brief", which summarizes
important data for quick and easy
reference. Includes numerous maps,
charts, and tables. Published
annually. C3.134.: Item 0150, ASI
2324-1 GPO, S/N 003-024-06572-0.
Superintendent of Documents, U.S.
Government Printing Office,
Washington, DC 20402
Also available online, free in PDF
format, at www.census.gov

**STATE AND METROPOLITAN AREA
DATA BOOK**, 1998 (Statistical
Abstract Supplement) Presents data
for 195 statistical items for the U.S.,
its regions, and each state, and 161
items for 277 Standard Metropolitan
Statistical Areas. C: 3.134/5: Item
0150, ASI 2328-54 GPO, S/N 003-
024-08827-4 Superintendent of Documents, U.S. Government Printing
Office, Washington, DC 20402
Also available online, free in PDF
format, at www.census.gov

U.S. SMALL BUSINESS

ADMINISTRATION

SBA PUBLICATIONS

The SBA (www.sba.gov) issues a wide range of management and technical publications designed to help owner-managers and prospective owners of small businesses. Each title gives guidance on a specific subject or management problem for owners and managers of all types of small businesses. Selected topics include:

EMERGING BUSINESS SERIES

Transferring Mgmt/Family Businesses. EB-1
Marketing Strategies for Growing Businesses. EB-2
Mgmt Issues for Growing Businesses. EB-3
Human Resource Mgmt for Growing Businesses.. EB-4
Audit Checklist for Growing Businesses. EB-5
Strategic Planning for Growing Businesses. EB-6
Financial Mgmt for Growing Businesses. EB-7

FINANCIAL MANAGEMENT

ABC's Of Borrowing. FM-1
Elementos Basucis Para Pedir Dinero Prestado FM-1S

Understanding Cash Flow. FM-4
A Venture Capital Primer For Small Business. FM-5
Budgeting In A Small Service Firm. FM-8
Record Keeping In A Small Business. FM-10
Pricing Your Products And Services Profitably. FM-13
Financing for Small Business. FM-14

MANAGEMENT AND PLANNING

Problems In Managing A Family-Owned Business. MP-3
Business Plan For Small Manufacturers. MP4
Business Plan For Small Construction Firms. MP-5
Planning & Goal Setting For Small Business. MP-6
Business Plan For Retailers. MP-9
Business Plan For Small Service Firms. MP-11
Checklist For Going Into Business. MP-12
Lista Para Comenzar Su Negocio. MP-12S
How To Get Started With A Small Business Computer. MP-14
The Business Plan For Home-Based Business. MP-15
How To Buy Or Sell A Business. MP-16
Business Continuation Planning. MP-20
Developing A Strategic Business

Plan. MP-21

Inventory Management. MP-22

Selecting The Legal Structure For Your Business. MP-25

Evaluating Franchise Opportunities. MP-26

Small Business Risk Management Guide. MP-28

Quality Child Care Makes Good Business Sense. MP-29

Child Day-Care Services. MP-30

Handbook for Small Business. MP-31

How to Write a Business Plan. MP-32

MARKETING

Creative Selling: The Competitive Edge. MT-1

Marketing For Small Business: An Overview. MT-2

Researching Your Market. MT-8

Selling By Mail Order. MT-9

Advertising. MT-11

PRODUCTS/IDEAS/INVENTIONS

Ideas Into Dollars. PI-1

Avoiding Patent, Trademark and Copyright Problems. PI-2

Trademarks and Business Goodwill. PI-3

PERSONNEL MANAGEMENT SERIES

Employees: How to Find and Pay Them. PM-2

Managing Employee Benefits. PM-3

CRIME PREVENTION

Curtailing Crime - Inside And Out. CP2

A Small Business Guide To Computer Security. CP3

For ordering SBA publications, write to U.S. Small Business Administration, P.O. Box 30, Denver CO, 80201-0030.
Also, most of these publications can be viewed online at www.sba.gov in a variety of formats.

COMMERCIAL PUBLICATIONS

CONSULTANTS & CONSULTING ORGANIZATIONS DIRECTORY (25th edition). In an increasingly complex and sophisticated marketplace, businesses are spending more on consulting services than ever before. Keeping up with this healthy, growing and dynamic segment of the U.S. and Canadian economies with Consultants and Consulting Organizations Directory. In this redesigned 24th edition, you'll find complete contact information as well as full, clear and concise descriptions of each organization's activities. Each entry furnishes: Street addresses or PO Boxes for headquarters and branches; Phone, fax, and toll-free numbers; e-mail addresses and Web sites; Notation of service to international clients; Notation of mergers and former names; and much more. More than 24,000 firms and individuals listed and arranged alphabetically under 14 general fields of consulting activity ranging from agriculture to marketing. More than 400 specialties are represented, including finance, computers, fund-raising and others. ISBN 0-7876-5278-4. The Gale Group, 27500 Drake Road, Farmington Hills, MI 48331 248-699-4253

E & P MARKET GUIDE Tabulates current estimates of population, households, retail sales and for nine major sales classifications, income for states, counties, metropolitan areas, and 1,500 daily newspaper markets. Also lists specific information on major manufacturing, retailing, and business firms, transportation and utilities, local newspapers, climate and employment, for newspaper markets. Includes states maps. Annual. Editor and Publisher Company, 770 Broadway, New York, NY 10003-9595

ENCYCLOPEDIA OF BUSINESS

INFORMATION SOURCES (17th Edition). Cut research and decision-making time in half when you find details on business information sources. The completely updated 16th edition of Encyclopedia of Business Information Sources lets you quickly identify more than 28,500 live, print and electronic sources of information listed under almost 1,200 alphabetically arranged subjects; e-mail addresses and URLs have been added to this edition. The Encyclopedia's broad coverage includes subjects of current interest, new technologies and new industries -- all arranged alphabetically to facilitate research. Also look for a convenient "Sources Cited" section that repeats all entries from the main body, but arranges them by title or organization name instead of by topic, making Encyclopedia of Business Information Sources a handy bibliographic guide. Entries provide title of the publication; database or organization; publisher of the information source; address, phone and price/availability. Fax numbers have now been added for thousands of entries. 1,600 pp., ISBN 0-7876-5876-6. The Gale Group, 27500 Drake Road, Farmington Hills, MI 48331 248-699-4253

1999 S&MM'S SURVEY OF BUYING POWER Few market strategists will make a decision without consulting the highly regarded Survey of Buying Power. Released annually in August, the Survey provides current figures on the population and demographics, effective buying income, customer spending patterns, retail sales breakdowns for major lines, and market quality indexes for state, county, city and metro marketsʸ everything you need for targeting potential customers in all geographic areas. This survey includes the following information:

1. Effective Buying Income figures are given for these categories: Total EBI, Median Household EBI, % of households by $10,000-$19,999 group, $20,000-$34,999, $35,000-$49,999, and $50,000 and over. These figures along with buying power index figures are given for each state, city, county, and metro area.

2. Population figures are given for these categories: Total, % of U.S., 18-24 age group, 25-34 age group, 35-49 age group, 50 and over age group, and by households. These figures are listed for each state, city, county, and metro area.

3. Retail sales figures are given for the following categories: Total retail, food, eating & drinking places,

general merchandise, furniture and appliances, automotive, and drugstore sales. Figures are listed for each state, city, county and metro area.

If you require an even more detailed breakdown of marketing information, see User's Guide to Demographics, USA 1993, listed below. Sales and Marketing Management, 355 Park Avenue South, New York, NY 10010.

1998 S&MM'S SURVEY OF MEDIA MARKETS This special complement to the **Survey of Buying Power** is published annually in October. It details the population, income, retail sales and buying power figures for television and newspaper markets in the United States. The data for the television markets reveal areas of dominant influence (ADI) while newspaper markets are identified both in terms of dominance and effective coverage. It also includes 5 year projections for growth in all U.S. metro areas and states, by population, income and retail sales. You'll also find U.S. metro market ranking tables covering retail sales for 10 merchandise lines. Sales and Marketing Management, 355 Park Avenue South, New York, NY 10010

USER'S GUIDE TO DEMOGRAPHICS USA 2001 Gives income levels, buying power, retail sales, age, sex and household demographics, market growth, rankings, projections and more for every county, and TV market in the country. You can quickly evaluate sales performance, spot potential crises before they develop, establish marketing plans based on hard information. Complete demographic and economic date including state and regional summaries, total percentages and rankings for population, age and sex, Effective Buying Income (EBI) retail sales, and Buying Power Index (BPI). Sales and Marketing Management, 355 Park Avenue South, New York, NY 10010

SALES MANAGERS BUDGET PLAN 1993 Published annually in February, this valuable compilation of selling facts and figures covers a lot of ground. It provides exclusive "selling cost index" and "cost per sales call" estimates for the leading metro markets across the county. It highlights the markets with the highest and lowest sales costs and outlines the sequence for preparing a sales cost budget. It will help you determine and control such selling expenses as sales training, meetings, travel and entertainment, compensation and sales support activities. Sales and Marketing Management, 355 Park Avenue South, New York, NY 10010

TRADE SHOWS WORLDWIDE, An International Directory of Events, Facilities and Suppliers. (18th edition). Trade show activity throughout the world continues to grow. More and more exhibitors are finding trade shows to be their most effective marketing tool. No longer seen as a "vacation" away from the office, today's trade show is considered one of the best ways to meet with current customers, reach previously unidentified prospects and offer goods and services to the international market. The new 16th edition of Trade Shows Worldwide contains the vital information needed by every segment of the trade show industry. Its comprehensive coverage of shows, their sponsors and organizers, convention facilities, service providers and sources of industry information provides the most accurate and current data available about the industry. Features of this new edition include: 710 new or previously unlisted trade shows; 100 newly discovered trade show sponsoring organizations; 600 new conference and convention centers; 900 new world trade services; Four comprehensive indexes. ISBN 0-7876-5904-5 The Gale Group, 27500 Drake Road, Farmington Hills, MI 48331 248-699-4253

PUBLICATION SOURCES OF INFORMATION

Publications such as Magazines in specific fields frequently publish considerable Market and Marketing information in the areas that they specialize in. They provide studies to their Advertising Clients and Agencies and this information is generally available to consumers. In addition, their editorial departments usually maintain complete files on past articles that have appeared in their publications on various subjects relating to their area of specialization.

Newspaper Display Advertising Departments frequently conduct Readership and Non-Readership studies in their trade areas. In addition, they usually have current market and trade area information on their specific community.

Magazines:

BACON'S 2002 NEWSPAPER /MAGAZINE DIRECTORY

Provides a Directory of publications in alphabetical order by subject. Developed primarily for Publicity and Public Relations releases. ISSN 0736-4644 Bacon's Information, Inc. 332 South Michigan Avenue, Chicago, IL 60604

STANDARD RATE AND DATA SERVICE, INC. Provides a Directory of publications in alphabetical order by subject. Developed primarily for advertisers. Includes information on Advertising rates, Circulation Data, Readership and Publication information. Standard Rate and Data Service, Inc., 1700 Higgins Road, Des Plaines, IL 60018-5605

Newspapers:

BACON'S 2002 NEWSPAPER /MAGAZINE DIRECTORY

Provides a Directory of publications in alphabetical order by subject. Developed primarily for Publicity and Public Relations releases. ISSN 0736-4644 Bacon's Information, Inc. 332 South Michigan Avenue, Chicago, IL 60604

STANDARD RATE AND DATA SERVICE, INC. Provides a Directory of publications in alphabetical order by subject. Developed primarily for advertisers. Includes

information on Advertising rates, Circulation Data, Readership and Publication information. Standard Rate and Data Service, Inc., 1700 Higgins Road, Des Plaines, IL 60018-5605

Radio/TV/Cable:

BACON'S 2002 RADIO/TV/CABLE DIRECTORY Covers all U.S. Radio and TV stations, including Cable, college stations, syndicators and more. ISSN 0891-0130. Bacon's Information, Inc., 332 South Michigan Avenue, Chicago, IL 60604

GALE DIRECTORY OF PUBLICATIONS AND BROADCAST MEDIA (136th edition). The longest continuously published directory of periodicals in America. This directory provides information on magazines, newspapers, journals, newsletters and special interest periodicals, and other periodicals published in the United States and Canada. This edition contains 39,000 entries. The geographically arranged directory includes Alphabetical and Classification Indexes, plus many special sections. 4,500 pp., ISBN 0-78876-3441-7

The Gale Group, 27500 Drake Road, Farmington Hills, MI 48331 248-699-4253

COMPANY AND PRODUCT INFORMATION

Thomas Publishing Company publishes detailed Registers including the Thomas Register of American Manufacturers and Thomas Register Catalog File--Company Profile which has an alphabetical listing by Company showing name, address, telephone numbers and listing of items manufactured and or supplied. The Company Profile Register also has in alphabetical order, a Trade Name Index of most trade names and the Products and Companies using the specific trade name.

THOMAS REGISTER OF AMERICAN MANUFACTURERS AND THOMAS REGISTER CATALOG FILE-- PRODUCTS AND SERVICES which provides in alphabetical order, a listing by products and/or services of almost all American manufacturers. Provides name of Manufacturer, address, telephone number, and approximate size when available. 24 Volumes. Also available on CD-Rom or DVD-Rom Thomas Publishing Company, Five Penn Plaza, 250 West 34th Street, New York, NY 10001

CHAMBER OF COMMERCE

Online, you can search for any Chamber of Commerce in the world at chamber-of-commerce.com/search.htm

WORLD WIDE CHAMBER OF COMMERCE DIRECTORY Provides

in alphabetical community order by states the name, address and telephone numbers of each Chamber of Commerce as well as International Chambers of Commerce. Johnson Publishing Company, Inc. 8th & Van Buren, Loveland, CO 80537

FRANCHISE INFORMATION

FRANCHISE OPPORTUNITIES

GUIDE Provides Companies, location, contact person, description of operation, capital requirements and other data. International Franchise Association, 1350 New York Avenue NW, Suite 900, Washington, DC 20005-4709

THE SOURCE BOOK OF FRANCHISE OPPORTUNITIES (7th

edition). Lists over 2,450 opportunities. Active franchise listings (2,070 American, 380 Canadian Franchisers). Source

Book Publications, 1814 Franklin Street, Suite 820, Oakland, CA 94612

ANNUAL FRANCHISE 500 ENTREPRENEUR MAGAZINE

Published annually listing the name, address, and other information on the 500 leading franchise operations as considered by the publisher. Entrepreneur, 2392 Morse Avenue, P.O. Box 19787, Irvine, CA 92713; or Entrepreneur, Subscription Dept., P.O. Box 50368, Boulder, CO 80321-0368

Also you can find this information online at entrepreneur.com

PROFESSIONAL & TRADE ASSOCIATIONS

Professional and Trade Associations are in a position to supply detailed and complete information, particular area and membership. Such information can include membership listing, market information on the industry, trade shows, research data, etc.

NATIONAL TRADE & PROFESSIONAL ASSOCIATIONS OF THE UNITED STATES DIRECTORY

Lists 7,500 national trade associations, professional societies and labor unions. Five convenient indices enable you to look up associations by subject, budget, geographic area, acronym and executive director. Other features include: contact information, serial publications, upcoming convention schedule, membership and staff size, budget figures, and background information. ISBN 1-880873-42-7. Columbia Books, Inc., 1212 New York Avenue, NW, Suite 330, Washington, DC 20005

STATE AND REGIONAL ASSOCIATIONS OF THE UNITED STATES. Lists 7,300 of the largest and most significant state and regional trade and professional organizations in the U.S. Look up associations by subject, budget, state, acronym, or chief executive. Also lists contact information, serial publications, upcoming convention schedule, membership and staff size, budget figures, and background information. ISBN: 1-880873-44-3 Columbia Books, Inc., 1212 New York Avenue, NW, Suite 330, Washington, DC 20005

ENCYCLOPEDIA OF ASSOCIATIONS Includes three Volumes. Volume 1: National Organizations of the U.S. Volume 2: Geographic and Executive Indexes. Volume 3: Supplement. Includes 110,000 associations located in the U.S. and throughout the world. You'll find descriptions of

professional associations, trade and business associations, labor unions, cultural organizations, chambers of commerce and groups of all types in virtually every field. Each entry provides detailed information on an association's scope and activities, size, budget, publications, committees, chief official, services, conventions and meetings, as well as complete contact data. Volume 1: ISBN 0-7876-4815-9, Volume 2: ISBN 0-7876-3113-2, Volume 3: ISBN 0-7876-3361-5. The Gale Group, 27500 Drake Road, Farmington Hills, MI 48331 248-699-4253

MAPS

This section lists (l.) maps that serve merely as a base for market analysis by providing geographic information and (2.) maps that themselves display marketing statistics. For ready reference, the maps are listed by publisher's name.

A WORLD OF MAPS The catalog describes the Business Control Atlas. The Atlas contains indexed maps for every state. The Atlas also provides a wealth of statistical and demographic information. Other Business Atlases & Maps are available. In addition, the catalog describes clear type and color print maps (includes plastic-surfaced maps for crayon presentations and maps on steel to accommodate magnetic markers). The company publishes U.S. maps for depicting sales, markets, territories, distribution, statistics, and traffic data; detailed State, county, zip codes and township maps; and several types of atlases for use in analyzing national markets. American Map Company, Inc., 46-35 54th Road, Maspeth, NY 11378

COMMERCIAL ATLAS AND MARKETING GUIDE Contains maps showing counties and cities, and statistical data on manufacturing, retail sales, and population. Standard metropolitan areas are shown. Includes a city index with information on transportation facilities, banks, and postal data. Rand McNally & Company, P.O. Box 7600, Chicago, IL 60680

COMPUTER AIDED MARKETING (MARKET PRO) A software tool with demographic database information that can be customized and displayed pictorially on maps. Market information includes information on households, average income, owner occupied, households with children, age groups, education, percentage moved, etc. Correlations and various presentations can be made by interrelating various data including zip codes, census tracts,

and supplied input data. Business Information Technology 4640 West 77th Street, Edina, MN 55435

CONGRESSIONAL DISTRICTS OF THE 103rd CONGRESS OF THE UNITED STATES Wall poster defining congressional district boundaries and numbers for each State of the 103rd Congress. Published in 1993. Poster, 72 X 110 cm. Shipped in a tube. C3.62/10:90/2. S/N 003-024-08693-0. Superintendent of Documents, U.S. Government Printing Office, Washington, DC 20402-9325

CATALOG OF TOPOGRAPHIC AND OTHER PUBLISHED MAPS. Published and distributed by the United States Geological Survey, National Mapping Program, Department of the Interior. Publishes a variety of maps that show state and city areas.

The following maps and a list of other available maps may be ordered from:

Maps of areas east of the Mississippi River, including: Minnesota, Puerto Rico, the Virgin Islands of the United States and Antarctica.
U.S. Department of the Interior, Geological Survey, 503 National Center, Reston, VA 22092

Maps of areas west of the Mississippi River, including: Hawaii, Louisiana, American Samoa, and Guam. USGS Branch of Distribution, Box 25286, Building 810, Denver Federal Center, Denver, CO 80225

Maps of Alaska USGS Earth Science Information Center, Box 12, New Federal Bldg., 101 Twelfth Avenue, Fairbanks, AK 99701

CONSTRUCTION INFORMATION

CONSTRUCTION AND REAL ESTATE REVIEW Annual Year in Review. Annual statistical review of construction activity in the United States for most all areas of construction including residential, commercial and industrial. Company publishes and maintains monthly and annual statistics in these areas. Dodge/DRI Construction and Real Estate Information Service, 24 Hartwell Avenue, Lexington, MA 02173

THE SWEET'S SYSTEM Complete index and listing of all types of materials used in construction with complete specification information. Complete Sweet's catalog is a series of several books listing this data. Separate Manufacturers Literature and Catalog File is also available. McGraw-Hill-Sweet's Group, 1221

Avenue of the Americas, New York, NY 10020

TRADE ASSOCIATIONS

Trade Associations are a valuable source of information on the industry which the trade association represents. Information which most trade associations provide include: names of members, statistical information on sales, product lines and projected growth.

Trade Associations usually will publish a monthly magazine, membership directory, hold an annual meeting and conduct market research studies as they relate to their industry.

Advance Medical Technology Association
1200 G Street, Suite 400, NW, Washington, DC 20005
(202) 783-8700; advamed.org
Advertising Mail Marketing Association
1333 F Street, NW., Ste 710
Washington, DC 20004-1108
(202) 347-0055
American Bankers Association
1120 Connecticut Ave, NW, Washington, DC 20036;
(202) 663-5000; aba.com
American Council of Life Insurance

1001 Constitution. Ste 700,
Washington, DC 20001;
(202) 624-2000 acli.com

American Electronic Association

601 Pennsylvania, North Bldg, Ste
600, Washington, DC 20004;
(202) 682-9110; aeanet.org

**American Financial Services
Association**

919 18th Street, NW, Third Floor
Washington, DC 20006;
 (202) 296-5544;
americanfinsvcs.com

**American Forest and Paper
Association**

1111 19th Street, NW., Suite 800,
Washington, DC 20036;
(202)463-2700;afandpa.org

American Health Care Association

1201 L Street, NW., Washington, DC
20005
(202) 842-4444; wahca.org

**American Hotel and Motel
Association**

1201 New York Ave, NW, Ste 600,
Washington, DC 20005-3931;
(202) 289-3100; ahla.com

**American Institute of Certified
Public Accountants**

1455 Pennsylvania Ave, NW, Ste
400, Washington, DC 20004
(202) 737-6600; aicpa.org

American Insurance Association

1130 Connecticut Ave, NW, Ste
1000, Washington, DC 20036;
(202) 828-7100; aiadc.org

American Petroleum Institute

1220 L Street, NW, Suite 900,
Washington, DC 20005;
(202) 682-8000; api,org

American Retail Federation

325 – 7th Street. NW Ste 1100,
Washington, DC 20004;
(202) 783-7971; nrf.com

**American Society of Association
Executives**

1575 Eye Street, NW, Washington, DC
20005
(202) 626-2723; asaenet.org

American Society of Travel Agents

1101 King Street, Suite 200,
Alexandria, VA 22314
(703) 739-2782; astanet.com

American Trucking Association

430 First Street, SE, Washington, DC
20003
(202) 544-6245; truckline.com

Association of American Publishers

50 F Street NW, Washington, DC
20001-1564
(202) 232-3335; publishers.org

**Associated Builders and
Contractors, Inc.**

1300 North 17th Street, 8th floor,
Arlington, VA 22209;
(703) 812-2000; abc.org

**Associated General Contractors of
America**

333 John Carlyle Street, Suite 200,
Alexandria, VA 22314;
703-548-3118; agc.org

**Automotive Parts and Accessories
Assn**

4600 East-West Hwy. Suite 300,

Bethesda, MD 20814;

(301) 654-6664; aftermarket.org

Automotive Service Association

P.O. Box 929, Bedford, TX 76095-
0929

(800)272-7467; asashop.org

Electronic Industries Association

2500 Wilson Blvd, Arlington, VA
22201

(703) 907-7500; eia.org

Financial Planning Association

5775 Glenridge Dr NE, Suite B-300,
Atlanta, GA 30328

(800) 332-4237

Food Marketing Institute

655 15th Street NW, Suite 700
Washington, DC 20005;

(202) 452-8444; fmi.org

**Grocery Manufacturers
Association**

1010 Wisconsin Ave, NW, Ste 900,
Washington, DC 20007

(202) 337-9400; gmabrands.org

**Health Industry Distributors
Association**

310 Montgomery St, Alexandria, VA
22314

(703) 549-4432; hidanet.org

**Independent Insurance Agents and
Brokers**

412 First Street, SE., Suite 300,
Washington, DC 20003

(202) 863-7000;
independentagent.com

**Independent Petroleum
Association**

1201 15th Street, NW, Suite 300,

Washington, DC 20005

(202) 857-4722; ipaa.org

**International Communications
Industries Assn**

11242, Waples Mill Rd, Suite 300
Fairfax, VA 22030

(703) 273-7200; infocomm.org

**National Association of
Broadcasters**

1771 N Street, NW, Washington, DC
20036

(202) 429-5300; nab.org

**National Association of Chain Drug
Stores**

413 N Lee Street, Alexandria, VA
22313

(703) 549-3001; nacds.org

**National Association of Convenience
Stores**

1600 Duke Street, Alexandria, VA
22314-2792

(703) 684-3600; cstorecentral.com

**National Association of Home
Builders**

1201 15th Street, NW, Washington,
DC 20005

(202) 822-0200

National Association of Realtors

700 11th Street, NW, Washington, DC
20001

(202) 383-1000; realtors.org

**National Association of Truck Stop
Operators**

1199 N Fairfax St, Suite 801,
Alexandria, VA 22314

(703) 549-2100; natso.com

National Association of Wholesaler-

Distributors

1725 K Street, Suite 300, Washington, DC 20006; (202) 872-0885; naw.org

National Automobile Dealers Association

412 First Street, SE, Second Floor, Washington, DC 20003; (202) 547-5500; nada.org

National Business Incubators Association

20 E Circle Drive, Suite 190, Athens, OH 45701 (740)593-4331; nba.org

National Industrial Transportation League

1700 North Moore Street, Suite 1900, Arlington, VA 22209; (703) 524-5011; nitl.org

National Lumber & Building Materials Dealers Association

40 Ivy Street, SE, Washington, DC 20003 (202) 547-2230; dealer.org

National Restaurant Association

1200 17th Street, NW, Washington, DC 20036 (202) 331-5900; restaurant.org

Printing Industries of America, Inc.

100 Daingerfield Road, Alexandria, VA 22314 (703) 519-8100; gain.org

Software Information Industry Association

1090 /Vermont Avenue NW, Suite 600, Washington, DC 20005

(202) 289-7442; siia.net

Travel Industry Association of America

1100 New York Avenue NW, Suite 450, Washington, DC 20005 (202) 408-8422, tia.org

Business Assistance Sites online

A guide to business-related Web sites.

There is virtually no end to the business and investment resource material available on the World Wide Web. This guide is by no means comprehensive, but it should provide a few starting points.

Business directories

Dow Jones Business Directory dowjones.com
The Dow Jones Business Directory is a free, thorough guide to business sites on the Web. Each site is rated on its content, speed, navigation and design. The categories reviewed are careers, companies in the Dow, financial, markets, government and politics, industries, personal finance, reference and small business.

Government FedWorld Information Network www.fedworld.gov A central point for accessing government information. Perform a keyword search for government reports, pick from lists of FedWorld databases (such as tax forms and instructions) and FedWorld-hosted Web sites. Users also can search all U.S. government Web sites, including its collection of links to business, commerce and economics sites at www.fedworld.gov/busin.htm

Services for Employers and Businesses
www.ssa.gov/svcs.htm
The Social Security Administration offers numerous resources for employers, such as a guide on year-end wage reporting, instructions on verifying names and Social Security numbers, tips on how to save time and money filing W-2 forms, and instructions on filing W-2 reports electronically. Also has news and international policies, including help for employers with overseas workers.

Small Business Administration (SBA)
www.sba.gov
Information on starting, financing and expanding small businesses. Includes special services, disaster assistance, legislation, a property-for-sale database and a very comprehensive list of other business-related Web sites.

U.S. Business Advisor
www.business.gov
One-stop access to federal government information available to businesses. Includes answers to frequently asked questions on taxes, exports, jobs, Social Security, environmental law, the U.S. Postal Service and small business.

U.S. Department of Commerce
www.doc.gov
General information about the Commerce Department. Search all the department Web sites or peruse a list of all bureaus. Includes information on the bureaus of Export Administration, Economics and Statistics Administration, Business and Trade, and Information and Business Services.

Bureau of Economic Analysis
www.bea.doc.gov
The BEA, a branch of the Department of Commerce, provides data and statistics on "economic growth, regional development and the nation's role in the world economy." The site is categorized into three areas: national, regional and international.

Bureau of Labor Statistics
www.bls.gov
Read Labor Department reports on the labor market, hours, wages,

productivity and prices. Also available online are BLS publications, research papers, surveys and programs on employment, productivity, living, working conditions and international conditions.

Conference Board
www.conference-board.org
Two major reports produced by the Conference Board are the consumer confidence index and the leading economic indicators index. These publications and other research reports are available for a fee. For free, users can get information on the board's conferences, councils, products and services.

Federal Reserve Board
www.federalreserve.gov
Information on the board of governors and on the Federal Open Market Committee. Read the official testimony and speeches from the board, including congressional testimony by Chairman Alan Greenspan. Summary of Federal Reserve regulations. Access to the Beige Book. Links to related Web sites, such as the Federal Reserve banks.

Resources for Economists on the Internet
econwpa.wustl.edu/EconFAQ/Econ

FAQ.html
An extensive guide to economic resources on the Net. Includes descriptions of each resource and a link to the site. Topics include United States macro and regional data, world data, financial markets and economic journals.

STAT-USA
www.stat-usa.gov
For a quarterly fee of $50, users have access to data on export and international trade and on economic indicator reports for such areas as construction, retail, manufacturing, employment, productivity, national income and personal income.

White House:

The Economic Statistics Briefing Room
www.whitehouse.gov/fsbr/esbr.html
The purpose of this service is to provide easy access to current Federal economic indicators. It provides links to information produced by a number of Federal agencies. All of the information included in the Economic Statistics Briefing Room is maintained and updated by the statistical units of those agencies. All the estimates for the indicators presented in the Federal Statistics Briefing Room are the most currently available values.

Federal Reserve Bank of Minneapolis

Minneapolis.org
Economic data for the Ninth District, including analysis, data and forecasts in the following areas: agriculture, banking, construction, exports, labor, natural resources, population and travel. Read information produced by the Federal Reserve, including the "fedgazette" and research papers. Search a Ninth District bank directory or review banking regulations.

Investing

Hoovers IPO Central
www.ipocentral.com
IPO Central compiles filings for U.S. companies conducting initial public offerings. Find an IPO by company name, industry, underwriter, state or metro area.

Securities and Exchange
Commission (SEC)
www.sec.gov
The SEC offers assistance to help investors avoid securities fraud, and it educates them about making wise investments. Read SEC news digests, speeches, studies, testimony and proposed and final rules. A section on the Litigation Releases explains its purpose and gives descriptions of current SEC civil suits, administration proceedings and decisions, investor alerts and

insider trading information. A section devoted to small-business information offers such items as a Q&A on small business and the SEC and small-business initiatives. From the SEC home page, users can search for non-EDGAR SEC documents (www.sec.gov/cgi-bin/txt-srch-sec) and the EDGAR archives (www.sec.gov/edgarhp.htm). The SEC filings are delayed 24 to 72 hours.

Standard & Poor's Equity Investor
Services
www.stockinfo.standardpoor.com
Use of the site is free, but registered members have access to more information, including market news, analyses, and Standard & Poor's stock reports and equity indices. S&P also has launched Personal Wealth, its personal investment site, at www.personalwealth.com

StreetEYE Index
www.streeteye.com
A searchable directory of investor-related Internet resources. Some of the topics are market data, exchanges, brokers, banks, personal finance and nonprofits.

Company info

The Annual Reports Library
www.zpub.com/sf/arl
Has information on how to read an

annual report and how to find reports online, as well as information for people who create annual reports or are interested in reports by nonprofit and charitable organizations.

EDGAR-Online

www.edgar-online.com

Users can do free searches for full-text SEC filings older than 24 hours by using the following criteria: company name, ticker symbol, form type, Central Index key, sector, industry, state, city and date range. Access to the complete EDGAR database back to 1994. Contains company information from other sources, such as quotes from PC Quote, charts from BigCharts and company capsules from Hoover's. For a fee, users can retrieve and download in real-time the current day's SEC filings and receive electronic notice when a company in which the user is interested files. A subscriber also has access to insider transaction filings.

FreeEDGAR.com

www.FreeEdgar.com

Offers free access to real-time company SEC filings. Search by company name, ticker symbol or SIC code. Create a "watch list" that notifies the user via e-mail when the SEC releases a filing by a company

on the user's watch list.

Hoover's Online

www.hoovers.com

Users can do free searches by company name, ticker symbol or keyword. Each return lists a brief company profile, the latest company news, stock information and 24-hour delayed SEC filings. For a fee, users can get the SEC documents in real-time and access Hoover's more than 8,000 detailed company profiles. Those contain information on a company's strategy, history, competitors, products and finances. Users also can set up custom searches.

Online business news

Barron's Online

www.barrons.com

The complete contents of the printed weekly newspaper are available online with the latest issue available Saturday morning by 7 a.m. "Weekday Extra" offers exclusive online commentary and features. Users can receive free e-mail delivery of the "Weekday Trader" after the stock market closes. A free, two-week trial period gives users access to Barron's Online plus The Wall Street Journal Interactive Edition and Smart Money Interactive. An annual subscription costs $49, or $29 if the user subscribes to any print edition of The

Wall Street Journal, Barron's or Smart Money.

Bloomberg Online
www.bloomberg.com
News, data and analysis of the day's top business and world stories and the latest market information updated 24 hours a day. Listen to audio clips of interviews with market experts -economists, analysts and strategists. Also includes news, latest scores, standings, game summaries and statistics for professional football, baseball, basketball hockey, golf, auto racing, boxing and some college sports. If you subscribe to the printed version of Bloomberg Personal, users can access its Web site for free and access information on more than 18,000 stocks and funds and set up a portfolio of as many as 50 securities.

Business Week Online
www.businessweek.com
Business Week puts the complete contents of its magazine online, including articles found only in its international editions. Also, get daily highlights of the U.S. and international markets. Get stock quotes, read charts of major market indexes, track your portfolio, or get information on mutual funds, currencies, banking and options

markets. Listen to hourly market and business news updates in RealAudio from Business Week's on-air correspondent. Search its archive back to January 1991, or browse by issue date selected stories back to October 1991. Some special reports are available exclusively online, such as "Women and Business" and "The Computer Room." If you subscribe to the printed edition of Business Week, the Web edition is free. For nonsubscribers, subscription plans start at $35.

CNNfn
www.money.cnn.com
Information on the U.S. and world markets, currencies and interest rates and the day's top business stories. Enter ticker symbols to get 20-minute delayed quotes for stocks, mutual funds and money market funds. Forbes Digital Tool www.forbes.com/ Forbes Digital Tool is a daily e-zine including stories on technology and the Internet, personal finance, startups and companies. It has the complete current issue of the magazine and archives from 1997 issues. Online-only supplements include Forbes ASAP, latest news, innovations and trends in high tech, and Forbes FYI, a quarterly guide to "living the good life." The Forbes lists are online, too; for example, use the Forbes 400 Hundred Query Page to

search the database of the richest people in America. Some of the search variables include net worth, state, age and source of wealth. You also can search the Forbes 500 list by selecting a company name or by selecting an industry or state.

Fortune
www.fortune.com
The Fortune e-zine contains free articles from its current editions, including the columnists, Smart Managing, Techno File, Small Business and Personal Fortune. Browse and retrieve articles from the Fortune archives back to September 1995. View the Fortune 500 list as ranked by revenues. Or select a CEO or industry list. Users also can search the database by company, CEO, industry or keyword.

NewsPage Home Page
www.individual.com
Build your own "page" of news based on your interests. Users need to register, but the service is free. NewsPage covers more than 2,500 topics and taps into more than 600 world news resources, including Reuters, the Associated Press and the Los Angeles Times. NewsPage uses an agent to filter and then prioritize articles of interest to each subscriber. Also available to subscribers is Company Link, which

offers news, financial data and contacts for 65,000 companies. Stock quotes are available without registering.

The Wall Street Journal Interactive Edition
www.wsj.com
The Wall Street Journal's online edition is by subscription only. It is updated throughout the day, with the next day's paper online by midnight the day of publication. Includes news coverage of business, the financial markets and technology. Users can access Briefing Book company news and reports or set up a Personal Journal to create a custom view of the news and investments. Searches in the Dow Jones News/Retrieval Publications Library gives users access to 5,000 trade and business news wires, magazines, transcripts and newsletters and an archive of The Wall Street Journal and other Dow Jones publications. The subscription includes access to The Wall Street Journal Interactive Edition, SmartMoney Interactive and Barron's Online. An annual subscription costs $29 for subscribers to the printed version of any Dow Jones publication, or $49 for non-print subscribers.

Financial markets

AP MarketsWeb

markets.ap.org/

The Associated Press offers financial market data primarily to newspapers. However, one area available to any user is the ticker lookup. Users can look for a stock or mutual fund by entering the ticker symbol or letters it contains, or by typing the partial AP stub name or the partial company name as it appears in the newspaper.

American Stock Exchange

www.amex.com

Get market summaries, the latest news and information on its 800 listed companies. And get data on the most-active issues on the NYSE, Nasdaq and world markets. All equities and options data are delayed 20 minutes. Site also has information on using options and investing in SPDRs (S&P depository receipts) and WEBS (World Equity Benchmark Shares).

Chicago Board of Trade

www.cbot.com

Plenty of background information on the CBOT, including a virtual tour. Market information includes intraday data, end-of-day data, market commentary and contract information. Futures quotes are delayed 10 minutes and options quotes are delayed 30 minutes. Get

information on trading Dow Jones industrials average futures and options at www.cbot.com/dow/home.htm

The Economeister

www.economeister.com

Read the day's top world and national market news. Search the Economeister for news on monetary policy, the markets, politics, the economy or portfolio management.

Nasdaq

www.nasdaq.com/

Users can search for as many as 10 securities listed on the Nasdaq, NYSE or AMEX and receive quotes on stocks and mutual funds. Also track any Nasdaq-listed security and get charts that provide daily and historical information, company descriptions, financial and trading profiles, quotes and SEC filings. Read market news and activity reports. Users can set up an online portfolio after filling out a questionnaire. The site also has resources for individual investors.

New York Stock Exchange

www.nyse.com

The site doesn't offer closing prices or delayed quotes, but refers users to links of NYSE-listed companies and offers a market summary of the previous day's activity. Also, its statistics archive has an excellent collection of free publications, including a history of the NYSE daily volume as far back as 1888, index closes back to 1966, and zip files containing market cap figures for NYSE-listed companies for the last three months in 1997. Also has profiles of newly listed U.S. companies and lists of all non-U.S. listed companies.

PCQuote
www.pcquote.com
Free, delayed stock quotes are available. For a fee, users can receive real-time data for stocks, options, futures, funds, research, news and indices by downloading PCQuote software. Prices for different levels of service range from $75 to $3,000. Another feature, called MarketSmart, gives users quotes, charts and portfolios in either real-time or delayed service, without a subscription fee. If the real-time service is chosen, the user pays the required exchange fees.

Lycos Inc.
www.finance.lycos.com
finance.lycos.com offers several subscription packages, which include real-time quotes and customized news. If a user registers but doesn't subscribe, some of the accessible information includes delayed security quotes for securities traded on U.S. and Canadian exchanges, earnings and balance sheet information on domestic equities; real-time and historical news headlines from more than 500 news sources; charts showing daily, weekly, or monthly price movements for individual securities and charts that reflect changing market prices.

StockMaster
www.stockmaster.com
Search for a stock or mutual fund to get a quote and chart. NYSE and AMEX quotes are delayed 20 minutes, Nasdaq quotes 15 minutes. Canadian stock quotes are available in Canadian dollars. A company can list a quote and graph of its performance by sending its Web address to StockMaster.

Miscellaneous

Economic journals on the Web
www.oswego.edu/~economic/journals.htm
A thorough index of economic journals available on the Internet, listed alphabetically. Includes national as well as international sites.

Chapter 8

Where to locate your business: Your site can save you

Selecting the best location for your business is one of the most important decisions you will ever make. Where you choose to run your business will affect your sales, operating hours, overhead costs, advertising, availability of good employees, volume of customer traffic and many other considerations that have a direct impact on your profitability.

> *In this chapter, you will learn:*
>
> 1. *How to think about your business in several different ways*
> 2. *You will learn how to choose the best location for your business or;*
> 3. *To make the most of the business site you have now.*

Successful retail store owners are especially careful about where they locate their businesses. When asked to name the three most important factors that contributed to their success, most will tell you; "Location, location and location."

Finding the best location for your business is important to non-retailers, too. For example, if you are planning to have a manufacturing company, it may be most important for you to locate near your sources of supply or near your customers. Or, it may be the type of business that requires large tractor-trailer pickups and deliveries. If this is the case, you have to be sure that these large vehicles are allowed in the area where you locate.

Or, if you go into a service business such as insurance or advertising, you may want to be in a location that presents a **SUCCESSFUL PICTURE** simply from its surroundings.

However, it may be that you will not be in a position to select the best possible site for your business. For example:

1. You operate your business from your home: Frequently when starting a small business, one begins in his own home. This is done in order to save money or save time.

2. There may be a pre-existing location of a business: When a business is purchased, its location is often already determined. It may or may not be the best location.

3. You may have limited alternatives: Often when one starts a small business, it is necessary to select a location which is "less than the best". This may be due to any number of factors, including cost and lack of space.

Should your business fall into one of the above three examples, this chapter will **still be helpful** regardless of your business location, you will still have to know the answers to such questions as:

*   Who is my competition?
*   Where are they located?
*   Who are my customers?
*   What services do they want?

How Important Is Your Location To Your Customers?

The horse-drawn carriage makers went out of business early in this century because they forgot what their real business was. It wasn't making carriages, although that's what they sold. Their real business was **transportation** - moving people from one place to another. If they had remembered that their customers depended upon them to get from here to there, they would have found something else to sell to meet that need. They forgot what was most important to their customers. As it happened, their customers moved on without them. Their customers found that automobiles and streetcars and trains gave them what they needed more conveniently and at a better price. Before you could say, "Going out of business sale," the market for horse-drawn carriages virtually disappeared.

This evolution of the market is Progress with a capital P. The strength of any business is its ability to meet the needs of its customers. The needs of customers are constantly changing, a fortunate fact of the marketplace that continually creates new opportunities for customer-oriented and future-oriented entrepreneurs.

We have already discussed how to identify new customer needs and new business opportunities; now, as you begin planning to implement your ideas, **REMEMBER YOUR CUSTOMER**. Now is not the time to fall in love with a store location because it's near your favorite shopping center; nor is this the time to satisfy your ego with an overpriced, trendy office complex address just to impress your friends.

Think about what is really important to your customers, and you will have the most important key to your business location.

Ask yourself: Why will or why do my customers come to buy from me? Is it for convenience, or perhaps because I am near their homes or a major thoroughfare? Is it because I can fill their orders faster and ship the same day? Is it because I deliver? Is it because they can walk in on their lunch hour? Is it my quality, and if so, are my customers so loyal that they will drive 10 miles out of their way to buy from me? Do a little careful research on your own and ask your existing customers or prospective customers why they buy from you. Listen carefully for patterns in their responses.

Once you have a clear idea of what's important to your selection of your business site. Do you have to be close to inexpensive labor and perhaps a bus line to continue beating your competition's prices? Do you need to be close to the airport for quick shipments? Do you need to be conveniently located in a luxurious shopping center and "bring your store to your customer"? Even if you are in the direct mail business or other business which theoretically can be run from anywhere, your rent or lease costs will affect your selling prices.

No matter what business you are in, business location will be important. You must plan to meet your customer's needs now and in the future. In order to illustrate some of the specific considerations in site location, we will use hypothetical retail stores and restaurants throughout the balance of this chapter.

Once you clearly determine the direction you want your business to take and what is most important to your customers, you are ready to actually begin exploring your market.

Where To Start Your Search

You can begin your search for the best site in your **local library**. By using local maps and reference materials, you can save a lot of time and discover what trends will affect potential sites. The reference materials you will need are: current data from the latest census (the last national census was held in 2000; some cities conduct their own population surveys and business surveys more often) and local statistical information. Your librarian is trained to assist you in finding the best information for your community.

Another source for maps and statistical information is a **local real estate firm**. These people know their territory. Not only will a good agent be able to describe the not-so-obvious characteristics about a neighborhood, but they may also know where the good business locations are.

Local banks also maintain good information about a community. The business they are in is PROVIDING SERVICE TO BUSINESSES AND

INDIVIDUALS. Therefore, they usually keep good up-to-date information on both population and business trends for their area.

Chambers of Commerce or local business organizations know what businesses are in town. They also know about new businesses which are planning to move into an area or established ones moving out. They probably can help you estimate how much business you may expect to do, particularly if there is or was a similar business in the area.

Still another source of good information is your **local newspaper**. The local paper makes it their business to know about your city. Talk to an editor about changes in the community. The Advertising Sales Managers are often the best source of good business information since they are "out on the street" every day.

Finally, there are **State and County offices**. Often these offices maintain an incredible amount of census and trend information about communities.

When searching out information for SITE LOCATION, there are **TWO KEY CONCEPTS TO KEEP IN MIND:**

- First**, it is best to locate your business near your potential customers.** Most retail businesses draw most of their customers from a predictable trade area around their location. Within this **trade area,** you must find your customers. Each type of business has a different size trade area. By knowing what size trade area your type of business generally has, you can draw a circle on a map of the city around each site you are considering in order to see where you will have to find your customers. It is the "convenience factor" that determines the size of your primary trade area.

Popular businesses, such as neighborhood restaurants and gas stations, draw most of their business from trade areas as small as one-half mile around them. Shopping centers can draw from a 35 mile radius. Trade areas don't have to be just geographical circles, however. You will attract customers from many miles away if your location is on a major thoroughfare, visible from a freeway, or close to a large office complex or university. You must be satisfied that you have made it as easy as possible for your customers to buy from you by locating yourself near them in a place that is easy to find.

- **Second, think like your prospective customer.** Forget your personal preferences. You have to please your customers, now and in the future, in order to make the most of your venture. This will call for some tough decisions on your part, and you must resist the favorite locations of your friends and family if such locations are not the best for your business. The most common reason people give for locating their store is that they "noticed a vacancy". Don't do it, most of these people go out of business within a few years! The stakes are too high when it comes to selecting your location, so don't take the first nice place you come across.

With these concepts in mind, let's look at the criteria you should use when researching a location:

CRITERIA #1: POPULATION

You must identify your customers in order to satisfy them. Remember that you are carving a niche for yourself in the market, and you have to know what kind of community you're getting into. You'll want to know the following information about prospective trade areas. Depending upon your business, these factors will have important effects on the success of your business.

Here are the most important population characteristics to consider:

1. **Cultural Characteristics**

    a. Ethnic characteristics, including the predominant racial profiles of the neighborhoods. There may be certain products more popular with one particular racial group than another. For example, a restaurant specializing in Mexican food could be more successful if located in or near a Hispanic neighborhood.

b.   Religious characteristics, particularly in communities where certain faiths are highly visible. A delicatessen with Jewish-style food would probably do quite well near a synagogue.

c.   National origin, particularly those of recent immigration such as Chinese, Vietnamese and Indian. What do these new Americans need? What products or services do they need?

Get a map of your city or your trading area. Make several copies of it. On one copy divide the area into neighborhoods which are predominately a certain cultural group (race, national origin, religion).

2.   **Income characteristics,** including average household income. This often reflects the average educational level, too. A trendy, high-fashion boutique with expensive clothes should be located near the prospective customers who can afford to pay more for their clothes. Likewise, a store selling work clothes and uniforms would do better in an area with a lower income level, assuming that blue-collar workers have a greater need for these types of clothes.

Income levels are extremely important to plot on a map of your trading area. Using another copy of your map, divide the area into several different income levels. Then refer to this map when you locate among the families you think represent the best potential. Use your map later if you plan to make mailings into the area.

3.   **Vocational characteristics,** including type of work and any large employers in the area. Do you want customers

in your trade area to be predominantly white-collar workers or blue-collar workers? How important is this factor to your business? It is a well-established fact in the liquor business that saloons in blue-collar neighborhoods sell more beer than wine or mixed drinks. Similarly, if you plan to sell personal computers in a retail store, you should locate the store in a community or neighborhood where the prospective customers have experience with computers at work. Ideally, they would also have professional interests and "sophisticated" hobbies (like astronomy or computer building) that would help justify such a purchase.

4.   **Age characteristics** are important because different ages have different buying patterns. If most of the residents around your store have young families, they are going to be buying the toys, home repair tools and yard equipment associated with starting a home. Older residents don't have the same needs they are spending their money on the finer things in life that they postponed purchasing while they raised their families. Expensive cars and travel tickets are more suitable for this kind of neighborhood.

What other characteristics are important to your business? Age of housing? Vocational or educational factors? Age of families? Age and make of cars owned? Property ownership? Usually, whatever information you need is available somewhere. A third map showing this information for your area will be most helpful.

5.   **Mobility characteristics**, or the likelihood that prospective customers will travel outside the trade area to make purchases. In an area with a high density of senior citizen high rises, it may be wise to have a delivery service if you run a convenience store. In less populated areas, the car is king and people don't seem to mind traveling greater distances to shop.   In the heavily populated areas, public transportation is much more available and commercial areas are closer together, so people are less likely to travel.   Generally, in the metropolitan areas throughout the country, customers in the suburbs

are more likely to drive than those in the city.

Your research into population information will help you answer questions including the following about your potential customers:

How many persons or families are in the trading area and how has it changed over time? Is the area growing in population or declining?

Where do they work? What do they do for a living?

How much money does the average household earn per year?

How many young people are there? How many older people are there?

How many families are there? How many have young people or small children?

How many single-family homes are there? Apartments? Condominiums?

How many families own their own homes? How many rent?

What is the value of the homes? What is the average monthly rent?

How many of the families own automobiles? How many own two?

How many other businesses are located in the trading area? What types of businesses are they? Will they attract potential customers to you?

Much of their information is taken directly from the CENSUS OF POPULATION AND HOUSING conducted by the U.S. Department of Commerce, Bureau of the Census. For more information, go to www.census.gov

CENSUS OF POPULATION AND HOUSING

Every ten years, the BUREAU OF CENSUS takes a census or count of almost all Americans. This census is taken in every county in all fifty states. The most recent Census was completed in 2000.

Statistical information is gathered about every person in two broad categories:

POPULATION questions are asked about sex, race, age, marital status, ancestry, children, occupation and vocation training.

HOUSING questions are asked about numbers of rooms, value of the home, ownership of telephone, air conditioning, television, dishwasher, clothes washer and dryer, plus the number of autos and vans.

Using the information from the Census Tracts, you can construct profiles of your market area. Depending upon what is important to you; your map can show income, cultural neighborhoods or types of housing.

All the answers to questions in the Census were then tabulated. In turn, the same information was compiled for the entire country, and then broken down by:

State
County
Metropolitan Area
Census Tract

The census tract is the smallest geographic area for which the statistics are published.

Let's look at a simple example of how you might use the Census information on Waterloo City, Iowa. Suppose you are considering starting a hardware store. If the average household spends $105 a year on hardware supplies (this figure was obtained from the National Association of Hardware Retailers), you can estimate the size of your market by simply multiplying households by average expenditure for hardware items times the percent of total business you expect at your location.

EXAMPLE OF CALCULATION:

29,808	X	$105.00	X	5%	=	$156,492
Total Housing Units		yearly estimated hardware purchase per household		Estimated market share		Sales

2001 Census Data Waterloo City, Iowa

HOUSEHOLDS BY TYPE

Total households	**28,697**	**27,958**	**29,436**
Family households (families)	18,213	17,568	18,858
With own children under 18 years	8,339	7,730	8,948
Married-couple families	13,082	12,414	13,750
With own children under 18 years	5,052	4,542	5,562
Female householder, no husband present	3,787	3,333	4,241
With own children under 18 years	2,600	2,216	2,984
Nonfamily households	10,484	9,839	11,129
Householder living alone	8,534	7,922	9,146
65 years and over	3,459	3,023	3,895
Households with one or more people under 18 years	9,135	8,511	9,759
Households with one or more people 65 years and over	7,293	6,709	7,877
Average household size	2.37	2.29	2.45

Average family size	2.95	2.87	3.03
HOUSING OCCUPANCY			
Total housing units	**29,808**	**29,216**	**30,400**
Occupied housing units	28,337	27,611	29,063
Vacant housing units	1,471	988	1,954
Homeowner vacancy rate (percent)	0.6	0.0	1.9
Rental vacancy rate (percent)	4.2	1.6	6.8
HOUSING TENURE			
Occupied housing units	**28,337**	**27,611**	**29,063**
Owner occupied	19,535	18,768	20,302
Renter occupied	8,802	8,066	9,538
Average household size of owner-occupied unit	2.47	2.37	2.57
Average household size of renter occupied unit	2.25	2.12	2.38

Thus, you have estimated your first year sales of $156,492 for hardware items in Waterloo City, Iowa.

CRITERIA #2: MARKET TRENDS

Once you have a basic understanding of the make-up of the city and neighborhoods around a potential site, you will want to evaluate the community from a broader, futuristic perspective. Essentially, you are striving to imagine what it will be like to do business in a particular location in the future.

Trends can be discovered most quickly by the following methods:

- Reading the local or neighborhood newspapers.

- Talking with other business owners in the area.

- Talking with the appropriate elected officials, including the Planning Department and the municipal body that is usually called the Promotion or Development Commission.

- Making use of information available through the local Chamber of Commerce.

- Population shifts: Is the population stable? If not, why are people moving? Where are they moving? How is the customer base changing?

- Progressiveness of the community: Is the community receptive to change? Will a new business be welcome?

- Distribution of wealth: Do most prospective customers seem relatively affluent? Have they bought other types of products or services from existing businesses that would indicate they have the desire and means to acquire new things?

- New construction: Where are the new developments being built? What types of developments are they? Again, the people who work for the city can provide a wealth of information; talk to the people in charge of zoning, permits and licenses.

- Business base: Is the community dependent on a single firm or industry? Is this industry or firm prospering? Do they have good relations with the community, or their union?

CRITERIA #3: COMPETITION

By now, you should be able to eliminate some of the site locations which you originally thought worth considering because they are not close enough to the people you think will be your best customers. Again, everything else being equal, location is important because you want to make it easy for your customers to buy.

Unless you are in a business without competition, your next concern is where your potential competitors are located. Naturally, your job will be more difficult if you locate just down the street from a successful, established concern. The time to find out about your competition is before you move in, not after!

PLUMBING SUPPLIES

Let's think about your competitors for a moment. What kinds of businesses would they be? If you want to see plumbing supplies, you will have to consider not only other plumbing suppliers, but also hardware stores and discount home centers. Be aware that the home care centers have a much larger trading area and a much larger advertising budget than you.

Don't kid yourself on this point. You are probably not the first person to think about servicing these customers in the way you plan, and you have to know who you are going to be up against in order to be successful. Pretending that there is no serious competition is like saying no one really needs what you are going to sell. What are people doing now when they want plumbing supplies or convenient shopping or clothing alterations or car repairs? These shopping habits will affect your sales.

NOTE: Draw up a list of all your potential locations and give each of them a letter code.

Now, you are ready for some work in the field. Your next assignment is to "shop" your competition for invaluable first hand experience with them. Remember, you are not competing against an impersonal store with products and fixtures, but rather the people who run that organization. How they think about their customers, how well they treat them and what types of products and services they offer are critical to your marketing approach. Since you have already narrowed your potential trading areas with the first two criteria, you should have a manageable number of competitors to shop. A personal visit is best, but some information can be obtained over the phone.

By "shopping" the competition, you are attempting to determine how well the customer base is being served. It is reasonable to conclude that if a competitor is providing high quality goods and services at a low rate and most people in the area are satisfied, you would be trying to build your success on his leftover customers and those are probably the customers he doesn't want anyway! In short, if there isn't room in a particular trading area, seek greener pastures now.

If, on the other hand, you discover that you are waited on by unknowledgeable or impolite salespeople, you may have detected a weakness in the competition. Similarly, the competition may be charging unreasonably high prices because they monopolize local business. The competitor's customers may jump at the opportunity to buy from someone else.

Here's how to "shop" the competition:

- Pretend you are a serious customer. As you walk in, note the appearance of the store or office. Do they appear concerned about their image? Is it clean? Is it easy and pleasant to shop?

- Take note of how long it takes for someone to notice you and offer to help. Explain that you are not going to buy today, but you need some information. Is the salesperson courteous and responsive? Give him or her reasonably tough question to answer, and give them every opportunity to solve it. Does he or she seem to know their business? Are the answers complete and do they include prices and options? Are you satisfied as a customer that you were treated well?

- Finally, take whatever literature, price lists or catalogs that are available on the company. You will need these later as you design your own marketing programs.

COMPETITIVE ANALYSIS EXERCISE

Here is an example that will help you analyze competition. With your own local resources and the competitor analysis form on the next page, complete the following activities:

1.   Using your map, identify the location of each competitor you want to visit personally. Plan an efficient route to see all of them, and then shop them all on the same day under similar working conditions. The following Competitor Analysis form will help you summarize what you have learned about each competitor. Complete a form for each competitor before moving on to the next one.

2.   At the same time, obtain a map of your local marketing area. On this map, use a colored marker to mark your potential location or the location where you would like to locate.

3.   Now, with a different colored marker, place an "X" at each

location where a competitor is located. When you have completed this, you have a much clearer picture of your competitor's potential impact on your business.

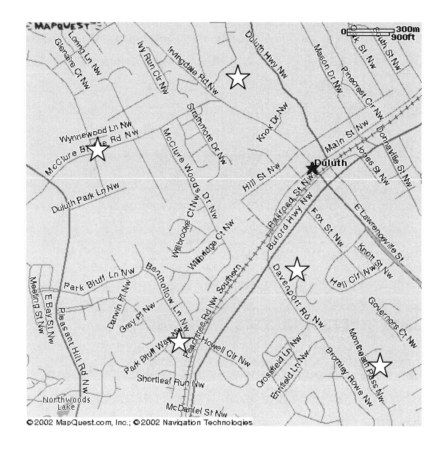

COMPETITOR ANALYSIS

Name of competitor: _____

Address of location visited: _____

Answer YES or NO for each of these factors.

High traffic area? _____   Easy access by car? _____

Adequate parking? _____   Free parking? _____

Easy to find? _____   Sign(s) used? _____

Store well lighted? _____   Well decorated? _____

Attitude of salesperson or proprietor? _____

Knowledgeable? _____

Services available: (Check as applicable, or if offered)

_____ credit sales   _____ coffee

_____ free estimates   _____ rush orders at no up-charge

_____ delivery available at extra charge of _____

_____ pick up available at extra charge of _____

_____ samples available   _____ literature

_____ variety of stock   _____ special orders available

_____ custom work available

_____ guarantees and warranties

_____ repair service available

Product selection: _____

Hours of operation: _____

Days open for business: _____

Price of item(s) shopped for: _____

Is price fair? Competitive with you? _____

Pricing policy (discount, high, varies, etc.)

Advertising:

____ TV ____ Radio ____ Newspaper

____ Magazine ____ Direct Mail ____ Catalog

____ Billboard ____ Other:

Your evaluation: _____

What can you do to be better than this competition?

_____

CRITERIA #4: LOCAL LEGISLATION

By now, you should be able to eliminate a few more site candidates from consideration because of a competitive situation. At this point, a minor concern with enormous implications should be double-checked: local zoning or closing ordinances.

For many of you, this will not be an issue because of the type of business you're in. But if you plan to open a restaurant, a social service facility like a day care center, a bar or liquor store, take the time to go to the municipal government and find out what will be required.

You can expect some differences between communities, particularly in suburban communities around a larger metropolitan area. Two or three miles away, on the other side of the municipal boundary, your situation may be more to your advantage. Or, if the ordinances have effectively screened out most of the competition, perhaps it would be worth your effort to comply if you could dominate the market.

CRITERIA #5: TRAFFIC AND ACCESSIBILITY

Traffic and accessibility are more important to some businesses than others. Think about how you sell to your customers; what kind of business do they expect you to run? What is really important to them? In this and the following sections, you will begin to balance the advantages and disadvantages of the specific sites you have identified as good for your business.

' CHOOSE RIGHT DIRECTION '

So far, you have identified the best neighborhoods or shopping areas for your business. Now, you are ready to begin looking at specific locations within these areas. Your first concern will be for traffic patterns and accessibility. You know that you will have a good customer base in any of these areas you've targeted; the trick now is to find the best locations within each area.

In central and suburban business districts, small retail stores depend upon the traffic generated by large stores. Large stores and small stores alike must attract business from the existing flow of traffic; the same is true for restaurants and other businesses that depend on the buyer who decides impulsively on the basis of convenience. If you run one of these kinds of businesses, every dollar you spend toward getting a better location saves you many more dollars in advertising you won't have to do.

Study the flow of traffic, especially around shopping centers and large stores. Note one-way streets, street widths, and parking lots. Look for the best traffic situations for your needs.

Determine how important traffic is to your business by considering the other criteria we have already discussed. When you have narrowed your site alternatives to your best few, determine how important traffic will be to your success. Depending upon how important you rank it, you will want to consider the following factors:

a.   **Public transportation**, which may be important for both your customers and employees; pay particular attention to locations in or near terminals.

b.   **Parking availability**, which will be important to all of your drive-by traffic. Cost and access to the lot or ramp are the most important considerations. Remember, it should be easy for the customer to stop and buy. Locating on a busy street will not help you if your customers can't stop to shop.

c.   **Distance from residential areas or other business areas**, will be important with some types of businesses.

d.   **Traffic congestion** can cause some people to actually avoid an intersection or shopping center. It is just like anything else: if it is uncomfortable or inefficient, it will hurt sales.

e.   **Side of street** is surprisingly important. Most of the research that has been done for gas station locations applies to many other businesses that would sell to the customer driving by. It has been learned that people want to buy certain things on their way to or from their homes. For example, newspapers and gas are bought on the way to work, while food and dry cleaning are purchased on the way home. The clever merchants locate their establishments on the side of the street that "their" rush-hour traffic travels on. If you sell better during the afternoon, cater to the afternoon rush-hour and locate on the side of the street that carries the outbound traffic going home.

f. **Width of street** is just as important. Street width indicates how well-traveled the road is or will be. Generally, the wider the road, the better the location. A main thoroughfare is better than a "feeder" street because it carries more potential customers per day. A wider road is easier for customers, too. Remember to think like a prospective customer in a hurry: Will traffic be blocked by a double-parked car?

g. **The part of the block** in which you locate may be important. The corner is more visible than a location mid-block because it can be viewed from the cross streets, and rental rates usually reflect this advantage.

h. **Neighbors** can be your greatest help if you choose your location well. Neighboring stores that are doing a lot of advertising to build their traffic will help you, too, because they will have to pass by your store on their way. With this in mind, many business owners pool a portion of their promotion dollars to fund merchant's associations that promote a distinct shopping district. Pick your neighbors well; stay away from neighbors that discourage your type of business, including X-rated book stores and theaters.

How to Take a Traffic Count

First of all, be sure you need one. As you have learned, there are other criteria that may be more important. While knowing about the type and volume of traffic is useful, it may not make any difference to your business. If you do decide that a traffic count is necessary, here are some tips to guide you:

- Many state and county highway departments maintain traffic counts on highways and busy commercial streets and roads.

- Simply look up the number for your county highway department in your local telephone book and call them. Or, you can write them a short letter, such as the following:

County Highway Department
XXX Street
City, State, Zip

Gentlemen:

    I am interested in receiving copies of your traffic count material for Sixth and Main Streets. Please provide me with the most recent traffic count information available. Thank you.

Sincerely,

John Doe
Address

Your objective is to count the traffic passing by your location, both pedestrian and vehicular, who are potential customers. If you run a men's clothing store, you obviously are more interested in counting the men between the ages of 16 and 65. By watching the people passing by carefully, you can get a sense of what kinds of people they are and even estimate their financial stature.

It is also important to classify the reasons people are passing by. Are they going to work? A nearby store? People are not always serious shoppers. You will have to conduct a number of random interviews with passersby to get accurate information, but if you explain that you are conducting a market research study (which you are), most people are glad to help.

Pick a period of time to make a traffic count that represents a normal shopping situation. The time of day, week, season, weather and even the time of the month affect traffic flow. People shop more during the end of the week and around the first and the fifteenth of the month because these are the times when they get paid. Let local custom be your guide, and select one day that is the most "typical". Then, divide your day into half-hour and hourly intervals, and count the traffic in these intervals during the store's normal operating hours. If it is not feasible to count for the whole day, make representative counts during the morning, afternoon and evening hours.

Use your traffic count information to compare the relative merits of one location versus another.

FORMULA FOR ESTIMATING SALES FOR A LOCATION

1. Number of people passing by each day: _____

2. Percent of people passing by who meet profile of prospective customer: _____%_____

3. Average number of potential customers passing by each day: _____ (Multiply #1 by #2. Remember, to qualify as a potential customer', a person must match your customer profile.)

4. Percent of prospective customers who would enter your store if it were there: _____ (This is based on your interviews, experience and industry statistics from your trade association.)

5. Average number of people entering your store to shop per day: _____ (Multiply #3 by #4.)

6. Percent of shoppers who would actually buy something: _____ (You can get this information from trade associations, prior experience and interviews.)

7. Number of actual customers per day: _____ (Multiply #5 by #6.)

8. Amount of average transaction: _____ (Based on trade association information.)

9. Estimated daily sales: _____ (Multiply #7 by #8.)

10. Number of days per year store will be open: _____

11. Estimated annual sales: $_____ (Multiply #9 by #10.)

You can divide the people passing a site into three categories: those who would just pass by; those who would look in the window and possibly enter the store; and those who would buy after entering the store. If, out of 1,000 people that pass by each day, 5% enter and each spends an average of $8, a store at that site, open 300 days a year, will have an annual sales volume of $120,000.

Obviously, you will have to make some assumptions and "guesstimates" to make these calculations, but if done at each site under your consideration, you will know which one or two locations are your "star" candidates. These are the ones with the most of your type of customer going by.

Other methods to calculate sales include talking to the competition "believe it or not", people will usually give you honest answers to honest questions and asking suppliers. Suppliers are particularly knowledgeable about who is doing what, how much is actually being sold of a particular line, who has expansion plans, what the potential is for growth, and the like. To them, you represent a potential customer. It is worth their time to help you get started the right way. For the price of lunch, you may be able to learn information that will significantly improve your plans.

For more information about sales forecasting and market potential, refer to the Forecasting and Budgeting Chapter.

Pick the Traffic Flow That Is Right For You

The site in the central business district that has the highest traffic

count of the "right" kind of people desired by a particular store is considered a 100% location. However, a 100% location for one store may be only an 80% location for another type of store with a different customer base. For example, a site that is a 100% location for a drugstore may be an 80% location for a men's

2005 Copyright of the American Institute of Small Business

store and only a 60% location for a paint store.

Pick the right traffic pattern and flow for you. It stands to reason that what's right for someone else will not necessarily be right for you. But with a good understanding of who your customers are, you will be able to identify the patterns that will help you the most to succeed.

CRITERIA #6: THE BUILDING OR
SPECIFIC ADDRESS YOU CHOOSE

When your potential locations are narrowed to a few, it will be necessary to visit each for a thorough inspection. Be sure to record your findings to questions like these:

1.   Age of building.

2.   Condition of building

3.   Condition and adequacy of all mechanical systems, including:

   a. electrical
   b. plumbing
   c. heating and air conditioning

(Note: If you find discrepancies or a borderline condition, it's best to hire a professional inspector.)

4.   Is remodeling necessary? At whose expense?

5.   Are doors large enough to bring in necessary fixtures or items you sell?

6.   Are public lavatories available?

7.   Is storage or warehouse space available if needed?

8.   Are there any potential safety hazards?

9.   Is security adequate? (Consider door locks, burglar alarm, fire and smoke alarms.)

10. Is the building insured adequately and under conditions you would impose upon it?

You may develop additional questions which fit your particular situation. Your investment of thought and time at this point will be of critical importance at a later date.

CRITERIA #7: MISCELLANEOUS FACTORS

By now, there are probably just a few sites that meet all of your criteria. Other important factors that must be considered include:

- Is the environment suitable? (Is it too smoky or noisy to be attractive to your customers? Is it too close to undesirable neighbors, such as bars, factories or garages?)

- Is the neighborhood suitable? (Is there adequate security, including police and fire? Are the sidewalks maintained? Is the building of quality construction?)

- Is the building ready to be used? Are you moving into a building that will complement your enterprise?

- Think like your typical customer: What does he or she expect? Is your business attractive enough, clean enough, conveniently located?

SPECIAL TIPS

Here are some special tips that will help you find that special location with that extra advantage.

Look for parallel businesses. We've discussed what types of businesses to stay away from; there are also some you should try to stick close to.

Ask yourself: Where else do my customers shop? Locating near a parallel business with an existing flow of customers will help you attract new customers faster. Radio Shack stores do best when located near a hardware store or men's wear because they attract men and do-it-yourselfers. Florsheim Shoe Company tries to locate near the financial districts because of the concentration of men who have to look good on the job.

Let Sears do the demographics. Despite its troubled sales record in recent years, Sears retains a first-rate reputation for picking good retail sites. The same is true for several other department store chains: Target Stores, Walmart and Fleet Farm.

These people know what they're doing. They have typically spent much more time and money in their research efforts than you will be able to do, and they have better resources to draw upon. Take advantage of what they know and piggyback on their research provided, of course you both sell to the same customer.

High traffic, high visibility, parking near-by, and proximity to shopping center make this the most ideal location, IF the other factors are acceptable.

Learn to use your local library reference materials. One of the best is the annual **Editor & Publisher's Market Guide**, which provides such tidbits as which supermarkets and department stores are in which shopping centers and what the deposits are at local savings institutions. Local newspapers, banks and Chambers of Commerce are also useful. Finally, the U.S. Census data can help you find information about your prospective sites that you didn't even know you were looking for until you find it.

Remember that demographics aren't everything. A crowded intersection is a good example. While the traffic count may be wonderful in theory, it may actually be a disadvantage because nobody will stop. In this case, the intersection is actually overcrowded for the purposes of the business owner.

Your store does not have to be near where people live; it could be near where they work. Wendy's, for example, has been successful placing stores across from light industrial plants and commuter college campuses. Big industrial complexes don't work as well, however, apparently because the tight security and rigid lunch hours make it too hard for employees to leave the grounds for lunch. However, bars usually do well at such locations.

Advertise. If you are in a mall or shopping center, your advertising does double-duty by attracting customers for your co-tenants as well as for you. In some situations, this makes you a more desirable tenant, and this is a valuable negotiating point when it comes time to sign a lease. While some tenants have to pay as much as 10% of gross sales in addition to their per-square-foot rental for space in malls, active advertisers may have to pay only 3% to 5%.

Make efficient use of your space. Strike a balance between the amount of space you would like to have and the amount you actually need. Design and redesign your floor plan until you are satisfied you are getting the most out of your space. It is better to start small and show a profit so you can expand later than to go broke quickly because you couldn't afford a crushing rent payment. Further, it is better to get a smaller space in the best location, even if you are a bit cramped, than to spread out comfortably away from the flow of traffic.

Ask for an excessive vacancy clause in your shopping center lease.
You can die on the vine if your big neighbor moves or goes out of
business. With an excessive vacancy clause, you can break your lease
if too much space is unfilled for too long. You need some market
muscle to get this position written in, but if the center wants you badly
enough, you can get it.

Try to locate in the center of the market. Don't let your
competitors head you off at the pass; force them to the extremities of
the market. If you know where the heart of the market is located, go
for it. Remember that markets have a way of shifting over time, and
that you want to be there just before your customers or your
competition.

One person's trash is another person's treasure. Radio Shack avoids
beauty shops, for example, because the parking space (especially in
small shopping centers) is taken up too long. Walgreen's, however, is
attracted to beauty shops because women come in to stock up on hair
care products after their hair is done. Walgreen's also likes
Laundromats because people with time on their hands are natural
browsers.

Note: By now, you should be able to identify your best one or two
locations. In a previous section, you learned how to evaluate and
negotiate a lease or rental agreement.

In this chapter, you have learned that:

1. *Choosing the right location for your business is one of the most important business decisions you will make.*
2. *Even if you have no control over your location, by obtaining information on your market, your potential customers and competition, you can run a better business.*
3. *You can obtain information on your population and market from you library real estate firms, local banks, local newspapers, Chambers of Commerce and even state and county offices.*
4. *In studying your market, it is important to get population information on the cultural, religious, national origin, income, vocations, age and mobility characteristics.*
5. *You can anticipate future market trends of the community by studying population shifts, progressiveness of the community, distribution of wealth, amount of new construction and strength and attitude of the current business base.*
6. *By shopping the competition, you evaluate customer satisfaction and your opportunity to succeed in each area.*
7. *You should determine the effect of local ordinances on your business.*
8. *By studying traffic flows, patterns and accessibility, you can select the locations with the amount and type of traffic best for you.*
9. *By studying business neighbors and their customers' needs, you can judge your neighbors' impact on your business.*
10. *By completing and evaluating the Where to Locate Your Business Quiz, you have determined one or two suitable locations to begin lease or rental negotiations.*

Chapter 9

Forecasting Sales

Dollars In, Dollars Out

By now you probably have some good ideas about what kinds of products and services will sell in your market. You are well along the way toward developing a plan for your business that will work as hard as you do. Good planning means success will soon follow.

Wouldn't it be helpful if you could estimate what your sales and expenses would be 6 or 12 months in the future? Just imagine: you would know how much inventory you would need to have on hand; you would know what your overhead expenses would be; you would even know how much money you were going to pay yourself!

With a little bit of imagination and a sharp pencil, you can do this kind of "fortune telling" for yourself.

Some people call it forecasting. Some call it budgeting. Your accountant probably calls it projecting or calculating a "pro forma". No matter what you call it, it means the same thing -- you are imagining what will happen in the future so that you can plan accordingly.

In this chapter you will learn:

1. Different types of forecasting methods; advantages and disadvantages of each
2. How to accurately forecast your sales
3. How to calculate your Fixed and Variable assets
4. How to project your cash flow
5. How to compare your forecasts to actual sales and expenses

---

THE ART OF FORECASTING

Financial forecasting is an art, not a science. No matter how carefully you think you have planned, you will not hit your projection exactly.

You can, however come very close.

Forecasting sales is like forecasting the weather. A sales forecast is no more (and no less!) than an educated guess as to how many sales you expect to make over a specified period of time. There are several ways of doing this:

1. You can use the LET-THE-BOSS-DECIDE Method, also known as the "jury of executive opinion" method. If this method were used at General Motors, the heads of its major divisions would pool their knowledge of the market to arrive at a joint opinion of how many sales to expect.

2. You can use the GRASS-ROOTS Method. This method is directed at your sales people and other employees who have the closest contact with the customer.

3. But since you are not a major American automaker, and you probably do not yet have a payroll, you had better consider the USER-EXPECTATION Method. With this method, you go directly to the consumer -- with questionnaires, on-the-street-corner surveys, telephone polls and any other opinion gathering device that will give you the story on what product or service sells (and why) and what doesn't (and why not).

Whichever method is used, the sales forecaster must consider seven elements

---

which are as important to the neighborhood auto mechanic as they are to General Motors. These are:

1. The SALES PERFORMANCE OF YOUR COMPETITORS.

2. The LEVEL AND TREND OF CONSUMER SPENDING, in general and for the specific products or services of your business.

3. The GENERAL TRENDS OF YOUR INDUSTRY OR PRODUCT FIELD.

4. Past, present and future ECONOMIC CONDITIONS.

5. MARKET TESTS.

6. KEY VARIABLES.

7. Prior SALES and PERFORMANCE PATTERNS of your business, if available.

Do these look familiar? They should. These are among the questions you raised while doing market research. The answers to your earlier market research questions now play major roles in your sales forecast. To do this forecast accurately, you need to carefully analyze your research results. You need to put them all together, like the pieces of a puzzle. But you must do it in such a way that the picture of the future you get is the most accurate one possible. Don't let your hopes get in the way. Look at the facts long and hard; see how they relate to each other; and let your head (not your heart or your pride) make the decisions.

LOOKING AT THE BIG PICTURE

One of the easiest ways to develop a forecast for your business is to get a grasp of the industry big picture. Suppose you are considering a television dealership which sells to all of Jefferson County. You will sell television sets, video cassette recorders, stereos, microwave ovens, radios, tape recorders, and various supplies.

By talking to potential suppliers -- either distributors or factory direct salesmen -- you learn what the national sales are for each of these products and how much moves at what price.

In addition, the good salesmen have industry-supplied figures for Jefferson County sales for at least televisions and video cassette recorders. With their help, you estimate the retail sales for your product line for Jefferson County. You learn which months are best for sales and which are worst. For example, you are told that a large share of your sales will be between Thanksgiving and New Year's Eve.

Thus, by looking at the total sales potential for the county, you have a good starting point for your sales forecast. Because many of these salesmen formerly sold at retail or have sold other brands, they can tell you a lot about your market and the industry. With their help, you devise marketing plans and strategies and estimate your share of the Jefferson County market. Because these salesmen have seen many new dealers enter markets in their territory (and some drop out), they can review your strategy and estimate your early monthly sales quite accurately.

These same salesmen can help you estimate your budget. They know average pricing and markups, county sales trends, credit policies, delivery costs, warranty opportunities, advertising expenses, inventory costs, and rebates. In addition, they can help you pick the best location because they know the strengths and weaknesses of retailers. If the salesmen know their business, they will make it easy for you to see a profit down the road. Remember, they want your business in order to fill in their weak market share areas.

But don't make a commitment to anyone at this point. Remember that you are just getting information. So, keep in control and make your own decision. Next week, your trusted salesman may be helping another entrepreneur get into business or converting your competitor to his line of products.

Not all businesses have such good statistics or easy access to competitive information. The following is a practical story of doing a survey to determine your sales forecast and establish a budget.

A SIMPLE STORY OF SUCCESS

To make this process as clear as possible, let's imagine a simple success story with you as the main character. In the beginning, long before you even saw a need to research your market, you did a lot of soul searching. You asked yourself what it was that you really liked to do and -- of equal importance -- what it was that you did best.

You always loved tools and tinkering. Over the years, you found much satisfaction in working with bicycles and, eventually, became the informal bike repair shop for the neighborhood kids and their parents. Even though your responsibilities at your regular job grew, you still spent your happiest hours putting bikes back together.

You never gave much thought to the idea of starting your own business though, much less a bike business, until the "get healthy" craze and gasoline prices both began to rise. You saw the trends before most: people once again were taking to the two wheelers. If you were going into a business of your own, you thought, it ought to be the bicycle business. When you caught wind of yet another layoff at the plant, you finally began to consider the idea seriously. Your head, however, told you that you had better think it through completely. Your heart beat faster at the thought of turning your hobby into a bona fide business.

Your head began to swim as you began to think about the details. Should you make your shop a repair shop, or should you sell new bikes at retail? What about used bikes -- you certainly could get your hands on a lot of them. Where is the best location, anyway? And how much could you really make in the bike business -- where was the money?

Now, imagine that you have a savings account of modest proportions (say $8,000) to start with, and you cannot afford to lose it by starting off on the wrong foot.

STARTING OFF ON THE RIGHT FOOT

Starting off on the right foot means getting the answers to those market research questions we discussed in the Market Research. And to do this, you know that you have to:

1. Ask the RIGHT questions of the RIGHT people.
2. Read the RIGHT material.
3. Survey the RIGHT customers.
4. Think clearly and cautiously.

So from your own home and on your own time, you set about researching your market.

First, ask the right questions of the right people who have at least part of the answers: You go to those already in the bike business, especially the retailers and wholesalers, and not surprisingly, find that bike sales are climbing and service jobs are up. Also, while there is not a noticeable increase in the number of bicycle shops, department store bike sections have clearly expanded.

Then, do the right reading: At your public library, you pour through back issues of "Bicycle Business News" and learn that today's big bike buyers are people over forty-five and people between the ages of eighteen and twenty-five. In the library's demographic and census materials, you discover that these people are found primarily in suburban areas; although a number of those in the lower age group also live near universities and colleges. You learn that this is true at the large state university a few miles from your home.

In the university's student newspaper, you read that an enrollment increase of nearly seven percent over the next five years is expected. Another article concerns programs aimed at attracting even more of the state's college-bound high school students.

In your city newspaper, you read that several schools that were once closed for lack of enrollment are being reopened. With more kids on the way, you correctly reason there will be the need for more bikes.

Next, survey the right consumers: Some clear thinking of your own tells you that the older folks want to steer clear of cardiac arrest.

Your oldest daughter, who has just begun her first year of college, also sheds some light on the buying habits of the second population group. With part-time employment and summer jobs as scarce as they are, she asks, how many college students have enough left to spend for a car? Not many. But for a good ten-speed? Quite a few. Besides, bicycle transportation for a college student makes good sense: no gasoline prices, no parking problems, no traffic jams, and you can take it almost anywhere -- even up four flights of dormitory stairs and into a room for one.

Add a dash of clear, cautious thinking: At this point, you begin to intensify your research. There is only one bike store in the university area, you discover; and this has been passed down from a father to a son. Casual chats with your daughter and her college chums, as well as a quick personal visit to the store, tell you that the father's out-dated and inefficient business practices have also been passed down. Customers wait weeks for simple repairs to be made; none of the more popular makes of bicycles are stocked; and apparently very little money is spent on advertising. People say the old man is hard to talk to, also -- a sure sign that people are not getting the attention they feel they deserve.

So far, the picture looks promising: there might just be room in the market for a bike shop with your strategy of featuring the latest models, the best repairs -- and QUICK delivery.

There is one dark cloud on the horizon, and it has snow in it. You live in an area where snow is on the ground at least three months of the year. This fact of life will hurt sales during this period of time, although it may be compensated for by more sales later on in the year.

There are several important conclusions that your research has led you to -- all of which seem to say: YOU CAN DO IT -- YOU CAN MAKE MONEY in the bicycle business.

After you are "reasonably sure" that there is a "reasonable chance" of success, you decide that it will be worth it to explore this business concept in more detail by putting some real numbers on paper.

Now you begin to construct your sales forecast for your imaginary bike shop. Basically, it is a process of elimination and decision-making; you need to answer the following questions in the following order:

- Are the trends right?
- Does the idea seem realistic?
- Would it all be worth it if you succeeded?
- Who is the customer?
- Where is the market?
- How big is the market?
- How many prospects will actually buy?
- How many of the buyers will buy from YOU?

Based on your research, here are the answers for your imaginary bike shop:

The time is right. By all indications, the present social and economic climate is favorable -- not the liveliest the country has ever known, but one well suited to the sale of bicycles. (Remember: a bad time for one industry, like the automobile industry, might just be a good one for another, like bikes.) People young and old want to stay fit, conserve fuel and save money -- and they are finding they can do it all with a bike.

The people are right. Based on a couple of conversations with the bike distributors you've bought parts from, you can conclude that the university area students and young professionals cannot get the prompt repair service that their fast lane lifestyle requires. What's more, they almost always go to those suburban competitors when they buy new bikes. One distributor told you, "The old guy doesn't seem to care about the new stuff. He only sells about six of our bikes per month." You know this distributor is tough to work with, and may just tell you

what you want to hear so he can sell you some bikes, too. So, you take his comments with a grain of salt. But he confirms what you have been hearing. The customers could do well, it seems to you, with an alternative bike store close at hand.

Finally, the icing on the cake. What really makes this picture glow is the hard data you get from your own informal market survey. With the help of your daughter and a couple of her friends, you set up a table on the university's busiest mall for a few hours (with the University's permission, of course -- a marketing instructor was very helpful in setting it up as long as a few of his students could help out and get some experience).

You attract your potential customers with a display of three of the latest models from Peugeot, lent to you from a distributor eager to please you as a potential new retailer. After some "bike talk" around the display table, you make sure that every student leaves with a postage-paid questionnaire in his or her backpack.

About 1,000 people walked by, and 180 stopped to look at the bikes and talk. These, you figure, are the "serious prospects" who are at least thinking about owning a bike in the near future. Of the 180 questionnaires you passed out, 136 are completed and returned within 10 days. (Ten days to two weeks allows enough time for everyone who is going to send them to do it. If you need to, you can raise the response rate by offering a discount coupon for merchandise or service if they cooperate.)

As you began tallying up the questionnaires that came back, you began to "meet" your potential customers. It turns out that 100 of these prospective customers actually live on campus; the rest drive to school from the suburbs. Out of this group of 100, 35 own bikes now. Seventeen bought their bikes new during the last 12 months, but only 9 of those 17 bought their bikes from the crotchety old man and his son.

You are becoming convinced that with a good location, adequate advertising and hard work, you can corner more than half of the area's market -- in other words, 5 of those 9 university area bike buyers. That's your conservative estimate. You really believe that you can probably sell a lot of those kids who go to the suburbs to buy their bikes. And you can probably even convince some people to buy that otherwise wouldn't have just because you're on campus and they see you every day.

But you don't want to get swept away by your own enthusiasm. You settle on 5 as the conservative number of sales you could make out of that original 100 students who lived on campus.

WORKING FOR THE NUMBERS, AND MAKING THE NUMBERS WORK FOR YOU

Now you are ready to translate your research into a sales forecast. Out of 1,000 people who passed by, 180 or 18.0 percent identified themselves as prospective customers because they were interested enough to stop.

1,000 X 18% = 180

This agrees with what you read in "Bicycle Business News" which stated that about 15% of the general population is bikers. This "litmus test" of your market test gives you confidence in your research. Had the number been very different, say 7% or 70%, you would have had to rethink your assumptions and, probably, find another way to get to talk to your customers. You are a little suspicious of the low number of people that appeared to own bikes already -- 35 percent or 3.5 percent of the thousand who went by. But then you remember that many of your potential customers were pedaling by on their way to class and were just too pressed for time to stop. You decide to count this group as a "fudge factor" and stick with the group you have "hard" information on because of the questionnaires.

According to the housing office and the university handbook, three out of every five or 60% of all students enrolled at the university lived either on campus or in the immediate vicinity. There is a total enrollment of 25,000; so that gives you a non-commuter, on-campus student market of 15,000.

$$25{,}000 \times 60\% = 15{,}000$$

Add to this the 5,000 young professionals who are said to live nearby, and you have a general market population of prospects of 20,000 people.

15,000 students + 5,000 young professionals = 20,000 prospects

Your informal survey -- which you have good reason to believe in -- tells you that, theoretically, 18 percent of those 20,000 people like bikes and own or want to own one.

20,000 X 18% = 3,600 "serious prospects"

How many of these serious prospects will actually buy bikes in a year? And how many will actually buy from you? Based on your research, you calculate that about 17 percent of these 3,600 serious prospects buy new bikes in a 12-month period (17 buyers out of every 100 prospects).

17% X 3,600 = 612 bikes

You know you can't sell all of them, but you conservatively figured that you could sell 5 out of the 17, or 5 percent (you can also think of it as 5 buyers out of every 100 prospects).

3,600 prospects X 5% = 180 bikes sold per year

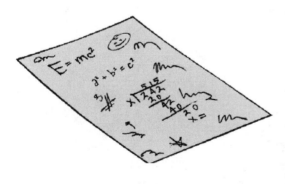

Let's now transfer this math into money. You are getting very close to your sales forecast! You are beginning to see what your business could look like!

You figure the average ten-speed bike sells for $350. But that's been marked up from the wholesale price of $200. So, for every bike sold, you'll realize a profit of $150. How many bike sales, once again, do you expect to make? 180, right?

$$\$350 \times 180 = \$63,000 \text{ Gross Sales}$$
$$\$150 \times 180 = \$27,000 \text{ Gross Profit}$$

In other words, from your first year in business, you get $27,000 in gross profit from sales of $63,000.

Now, what other ways can your bike shop make money? How about those repairs? What about accessories? Based on the industry guidelines that you read about in the trade journals, you figure that for every thousand dollars in new bike sales, you will have $200 in service calls and accessories.

$$\$63,000 \ / \ 1,000 \times \$200 \text{ new sales} = \$12,600$$
$$\$63,000 + \$12,600 = \$75,600 \text{ Gross Sales or Revenue}$$

Sixty-three (for $63,000 in gross sales) multiplied by 200 equals another $12,600 in revenue per year.

Not bad for a beginner! At least, that's the way it looks right now. Gross profit is the difference between the cost of the goods you sold and your selling price. It does not take into account your overhead costs. We will discuss this relationship a little later in this chapter when we look at budgeting expenses.

NOW COMES THE FORECAST

Now comes the crystal-ball part of forecasting. When during the year are you actually going to see the money for those 180 bikes? Now you have to think about all of those variables that can affect sales during the year, including the weather and the competition. What if the weather is great, but the old man gets his act together and starts to advertise like crazy? What difference will that make to your sales?

Sales are sure to be healthy during the spring, for example, with the anticipation of the warmer, bike-riding months of summer in the air. Summer sales should be good, too, although not as high as those during the spring rush. It is during this period, however, that riders get the most use of their bikes, even though school is closed. The greater the use of bikes means more flat tires and other repair jobs. Income from repair jobs, you hope, will see you through to the fall, when the students return eager to spend their summer savings. In this season of falling leaves, you expect to see your profits rise.

Finally, there is no getting around slow sales in winter -- or is there? As it looks now, the winter months will be tough to weather. You will have to keep this in mind during those peak periods of healthy earnings. Instead of buying that new compression pump you may want, it may be wiser to save those peak season profits for the rainy (or snowy) days of the off-season.

It's time now to put your sales forecast for the upcoming year on paper. Using a ruler (neatness is important because you want to be as precise as possible), prepare a grid as shown.

The precise numbers of the sales forecast can be assigned month-by-month to a "spread sheet" like the following:

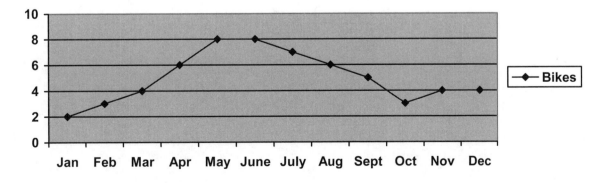

My Bicycle Shoppe

2005 Copyright of the American Institute of Small Business

Congratulations! You have just completed a model sales forecast! You can do this for your real business, too, just by following these simple guidelines:

a. Base your forecast on "hard" information about your ACTUAL prospects.

b. Anticipate changes in your sales levels during the year, taking as many variables as possible into consideration.

c. Be conservative.

One decision you can already make for your imaginary bike business based on your sales forecast is when to open for business. Since winter is so slow, you should put as much of that time behind you as possible. You should probably open just in time to advertise your spring sales and the new models so you can be in the right place, ready and waiting, when the best sales season begins. DO NOT open in the fall unless you have enough cash to carry you through three or four months of overhead expenses without sales. And why would you want to do that anyway?

BUDGETING YOUR EXPENSES

Money flows in when you sell your bikes or other products or services, and money flows out when you pay your expenses. What stays behind -- the difference between the two -- is your net profit. This is what you are working for: cash to use as you please. This is "new money" that your business has earned for you. You can and should be very proud of this amount.

Of the hard earned $8,000 that you have in your imaginary savings account for your imaginary bike shop, you had better plan on spending most of -- perhaps $6,000 -- before you even open your doors for business. This is typical; you usually have to spend some money and take a financial risk before you take in any money.

There are two kinds of expenses -- variable and fixed.

VARIABLE EXPENSES

Your sales projections are based on how much you sell. Depending on how much you sell, you are going to have variable expenses that are a percentage of your sales revenue. These variable expenses are often referred to as "costs of sales".

Your largest single variable expense, if you are a retailer, will be your inventory. Logically, you have to buy something before you can sell it. If you are going to have an **inventory** in your imaginary bike shop, you have to purchase it from a wholesaler or a distributor. The faster you sell the inventory (called "sell-through" or "turning the inventory"), the faster you get your costs back plus your profits. That's why it's so important to select merchandise that people want to buy.

Labor may be your single largest expense if you are in a service business, unless you put all of your employees on salary, in which case they become a fixed expense. Most of the time, small businesses link their personnel needs to the amount of work to be done. As a plumbing contractor moves into his busy season, for example, he hires more plumbers to service all the calls. When the business dies down, the extra help are laid off.

Variable expenses, of course, are not as predictable as fixed ones. But you CAN make good guesses because VARIABLE EXPENSES ARE LINKED DIRECTLY TO SALES. Take an average month's sales and calculate what percentage of the selling price was made up of variable expenses. That percentage is a useful tool in projecting what your expenses will be in the following months. Presuming that you meet or come close to your sales projections, you should hit your variable expense estimates very closely as well.

When they are graphed, variable expenses should look similar to the sales forecast curve.

Notice that the variable expenses came due slightly before the money from sales. This is because you usually will have to actually pay for the merchandise (or labor) before you can collect the selling price. The closer these two curves are to each other, the healthier the business is because it has less money sitting idle in the form of "owned" inventory. Ideally, a small business should buy on credit as far into the future as possible -- say, 60 or 90 days -- and sell it all before the bill comes due.

This is what the spread sheet looks like after the variable expenses are added.

My Bicycle Shoppe

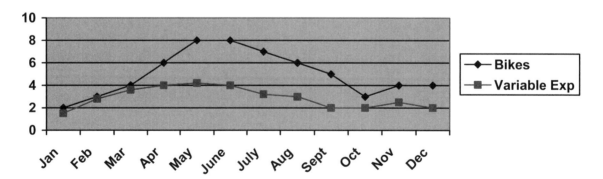

FIXED EXPENSES

As the name suggests, fixed expenses are those that remain fairly steady and predictable. These expenses may rise with the tide of inflation, but they will not fluctuate as your sales will. Nor are they influenced by your volume of sales.

Your fixed expenses are those overhead essentials you need to stay in business. For example, the rent money you pay for that prime corner location (which, you believe, will give you the edge over your side-street competitor) is a fixed expense. In the case of your bike shop, this will cost you, say, $750. Your phone is another fixed expense. So is your salary; although you may want to base that on how strong your sales are. Whether you sell one bike, no bikes, or a hundred, fixed expenses are going to stay the same and HAVE to be paid.

Fixed expenses are very easy to portray visually. All you need is a straight line. This shows up on your forecast or spread sheet like this:

My Bicycle Shoppe

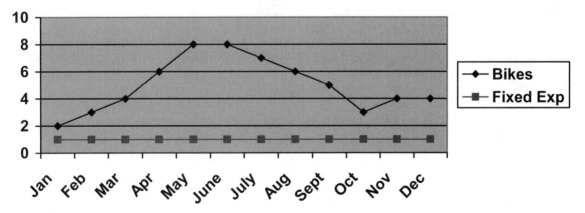

Now we can combine the variable expenses with the fixed expenses to get a clear picture of total expenses.

Here's what this combination of sales and expenses looks like on the spreadsheet.

My Bicycle Shoppe

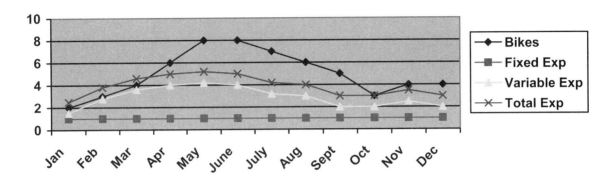

PROJECTING YOUR CASH FLOW

Up to this point, we have discussed the money you expect to make (from your sales) and the money you think you will have to spend (on expenses). To get the most accurate picture of your cash position and your financial health, however, we must link the two together. All those wavy lines add up to a cash flow projection -- a prediction, in fact, of where your money is coming from, where it's going, and what you're left with in the end. On paper, in black and white, where you can read it and understand it, this is called the CASH FLOW STATEMENT. It is, perhaps, the most useful planning tool you will ever have (or need) to monitor the health of your business.

Each month on your spread sheet reflects what you think your Income Statement (also known as a Profit and Loss Statement) will look like for those months in the future. Side by side, they give you a very good idea of what the trends are in your business.

Here's one of the ways to use your forecast: look at the next-to-the-bottom line on the cash flow statement. These are your projected profits (or losses) on a month-by-month basis. By adding them together horizontally and keeping a running total on the last line of the spread sheet, you can tell how far ahead -- or into the hole -- you really are. This is called the Cumulative Total, and is THE REAL bottom line.

Projecting your cash flow in this way would not be of much use to you, however, if you discovered your business was in financial trouble and on the verge of bankruptcy. For this reason, you probably will want to chart the difference between what you THOUGHT would happen (this is your projection) and what will ACTUALLY happen (these would be your actual sales and expense figures as they occur).

This can be done using a form similar to the one below as a kind of early warning system. Each month you can see at a glance what your actual sales, expenses and cash position are, compared to what you thought they would be.

	February				Year to Date		
	Actual	Forecast	Difference		Actual	Forecast	Difference
Beg Cash	4.2	4.5	-0.3		5.0	5.0	0.0
Sales	2.7	2.5	0.2		4.3	4.5	-0.2
Expenses							
Variable	2.3	2.2	-0.1		3.7	3.7	0.0
Fixed	1.0	1.0	0.0		2.0	2.0	0.0
Total	3.3	3.2	-0.1		5.7	5.7	0.0
Net Profit	-0.6	-0.7	0.1		-1.4	-1.2	-0.2
End Cash	3.6	3.8	-0.2		3.6	3.8	-0.2

The first set of three columns shows the current month, and the second set shows the year-to-date figures. The first column, called "actual", is how you actually did. The second column, "forecast", is your earlier estimate of how sales and expenses would go. The third column, "difference", is just what it says - the difference between what you did and what you thought you would do. It could show the difference in terms of dollars or percentages.

By preparing and evaluating comparisons each month, you'll be able to detect problems before they get out of hand. The third column tells you how accurate and/or realistic your projections are. And, hopefully, you'll get better and better each month at forecasting the future.

Forewarned is forearmed. And preplanning, based on what your forecasts reflect, will go a long way toward keeping you out of trouble.

For example, imagine that in five years your bicycle business has grown to the point where you have four full-time employees on the payroll. Not surprisingly, your cash flow chart has grown considerably, too. Now, you have three lines for repair supplies alone. One of these is reserved for expenses involved in purchasing tire patching kits. Since your time is now almost always spent in the back room with the books of the business, these particular expenses come to you from the employee responsible for such purchases. Three months into the new year, you realize (by comparing "Actuals" with "Estimates", the third column shows "+100%") that you are spending twice as much each month for patching kits as you thought you would.

This would not be a problem if these unexpected expenses were offset by unusually high sales in the area of patching kit sales. You check and see that this is not the case. You have a problem: your business is leaking cash and the leak must be patched as quickly as it is discovered. Now you can ask the right person some straightforward questions, such as: "Have you switched to a different wholesaler? Are you purchasing a more expensive kit? Has the price of patching kits increased since last year? WHY are we spending MORE on flat tire patching kits than I PROJECTED we would?" If there is a good reason, you can change your projections -- and the rest of your plans -- accordingly to accommodate the new information. If there isn't a good

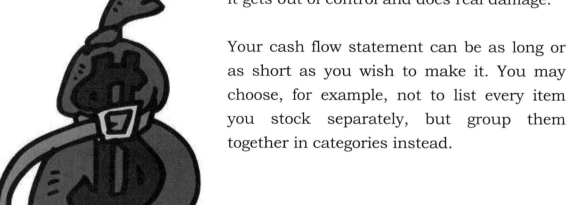

explanation, you can nip the problem before it gets out of control and does real damage.

Your cash flow statement can be as long or as short as you wish to make it. You may choose, for example, not to list every item you stock separately, but group them together in categories instead.

A FEW CLOSING WORDS ABOUT BUDGETS

Whether it is for a complex business or for a family of four, there is really no mystery to it. A budget is not money itself, but it is about money. A budget

---

is made up of a lot of assumptions. For you, the bicycle businessman, it is whether or not you will be able to buy that new compression pump, whether or not you will be able to put the neighbor boy on your payroll for the summer, whether or not you can open a branch store, whether or not you can pay off a debt (or take out another bank loan), whether or not you can take a vacation this year -- or give yourself a raise. Your budget is the financial well-being (or ill health) of your business. And your cash flow statement is none other than the visual representation, on paper in black and white, of your budget.

A budget is no longer a luxury, if ever it was. For businesses, large or small, it is a necessity.

Now you are prepared. Your forecast is your budget. You can run your future business by getting yourself "on plan" or "on budget" today. If you aren't on budget, your forecasts tell you where to make the changes. What's out of balance? If one "actual" is significantly higher than the "projected", your objective should be clear: do what you have to do to lower it.

There are those owners of small businesses who have very little to say about budgets, and there are those who do not even have them. But they are hard to find. There are many, on the other hand, who could probably talk your ears off about the merits of a budget.

In this chapter, you have learned:

1. *A budget PRESENTS YOU WITH A DEFINITE BUSINESS OBJECTIVE. It gives you an idea of where you are headed financially.*
2. *It ACTS AS A SAFETY SIGNAL. If there is trouble ahead because your buyer is spending too much for a new kind of flat tire patching kit, you will know about it in advance to do something about it.*
3. *It PLACES RESPONSIBILITY. If there is a problem, you will know where to look to correct it.*
4. *A budget HELPS YOU PREVENT WASTE. More than any other tool you have at your disposal, your budget tells you where you are paying too much or getting too little.*
5. *Sales forecasts, cash flow statements, and budgets will keep you moving steadily toward your long-term success. They keep both of your feet firmly planted in reality. What you don't know can put you out of business. But if you plan with good projections, you can succeed even faster.*

Chapter 10

Finding Money

Happiness is not in the mere possession of money; it lies in the joy of achievement, in the thrill of creative effort.
- Franklin D. Roosevelt

In this chapter you will learn:

1. *How much money will you need to start?*
2. *Four steps to obtaining a loan.*
3. *The two general categories of financing.*
4. *Where can you borrow money?*
5. *How to prepare a loan proposal.*

MONEY is obviously important to starting a business. You have to want it in order go get more of it, and you have to be organized enough to keep it and manage it once you get it. Unless you have successfully managed a small business before, brace yourself -- because you are going to learn a whole new way to think about money!

First and foremost, forget all those discouraging words you heard from the pessimists in your life. You CAN get the money you need to start and successfully run your business -- IF you follow the plan we lay out for you in this chapter. It may be of interest to you that more than 500,000 new businesses get started each year. Each one of them started the same way -- with an idea and a little money.

Money is why a person goes into business in the first place. Money means freedom to the small business person. It means power, too - power to do the things you always wanted to do. Money can do a lot for you, if you learn to manage it early.

These are the SIX MONEY KEYS you will have to keep in mind:

1. YOU MUST WANT TO MAKE MONEY.
2. YOU MUST KNOW HOW TO SPEND MONEY.
3. YOU MUST KNOW HOW TO USE OTHER PEOPLE'S MONEY TO FINANCE YOUR BUSINESS.
4. YOU MUST KNOW ALL ABOUT THE FEATURES AND BENEFITS OF THE PRODUCTS OR SERVICES YOU SELL.
5. YOU MUST KNOW HOW TO GET MONEY FROM THE CUSTOMER'S POCKET INTO YOUR POCKET.
6. YOU MUST KNOW THE MOST SUCCESSFUL COMPETITORS MAKE THEIR MONEY.

Let's look at each of these. **Key #1 is the most important: you must want to make money.** Surprisingly enough, some people are content to just work on the "fun" parts of their business and ignore the financial side. Naturally, this can't go on forever. Money travels a two-way street; it can go out just as fast as you bring it in, if you let it. Remember that money buys you a certain amount of freedom to do those things you like, but only when you take care of it.

You may find it helpful to write down your answer to one question: **WHY** do you want to make money? Some people are looking for an extra bit of cash each month to buy themselves some security, and so they put what they make into a retirement account. Others want a business that is a tax shelter to protect their other income. Some want to buy personal 'toys'; still others want to "make a million" so they can buy a new home for their family and retire early. Whatever it is, keep your goal in mind. It will help motivate you and keep your business senses sharp.

We are not suggesting that you make money your sole objective. For everyone's sake, don't change your value system now! However, WE ARE STRONGLY RECOMMENDING that you GET SERIOUS about money now. Making money is a way of keeping score in the game of life, and it can warn you when you are getting into trouble. No one wins if you go broke, even if you enjoyed spending your cash and wasting your time in the process! Being conscious of money forces you to run your business better.

Key #2 is: you also have to know how to SPEND money. Since more small businesses run short of operating cash at one time or another, small business people who are successful are of necessity very resourceful individuals. They are masters of "have-not" financing, and  are somehow able to make every dollar work like two. They can do this because they have paid attention during the time they were learning their business; consequently, they know how to cut the right corners. They know when to spend money for new inventory; they know when to buy the new truck. They are very careful about hiring the right people, and they avoid paying high interest rates on debts like the plague. In short, they think things through before they waste their hard-earned cash.

 **Key #3 is: Finance your business with other people's money.** Don't let this notion surprise you; joint ventures between people with money to invest and people with ideas is a cornerstone of the free enterprise system. It does take money to make money. You need it to pay the bills before you make a profit (this is called 'operating' money because it pays for the day-to-day operations), and you need it to buy equipment (this is called 'capital' or 'long-term' money

because these purchases are large, one-time expenses that are paid for over a long period of time).

THERE **ARE** MANY PEOPLE WHO WILL INVEST IN YOUR BUSINESS WITH YOU. There are people like this in every community -- people who have made a few dollars and want to keep making more, but by letting other people do the work instead. For their part, they will provide the money to get the business started. Their business is to share the risks with you. They are motivated by the desire to make more money, just like you.

Investors in small businesses hope to reap larger than normal rewards because of the higher than average risks. Just like you, they want to make a lot of money. They know that they don't know enough or care enough about your particular business to make it successful without you, so they depend heavily on you to run the business well. In many regards, they feel like they are investing in you, not necessarily your business. The quality of your ideas and your hard work makes you an equal with them. You need their money, and they need your business.

In short, the way to share the risks of small business ownership is to use other people's money -- and the way to get them involved is one of the purposes of this chapter.

Without enough money to get you started and pay the bills until you show a profit, you will go broke. When this happens, a business is said to be undercapitalized. Being undercapitalized is one of the most common reasons a business fails. We believe that an undercapitalized business is really just an "under-planned" business. In this chapter you will learn how to prepare, package and present a financing proposal for your business so that you can start with enough money to make it work profitably.

Key #4 is: Know your products features and benefits. To be successful a small business person you must be an expert on the product or service that you sell.

Suppose a customer comes into your store looking for a 27" TV. Why should they buy from you instead of someone else? First review the product's features. Suppose your TV can show up to 10 channels on the screen at once and that it has an automatic color system that maintains a perfect picture better than the competitor's TV. These features represent valuable benefits to the customer. Being able to see multiple channels on the screen helps the user decide which to watch and helps ensure that no program is being missed. The automatic color system adds value to this particular set.

Other dealers probably carry the same TV set, so your challenge is to give your customer a good reason to buy from you. It is often said that a good salesperson sells the sizzle, not the steak. But before you can sell the sizzle, you have to be an expert on the "steak" or the products you are selling. You may be able to offer your clients additional services like product delivery, education, maintenance plans or special financing.

Key #5 is: Know how to get money out of your customer's pocket. To accomplish this, you have to know your market. Who are your customers and prospects? Are they women, men, teenagers, senior citizens or do they represent a cross-section of all ages? How big is your market? How many customers or prospects are in your market?

Once the market is defined, the successful small businessperson must attract these customer and prospects to his or her place of business. What type of advertising appeals to your prospective customers? Which media or form of advertising?

Know what appeals most to your customers and prospects. What are their "hot buttons"? Once you get their attention, you need to offer products and services that solve problems for them. Solving problems is what makes people take money out of their pocket and put it into yours.

Key #6 is: Know how your most successful competitors make their money. Someone once said, you never invent the wheel, you simply reinvent it. Why not use some of the same tactics of your number-one competitor and then go one step farther? Look at McDonald's, one of the early entries in the field of fast food. Now they are the biggest in their field, but were are they first? No. White Castle, A&W Root Beer, and others came before came before McDonald's. Ray Kroc, the man behind McDonald's, simply copied what they did well, and went several steps further. Then Wendy's, Burger King and Arby's and others came into the field with various levels of success. They simply copied one another and added a new twist here and there.

If you want to be successful, look at your competition:

Where are they located?
How do they advertise?
What additional services?
What hours are open?
What days of the week are they open?
What product lines do they carry?
How do they sell?
How big of an inventory do they have?

Using information from your competitor's will help you, as a small business, make better use of your time and money.

The goal of this chapter is to prepare you to write your first loan proposal and present it successfully. We'll begin at the beginning.

WHAT WILL YOU USE THE MONEY FOR?

Few people have difficulty spending money. Every entrepreneur, however, should be familiar with and prepared for some very important uses of money. Below are typical uses of money.

Working Capital

This money is used to buy inventory, pay salespersons, make lease payments and handle unexpected costs until customers buy and pay up in large enough amounts to keep your business up and running on its own.

Inventory

Because inventory can consume large amounts of working capital, make sure you buy the right amount of inventory. In retailing, for example, too small quantities may lead to empty shelves and lost customers. Too large a stock, on the other hand, can raise your costs due to excess inventory and obsolete merchandise.

Excess inventory is a nonworking asset. As long as it sits on shelves, inventory ties up cash while producing no return. If your inventory is financed, you're actually paying someone for your stock to gather dust. To reduce inventory, some companies are turning to "just-in-time" systems. Instead of overstocking raw materials to ensure fast delivery, a just-in-time system shifts the burden to vendors through contracts that guarantee rapid shipments to fulfill customer orders.

Capital Equipment Purchases

Whether you start a business, buy one or get into a franchise, some of your largest expenses will be capital equipment. One important consideration when building a budget is that loans for machinery, technology including telecommunications systems and computers and other types of capital equipment are generally easier to get because they are secured by the equipment itself as the collateral. Because of that, loans are based on the life of the equipment but generally not for more than ten years.

Research and Development

Ideas form the basis for most businesses, large and small. One idea may be enough to start an enterprise, but it is not enough to maintain growth. The importance of improving existing products and developing new ones has never been more evident than it is today. Campbell Soup Company never stops developing new varieties and uses for their soups; Hershey Chocolate eventually diversified into other candy products, building on the success of its original Hershey Bar to keep its share of an increasingly competitive market.

The lesson to be learned is that research and development is a continuing need for many businesses and that funds must be allocated or found for product development on a continuing basis.

Expansion

A good idea can't be held down. If a retailing idea is good in one location, two stores will be even better and ten stores will create a commanding purchasing situation. The same holds true in other marketing fields. If you=ve put together a hot selling organization for one line of products, chances are you can take on another line or two and be that much more successful.

Naturally, expansion always brings with it extra costs, but additional financing should be easy to come by if you have a successful record to show for your efforts.

Purchasing a Business

You never know when the opportunity to acquire a good company will come along, whether in your own business or in an allied field. Many entrepreneurs have made a career of going from success to success by keep keeping their eyes open for the right opportunities. Naturally the better record you establish in your main business, the easier it will be to get financing for a new acquisition.

HOW MUCH MONEY WILL YOU NEED TO START?

The answer to this question is easy to understand, but hard to calculate. A new business needs:

1) Enough to buy the equipment, tools, raw materials, inventory or whatever else it needs to build the products or provide the service it sells;

2) enough to pay the day-to-day operating expenses until the profits begin.

Most entrepreneurs are proud, resourceful people; they feel uncomfortable asking for money. Their initial tendency is to ask for too little money. Being as optimistic as they are about the future of their enterprise, they assume that they can make everything work the way they want it to. As a result, they start their business with less money than they need.

Buck's painting service is a sad, but true, case of poor planning. He thought he could get started on the money he planned to make from his first job. He bought the business cards he needed and his first order of paint on credit, figuring that he could collect the money before the bills were due in 30 days. He didn't plan on having to buy an extra ladder, but he felt pretty good about the amount of money he was making; so he went ahead anyway and put it on his charge account with the paint supplier.

The job went reasonably well: he finished on time, even though he had to go back and get two more gallons of paint to get the right coverage. The customer paid him in full when he was finished, too. Unfortunately, on the way back from the job, his truck finally lost the exhaust pipe he had been patching together for the past few months. It took $187 to get it replaced, and that was $187 he didn't have. Since he wasn't working his regular job anymore, all of his regular expenses had to be picked up by his business in addition to the expenses for his first job. He was too tightly budgeted, and all it took was a bad bump on the road to throw him off.

In less than a month of business, Buck had already dug himself into a hole that looked deeper every day. He got so worried, he went back to his old job because of its regular income. Because he wasn't out soliciting new customers and he wasn't available to answer the phone or make estimates, what little business he did have trickling in dried up

almost immediately. By the third month, Buck was out of business, vowing never gain to do anything that crazy.

Imagine another small business -- this one a word processing service -- that started with a good deal of planning up front. Judy thought carefully about where her customers were going to come from, how much they probably would spend with her each month and what kind of equipment she would need to service them. She took time to shop the market, get the right equipment to begin with and even approached a few of the customers to find out what kind of jobs they were interested in. She was pleasantly surprised to find a small publishing company that had overload work every July for about six weeks, and they needed it done in a special typeface. She said she would prepare to handle the work at a pre-arranged price if they could assure her of the contract.

As a result of doing her homework, Judy was able to predict very accurately what her monthly income was going to be. She felt very confident about her figures for the first six months, and reasonably confident about the second six months. Based on these estimates, she was able to calculate her start-up costs and her operating expenses. The moral of the story is simple: when she got the biggest projects of the year - as planned - she was ready for them. She had the cash she needed to pay an extra typist to work overtime on a rented word processor and she could afford to buy the new typefaces she promised the customer to get the job in the first place.

What is the difference between Buck and Judy? Very simply, one planned the financial side of the business, and the other didn't. One is still in business, and the other isn't.

You CAN do it! There is nothing magical about financial planning, and you don't need a lot of formal training to do it. All you need to do is look ahead and imagine what is going to happen in your business, and then use your common sense!

Buck is statistically more typical than Judy. Planning the finances for a business is hard work, and not everyone likes to do it. Not everyone realizes how important it is. Then, four or six or twelve months later, just as things are starting to get going, they run out of money. Instead of concentrating on delivering products and services to their customers, they're running around town trying to arrange financing to pay their suppliers and the phone bill so they can stay in business. Since they can't take care of the customers at the same time, the customers get frustrated and begin to drift away. Sales and cash flow go down. As the situation gets more desperate, the small business owner runs faster and faster, trying to keep it all together. It becomes increasingly difficult to reverse this downward spiral; ultimately, the business runs out of time with the creditors and the entrepreneur runs out of energy and excuses. The poor management decisions lead to the initial undercapitalization, and the undercapitalization finally causes the business to fail.

It doesn't have to end this way, however. Undercapitalization is just "under-planning"; with a little more planning at the beginning, the small business can get a little more money up front, and that can make all the difference.

Here's how to do it: to calculate how much you will need, you must construct a CASH FLOW PROJECTION, sometimes referred to as a PRO FORMA by your banker. **This tool is better than a crystal ball!** It is a wonderful planning tool because it can  help you imagine the future. By imagining, or projecting, what you think you are going to sell and spend during the upcoming months, you can see problems coming while there is still enough time to do something about

---

them. Losing money on paper is a lot easier to take than losing real money -- especially when it's your own!

To construct a cash flow projection, all you need to do is estimate what it is going to cost to keep your business going month-by-month during the next year or 18 months. You can think of it as all of your monthly income statements side by side. (Your income statements are the statements that list your sales income, sales costs and overhead expenses, thereby giving you a monthly profit or loss figure.)

By adding together all of the "bottom lines," that is, the monthly profits or losses, you will be able to see your cumulative cash flow. Look at how the bottom line changes in the example which follows.

Frank's Snow Plowing and Lawn Care Service
Pro Forma Cash Flow Statement
For the Twelve Months Ended December 31, 20XX

	Apr	May	June	Jul	Aug	Sep
Sources of Cash:						
Sales	**2,500**	**3,000**	**3,500**	**500**	**500**	**1,000**
Uses of Cash:						
Cost of Sales	1,175	1,350	1,575	275	275	450
Operating Expenses	1,443	1,555	1,668	893	893	1,055
Total Uses:	**2,618**	**2,905**	**3,243**	**1,168**	**1,168**	**1,505**
Increase (Decrease)	(118)	95	257	(668)	(668)	(505)
Cumulative Cash Flow	**(118)**	**(23)**	**234**	**(434)**	**(1,102)**	**(1,607)**

	Oct	Nov	Dec	Jan	Feb	Mar
Sources of Cash:						
Sales	**1,000**	**6,000**	**6,000**	**12,000**	**6,000**	**6,000**
Uses of Cash:						

Cost of Sales	450	900	900	1,800	900	900
Operating Expenses	1,455	2,380	2,380	3,530	2,180	2,330
Total Uses:	**1,905**	**3,280**	**3,280**	**5,330**	**3,080**	**3,230**
Increase (Decrease)	(905)	2,720	2,770	6,670	2,920	2,770
Cumulative Cash Flow	**(2,512)**	**208**	**2,928**	**9,598**	**12,518**	**15,288**

What does this cash flow projection tell us about Frank's business? First, it tells us a lot about how he spends his money and is very helpful in determining how much he will need to run his business.

Here is a list of the equipment Frank's company will need before he even gets started:

	Cost
Truck (4-wheel drive) for snow plowing and hauling mowers	$0
Snow plow attachment	1,700
Snow blower	1,000
Gasoline tank for extra gasoline	50
Snow shovels (2)	200
Ice axe	75
Lawn mowers (1 riding, 1 push)	2,000
Grass bagger	100
Rakes	50
Shovel	30
Chemical sprayer	150
Hoses (3)	95
Pruning shears	50
Total	$5,500
Fertilizer	800
Office Equipment	1,000
Total	$7,500

In addition to the $5,500 for equipment, Frank needs $800 for fertilizer and insecticides, $1,000 for office equipment and $200 for office supplies. Thus, his total start-up expenditures will be $7,500.

Frank's start-up costs could have included the amount of his original equipment investment to get his truck but since he was able to buy it over time and pay cash, it does not have to be counted as a start-up expense. He sold the truck to his company for $10,000 and enjoys some very nice tax benefits.

This was a smart way to get himself some of the equipment he needed because he can now count it as an asset without debt, but it wasn't the only way. The truck could have been financed through a local banker.

What else can we learn from Frank's pro forma cash flow? We can see just when he gets his income, and at what levels. Notice that Frank's cash flow has dramatic seasonal fluctuations: in the winter and spring, he is taking in a lot of cash. However, there a few months between seasons when the grass isn't growing and the snow isn't falling, so he isn't making much money. Actually, during these months, he is taking in very little and must live off what he has already earned.

So how much does Frank need to start? It's simple: he needs enough to pay his start-up costs plus the extra amount he needs to get himself through the slow months of low income.

The lowest point of Frank's cumulative cash flow is in the seventh month (October) when he is "down" $2,512. At this point, he has paid all of his bills, but still has more money going out than coming in. If it kept up like this,

Frank would soon be out of business. However, Frank knows that it takes this long to establish himself in the market and build up his accounts.

Now, most entrepreneurs would say, "It looks like I need about $10,000 to start my business -- $7,500 for start-up costs and $2,500 to cover expenses that exceed my income through October." But Frank is a little smarter than that -- he knows that if it doesn't snow as expected, the money from his plowing contracts will start late.

Instead of getting "just enough" to get started, Frank uses a good rule of thumb he learned from his banker: he is going to begin his company with enough money to purchase his initial equipment and supplies ($7,500), plus one and one-half times the amount he thinks he needs to cover his expenses in the early months.

$$1.5 \times \$2,500 = \$1,250$$
$$\$1,250 + \$2,500 = \$3,750 \text{ for operating expenses.}$$

Rather than getting "just enough" -- which was probably just enough to get himself into trouble -- he is getting enough money to succeed. He has planned extra money for those unexpected problems that come up. Now, if he

needs to make repairs on his truck, or if the price of gas goes up, or if it doesn't snow as planned, he will be able to ride out the situation and be around to profit another day.

You **must** do this for your business, too. Before you start looking for ways to cut corners or start operating on less than you should, find out how much it would realistically cost to run your business the right way. Remember -- multiply the lowest point in your cash flow by 150% (1.5) or even 200% (2) and you will be very near the actual amount you will end up spending. This is the ACTUAL amount of money you need to get your business started. If you follow this rule, and you have carefully thought through all of the expenses to include on your cash flow projections, you will not suffer from undercapitalization.

Frank's goal now is to raise the $7,500 he figures he needs for start-up and the $3,750 he needs for operations, a total of $11,250.

$$\$7,500 + \$3,750 = \mathbf{\$11,250}$$

FOUR STEPS TOWARD A LOAN

Unless you are able to write your own check to start your business, you will have to get at least a few other people involved. Even if you are able to do your own financing, you may want to get someone else involved anyway because of their skills, business contacts or experience.

One of the principles of small business that you should become familiar with now is the notion of using other people's money to begin a new venture.

Remember, this is the third key to understanding money that we discussed at the beginning of this chapter. This is referred to in the financial community as 'sharing the pie'. When you use other people's money, you are saying to them, "If you let me use your money in the beginning to get started, I'll share my profits with you later." In this way, you both make more money. Economists call this the creation of wealth, and it's one of the fundamental components of our free enterprise system.

Getting someone else involved is a decision that you must think about carefully. The easiest or the cheapest source of money is not always the best. There may be "strings" attached or unreasonable conditions.

Once you have decided how much you need, you will be almost ready to start discussing your situation with people who can help you. First, you have to **PACKAGE** your idea. In a way, you have to sell someone else on your dream -- and in order for them to be persuaded to part with their cash, you have to convince them that you are worth the investment.

Where you get your money is largely dependent upon how much you need. Different sources are comfortable with different amounts. Generally, the more money you want, the more "packaging" you need and the more lengthy your written proposal.

Yes, you **will have to write your proposal**. For obvious reasons, this is still the best way to get your story in front of a lot of people quickly, professionally and in a consistent way. But don't despair if you aren't the world's greatest writer or a born "typewriter jockey" -- you can get plenty of help from secretarial services, someone you know with a word processor or a student

looking for part-time work. The important parts are your ideas; so if you can't do it alone, find someone with whom to work. Look at it this way: being able to meet this challenge is one of your first managerial tests!

There are basically three stages in financing a business. These reflect the three basic life cycles in a business.

First, there is **seed money** that is used in the very preliminary stages of a business. The amount of money needed here can be quite small. It is used to organize and plan the project. Frank used his personal money for this

---

324

stage to drive around town talking to building owners about his contract plowing service. It cost him several hundred dollars in travel expenses, lost wages from his regular job, lunches, letters, postage, letterhead and the like. A restaurant entrepreneur might use this time and money to make a site selection and have an architect do some preliminary drawings of the restaurant.

The second stage of financing is the **start-up** financing. This is the money it will take to get the doors open and get the business started. Frank needed his $11,250 for this stage.

The third stage is **growth** financing, and is usually needed after a year or so of successful operation. Frank might want to buy a few more trucks or set up a similar type of operation in a nearby community once he's got all the bugs worked out and has turned the corner of his one-truck operation. ("Turning the corner" means he is showing consistent profits.) The restaurant entrepreneur might want to open another location or two, or even start franchising his idea if it turns out to be profitable.

HERE'S HOW YOU PACKAGE OR PRESENT YOUR SITUATION TO A POTENTIAL INVESTOR OR LENDER:

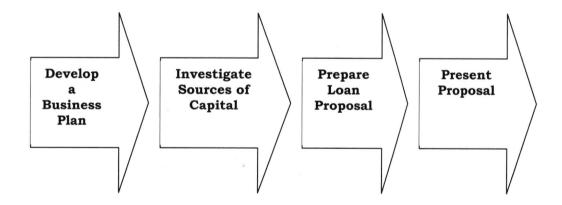

STEP 1: Develop a business plan. In the financial community, this is THE tool you need. It is a typewritten report that tells the investor or lender that you have thoroughly planned your business. It is designed to give them

confidence in you. IF you don't need very much money, say $15,000 or less, you may not need to write a complicated plan, but you should have at least thought enough about each of the aspects of the business plan to be able to discuss them with an investor or lender. The Business Plan is discussed in detail in the last chapter of the book.

Basically, the business plan answers the following questions in a logical order:

1. What is a business?
2. Which will be the most profitable products?
3. What are the major markets and competitors?
4. How will you pay back the monies you borrowed?

It also presents the budget and cash flow projections for at least the next 12 months.

The details of writing a business plan are presented later in this book.

Frank's proposed loan of $11,250 was a relatively small amount of money for relatively straightforward needs. Although he did not write a long formal business plan, he did think about each of the components thoroughly because he knew that some people would push him just enough to find out how much he really knew about his business.

STEP 2: Investigate potential sources of capital. After you have done your basic planning and have prepared your loan proposal of up to 10 pages, you can start looking for the best source for the amount of money you need. Frank's snow removal and lawn care business needed $11,250; this is a lot of money to some people and not enough to trouble with for others. We will discuss several of the best sources of money a few pages from now.

STEP 3: Prepare a loan proposal. This is ABSOLUTELY REQUIRED for all but the informal financing arrangements. It is like a mini-business plan, is about 10 pages long, and is tailored specifically to a single investor or lender. Because it is short, each one can be customized to show each prospective lender or investor the information that is needed or requested. This becomes the "talking tool" in your negotiations for money. It has the following information:

1. A very brief summary of your business, including what your business is, what products you sell and the general types of competition you have.

2. A brief history of yourself and your business to date, including any other financing.

3. An explanation of the proposal: what amount of money you need, what terms are preferred, repayment preference, collateral available, equity options available and any other information that is relevant to your specific request for funds.

4. The appropriate financial statements must be included: balance sheet, earnings history (if any) and financial projections for three years.

5. Credit, personal and business references.

Frank put together a very successful financing proposal for his business. It did its job -- it got him the money he needed on terms that made sense for him. Later in this chapter, we will take a close look at a typical loan proposal so you can see exactly how to put yours together.

STEP 4: Present your materials to your prospective lenders or investors. This can be a formal presentation or an informal discussion, depending upon who you are meeting with. One of the people who expressed interest in Frank's business turned out to be his barber -- he was interested in investing the whole $11,250. When Frank made his presentation, he did it over coffee at a restaurant near the barber shop. Later, when he made a presentation to a loan officer at a bank downtown, it was much more formal.

That's all there is to it: 1-2-3-4, and you've got the money you need to start and run your business. YOU can do this, too -- literally hundreds of thousands of people are getting millions of dollars to start and run their dreams every year.

For the rest of this chapter, we will concentrate on filling in the rest of the "how's" related to getting money, such as:

- How do you find people who are able to lend money or invest?
- How do you approach them and ask them if they are interested in your proposition?
- How do you make a successful presentation?

By the time you have finished this chapter, you will be fully prepared to get the money you need. You will be able to hold your own in conversations with other business people, investors and lenders. In short, you will have learned what it takes to put money behind your dreams. Rather than just being a bystander, you can be an active contender.

THE TWO CATEGORIES OF FINANCING

Obviously, there are as many different ways to structure a deal as there are people to make the deals, but they all fall into two general categories: debt financing and equity financing.

DEBT FINANCING is the simplest way to raise money. Basically, it describes any kind of loan. The person or organization loaning you the money makes his money on the interest you pay. As long as you continue paying the loan payments, he will leave you alone and let you run the business as you see fit. The interest rate is agreed to in advance. The loan-maker knows how much he will make on the deal before he loans you the money, and his chief concern is whether you will be able to pay back the loan on time.

Your ability to repay makes the difference when you convince someone to loan you money. Depending upon whether it's your bank or your brother, you have to satisfy different criteria. Your prior history of repayment (your credit record) and the viability of the business are key elements. Obviously, if you still owe your brother from the last $500 he loaned you and he thinks your business idea is pretty shaky, he is going to doubt your ability to repay. If the business goes bad, how will you pay him back?

If you talk to your bank, the same concerns are present. What assurances and evidence can you give that indicate that you can pay back tomorrow what you borrow today? If your business idea seems shaky, the bank may ask you to pledge your car or even your house as collateral in case you can't make the payments. You may want to think twice about what you pledge and how much you pledge. If the unthinkable happens and you lose the money in the business, you risk losing some of your own assets. Sometimes bankers ask you to pledge collateral to lower their risk by taking on more of it yourself; in essence, they are saying, "We will let you use our money so you don't have to sell your assets to raise the money. But we want to be sure of getting our money back and we want to see how committed you are to this new business of yours. We want you to put up your personal property as security for us."

EQUITY FINANCING is different. Selling equity means you sell a part of the business to someone else. What they are purchasing by investing in you is the possibility that you will make a success of the business. They are gambling that, in the long run, their share of the business will be worth many times more than the amount of their original investment.

You have to decide two things: what you WANT (in other words, what would be the best deal for you) and what will WORK. You may have to settle for a

"less than ideal" arrangement. You must think through beforehand how much risk you want to take yourself, how much you want to share with an outside investor, how much control of the day-to-day operations you want to share and how much of the "pie" you want to share, if any. Many small business people eventually conclude that sharing a larger pie and sharing the risk is worth giving up part of the profits and some control.

The right investor can be an angel, but the wrong kind can have a very negative influence. If the investor brings valuable management expertise or skills to the business, everyone wins. However, if the investor is a 'meddler' or egomaniac, it may be better to look for another investor - a silent partner - who will stay in the background.

Sometimes you can combine debt and equity financing. This is called a convertible debenture. This begins as a loan, and then is converted to a share in the ownership of your business, if and when the business is successful. It is particularly attractive to friends and relatives and certain business investors. If the deal goes sour, they fall back on the provisions of the loan. If it is successful, they can convert their loan into stock or part ownership of the business at probably a much better profit or gain than through an ordinary loan with interest.

WHERE CAN YOU BORROW MONEY?

There are many different sources of money. Each of them can be considered a possibility for the person who will need money to either start a small business or to help an existing business. These sources can be divided between traditional and nontraditional sources.

Traditional Sources

Yourself. For the individual businessperson the most logical place to look for financing is his or her own assets. These sources include money in bank accounts, certificates of deposit, stocks and bonds, cash value in insurance policies, real estate, home equity, value of hobby collections, automobiles, pension fund, Keogh or IRAs.

Obviously, if you had sufficient capital, there would be no need to turn to other sources for your needs. But, as noted before, in order to be successful in a business, most people must know how to use other people's money to finance the new or expanding business.

One word of caution. In today's fast moving economy, most of us have one or more credit cards. It is tempting to take advantage of the availability of money simply by using these cards. Remember, most credit card companies advance money at a much higher rate of interest than you could normally pay a bank or some other financing source. Equally important, although your monthly payments may appear to be small, because of the high interest, your debt compounds and rises quickly.

Family or Relatives. If you are fortunate enough to have family or relatives who have money to invest or loan, then sometimes they represent an excellent lending source. Exercise great caution, however, when borrowing money from a relative. There is an old saying: NEVER MIX BUSINESS WITH PLEASURE.

For every family loan that goes sour, there are probably two sweet ones. Before seeking out a loan from a relative, consider what future effect a loan may have on the relationship.

One source of money often used is family and relatives. Too often, however, money gets in the way of good family relationships. Therefore, extreme care must be used in determining whether or not a family member or relative should be approached.

One way you can avoid future problems and disagreements with relatives who lend you money for your business is to have a written agreement. Spell out clearly what you and your relatives have agreed:

> * Date of the loan
> * Loan amount
> * Date the loan will be repaid in full
> * Dates of loan payments
> * Frequently of payments? Monthly, quarterly, etc.
> * Amount (percent) of interest
> * Collateral, if any.
> * Signatures by both parties

One important note: It may be wise to make sure the relative from whom you are borrowing has notified his or her spouse. That way, you can ensure that no future problem arises due to any miscommunication.

Friends. Friends, by their very nature, trust one another. And they often are in a position to aid in a financial situation.

Again, as with relatives, one has to be careful to assure that the friendship will not be put into jeopardy in the event the friend will require a sudden payback. Use the same caution as you would borrowing from a relative.

Your Own Company. If you already have an established company and are in need of money, one of the first places to turn is to the company itself. An established company or business has several options available. These include taking a first or second mortgage on any real estate or property that it owns, borrowing money against machinery or hard assets such as equipment or motor vehicles; borrowing against inventory that is considered liquid.

Pledging Accounts Receivable
A common method by which companies can obtain a loan is by pledging the firm's accounts receivable in return for a loan. This means that your receivables are pledged or turned over to the bank or loan company that makes the loan. Then, as the receivables are paid, the firm deducts a certain amount of each payment until the loan is paid. Essentially, what the bank or loan company is doing is using your accounts receivable as collateral against the loan.

Factoring
Factoring is another way of using your receivables in order to raise badly needed cash. In factoring, one goes to a factoring company which actually

buys your accounts receivables.

Assume, for example, that you have $50,000 in accounts receivables and it is a particularly slow time of the year in which you have very little cash flow. The factor will buy your $50,000 in receivables. Possibly they will give you $30,000 or $40,000 for them. The factor then owns the receivables. The amount of discount that the factor takes depends on such things as how old your accounts receivables are, who owes you the money, what you sell, how long you have been in business and so on. You can find a listing of factors in the Yellow Pages. You can also get a list of such companies from your banker.

Commercial Banks. Commercial banks are the largest single source of loans

to both small and large businesses. Banks are in the money business. They make money by lending money. Many banks have a special department that focuses on small business loans.

At the end of this loan source listing we will describe in considerable detail how to prepare a BANK LOAN PROPOSAL.

Savings and Loan Associations. These are like banks, but are organized under a different type of charter. Originally established to facilitate the lending of money for home mortgages, they have gradually evolved into full-service banking operations. There are some government restrictions on where and how they can operate as compared to commercial banks. Like banks, their charge for loans is based on the prime rate or some variation of it.

During 1991 and 1992, the savings and loan industry was rocked by a great number of scandals involving poor-risk loans. As a result, the remaining savings and loans are taking a very careful look at any business loan application. Many are now requiring any loan to be backed up by an equivalent amount of collateral.

Loan Companies. Loan companies, which exist in most U.S. cities and communities, represent one of the largest sources of money in the country. Unlike banks which obtain their funds from many different sources, loan companies have to rely upon their own capital or raising money, just as other businesses do. Thus, their interest rates are usually higher. In some instances they can be several percentage points above the prime rate.

Loan companies are considered collateral lenders, that is, they rely heavily upon the borrower's ability to back up every dollar of their loan with an asset. For example, a borrower may have to pledge accounts receivable, put up the mortgage on the company's building, or assign the value of an insurance policy, stocks or bonds.

Loan companies often have different operating policies, and the interest rate they charge may vary as much as five percent from one firm to another. Therefore it is prudent to shop around before you settle on a particular loan company. A listing of the loan companies for your area can be found in the Yellow Pages.

Small Business Investment Companies (SBIC). These are privately owned companies licensed and insured by the Small Business Administration (SBA) to provide capital to small firms. SBICs focus on specific industries such as medically-oriented high technology enterprises, or agricultural, manufacturing or real estate companies. Normally these firms have proprietary and high growth potential products.

Community Development Companies. These are companies that have been established by local communities to attract business into their community. The most popular type of CDC is one which develops a shopping mall or business development center. An example of the latter would be a geographic area set aside in a community for a commercial or industrial park.

Insurance Companies. An often overlooked source of money is your own insurance company. You may find that you can use your life insurance policy as collateral in obtaining a loan. Insurance companies often have a large reserve of cash and are constantly looking for good investment opportunities.

Small Business Administration (SBA). In most states the SBA has a Lender 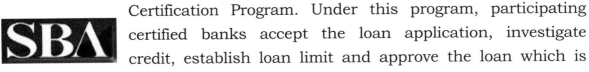 Certification Program. Under this program, participating certified banks accept the loan application, investigate credit, establish loan limit and approve the loan which is guaranteed by the SBA. The procedure takes three to six days. Non-certified banks may take four to six weeks, if they participate at all in the SBA program. The bank will help you decide what SBA loan programs may fit for your needs.

Farmers Home Administration. This government program guarantees loans up to 90% of loan value for businesses located in towns of less than 50,000 population. Amounts borrowed are normally larger than under the SBA, and the borrower must show how his new or expanded business will benefit the community.

Nontraditional Sources

Nontraditional sources are unlimited in number and type, but you need to be creative to acquire the necessary funds from them for your start-up or expanding business.

Customers.   Customers or potential customers can be an excellent source of funding. Consider the following examples: Two engineers work together at the same company. On their own time, they develop a new plastic, the

manufacturing of which require a very large capital investment. When used as raw material their plastic is one-third the cost of the product companies or customers are currently using. The engineers contact a very large potential user, who realizes that the new plastic can reduce her raw material costs significantly. Subsequently, she lends the two engineers the necessary money to start their own business. In return for her investment, the user receives a contract assuring her company of getting 75 percent of the manufacturing output of the new plastic.

Another typical example, is that of a cosmetologist who wants to open her own salon. In conversations with a customer, it turns out that the customer likewise wants to have her own business. The customer invests in the salon and the two form a partnership. The cosmetologist manages the salon and the other employees; her partner participates in the day-to-day affairs of the salon, handling bookkeeping, advertising and customer service.

Suppliers. Depending on the type of business you plan, your suppliers could be an excellent source of money.

For example, a family in a medium-size southern city decided to open a convenience food store. They went to their food wholesaler who made arrangements to borrow enough money to pay for their shelving in exchange for a promise from the store owner that he would make at least

80% of his purchases from the firm, providing the prices were fair.

This same small businessman also went to his meat supplier who made arrangements for him to borrow money to purchase his refrigerated meat display cases.

Thus, he was able to purchase all of his display cases and shelving with money borrowed on a promise to purchase a certain percentage of his needs. Further, he signed agreements assuring that he would not be overcharged when making his purchases.

Leasing Companies. One way people have been able to finance their business is through a leasing company. Instead of actually borrowing money, you would make arrangements with a leasing company who would purchase items you need for your business, such as a truck, office furniture or computer equipment.

Then, you lease the items from the leasing company over a certain period of time. Title to the goods or property is retained by the leasing company.

Business Brokers and Investors. Some individuals specialize in making small business loans either on a straight interest basis or a shared equity basis. Often these people will advertise in the classified section of the Sunday newspapers and in the yellow pages of the telephone book.

If you elect this method of financing, be certain you are dealing with someone who is reputable and has a good track record with such loans. If they want a piece of your business, would you want them as a "partner"?

Invoice Discounting and Factoring. There are many companies out there to help you with your short term financing needs. If you have or can generate invoices to customers for future services, there are companies that can help

---

you. Look in your local yellow pages for factoring companies or search the Internet. For invoice discounting services contact the Interface Financial Group at 972-562-8512. They are the leaders in invoice discounting.

Advertise for Money

You can actively seek funding by running a display advertisement in the business section or under the appropriate heading in the classified ads of your local newspaper. Specify the amount of money needed and the type of business for which it will be used. Check the "Business Opportunities" in your local paper for samples. Confidentiality for both parties can be maintained through the use of a post office box or newspaper box number.

Grants

Grants for FREE money to start businesses are hard to find. There are a few people out there that would make you think that grants are easy, but it is just not the case. Most grants from the U.S. government are for non-profit entities, high technology companies or other government agencies. Grant programs come and go frequently and it is hard to keep up on all of them by state. To find grants, call your local city hall, county offices, state office and economic development agencies and ask if they have any current grant programs. Be aware that applying for grants can be a long and complicated process. If they have an application form, be sure to fill it out completely. Many grant providers will reject your request if you don't fill it correctly.

Here is some information on our grant program:

The American Institute of Small Business (AISB) Grant Programs –
AISB is the publisher of this book you are reading. We also have classes that we teach that are phone based with a live expert instructor. The two grant programs that we offer give entrepreneurs between $500 and $10,000 for either 1) starting a business or 2) expanding a current business. The grants are awarded annually in early January. The deadline for applications is December 17th of each year. To be considered for an AISB grant fill out the appropriate application form on-line at www.aisb.biz.

HOW TO PUT YOUR LOAN PROPOSAL TOGETHER

No matter which source of money you approach, you will need to sell them on your concept. As we discussed before, you will need a loan proposal as your best tool to tell your story. This is true even if you plan to use a more complete business plan as outlined in Chapter 18 because you need a larger sum of money.

Your loan proposal is so common in the marketplace and so important to your success that you must make the commitment it takes to settle down and write it. No part of it is more than a page or two; so if you break it into bite-sized pieces, you should be able to at least put it into a rough draft stage with a few evenings' work.

Your proposal must fit your needs, wants and background. It must also fit the needs and interests of the investor or lender to whom you are applying for financing.

Be brief and to the point in your proposal. Most will probably spend only 5 to 10 minutes reviewing it. If your key points and plans are not immediately evident and clearly presented, keep working at it until it is tight and well-written.

Guidelines

Here are some simple guidelines to keep in mind as you begin writing:

1.   Say it straight. Your loan proposal should be realistic and honest.

Anticipate any negative reactions and address them squarely.

2. Match each proposal page to suit your reader. If you are asking for a loan from one group and an equity investment from another, parts of the proposal will change for each.
3. Write in a smooth, comfortable style.
4. Don't rush and don't write when you are too tired to think clearly.
5. Don't overstate figures or purposes.
6. Follow the outline below.
7. Do not write out your loan proposal.

Let's look at exactly what your financial proposal should look like:

PAGE	SUBJECT MATTER
Cover Page	Loan Proposal to which bank, from whom, and date
1	Loan amount and use of funds
2	Description of the business (or proposed business)
3	Specific use of funds
4	Catalog pages, literature, quotations supporting the use of the funds, how finds will be spent
5	Projected Income Statement for the business covering one year
6	Projected Balance Sheet for the business after one year
7	Source of funds to be invested in business in addition to the proposed bank loan
8	Personal financial statement of owners
9	List of credit references
10	List of present and past business associates
11	Personal background of applicant
12	How and when loan is to be repaid

Using SMITH'S SNOW PLOWING AND LAWN CARE SERVICES as an example, we have developed a complete BANK LOAN PROPOSAL.

All you have to do to develop your own Loan Proposal is to substitute your own name, business, money needs, etc. in each applicable page as you prepare your own.

Loan Proposal to

FIRST NATIONAL BANK OF ANYWHERE

from

SMITH' SNOW PLOWING AND LAWN CARE SERVICES

September 10, 200X

May 1, 20XX

Example Loan Proposal

(Page 1)

LOAN AMOUNT AND USE OF FUNDS

Joe and Doris Smith, owners and operators of SMITH'S SNOW PLOWING AND LAWN CARE SERVICES, request a loan from the FIRST NATIONAL BANK in the amount of $20,000. This money will be used as follows:

Working Capital-Payroll	$ 4,000
Truck	10,000
Lawn Mower Purchases	3,500
Office Furniture	1,500
Computer	1,000
Total	$20,000

SMITH'S SNOW PLOWING AND LAWN CARE SERVICES

SMITH'S SNOW PLOWING AND LAWN CARE SERVICES is being formed by Joe and Doris Smith. The Company will provide lawn cutting and lawn care services during the spring, summer and fall to both homeowners and commercial customers. In the winter, the Company will provide services to these same customers, plowing snow from their driveways and parking lots.

The Company plans to rent a double garage-type warehouse space at the Mini Warehouse located at 3500 East Superior Boulevard. At the outset, Joe and Doris Smith will operate their business from their home and set up an office in the newly remodeled basement of their home.

Recognizing the fact that most people living in the western suburban area of Anywhere own their own homes and also knowing that there is a serious shortage of good lawn care service companies as well as snow plowing services, Joe and Doris are establishing this company.

They have canvassed the neighborhood extensively and have already signed contracts with 22 homeowners for lawn care services this spring. They also have commitments from nine (9) of these homeowners to plow their driveways in the winter and from five (5) business firms to plow their parking lots during the winter.

Example Loan Proposal
(Page 3)

SPECIFIC USE OF LOAN FUNDS

Payroll		$2,400
Insurance		650
Office Supplies		350
Gasoline	100	
Tools	500	
Business Supplies		600
Total Working Capital		$ 4,000
Used Pickup Truck Purchase, Toyota		$10,000

Lawn Mower Purchases

2-Toro Riding Mowers, Commercial	2,300	
1-Toro 21-inch self-propelled	1,000	
Other Toro Accessories	200	
Total Mowers		3,500

Office Furniture

1-Office Desk	800	
2-Office Chairs	250	
2-4-drawer Filing Cabinets	450	
Total Office Furniture		1,500

Computer & Software	1,000
Total Funds Needed	**$20,000**

Example Loan Proposal
(Page 4)

SMITH'S SNOW PLOWING AND LAWN CARE SERVICES
April 29, 20XX
1423 Pender Road
Anywhere, USA 12345

QUOTATION NUMBER 7589

2 Toro Riding Mowers, Commercial 11 HP Model 30111	$2,300
2 Toro 21-Inch Self-Propelled Mowers	1,000
Toro Accessories	200
Total	$ 3,500

SMITH' SNOW PLOWING AND LAWN CARE SERVICES
PROJECTED INCOME STATEMENT
FOR THE YEAR ENDED APRIL 30, 20XX

SALES

Lawn Services	$60,000	
Snow Plowing	40,000	
Total Sales		$100,000
COST OF SALES		32,000
GROSS PROFIT		$68,000

OPERATING EXPENSES

Salaries	32,000	
Payroll Taxes	3,000	
Rent	2,000	
Advertising	1,100	
Insurance	1,500	
Car/Truck Expenses	5,000	
Telecommunications	600	
Office Supplies	900	
Repair/Maintenance	3,000	
Miscellaneous	550	
Depreciation	5,500	
Interest	2,850	
Total Operating Expenses		$58,000

Income before Taxes $10,000

Example Loan Proposal
(Page 6)

SMITH'S SNOW PLOWING AND LAWN CARE SERVICES
PROJECTED BALANCE SHEETS
AS OF MAY 1

ASSETS

	YEAR 1	YEAR 2
Current Assets		
Cash	$5,900	$12,500
Inventories	600	1,000
	6,500	13,500
Furniture, Fixtures, Equipment	$27,500	$27,500
Less: Accumulated Depreciation	-	5,500
Total Assets	$34,000	$35,500

LIABILITIES & STOCKHOLDERS' EQUITY

Current Liabilities		
Accounts Payable	0	$1,000
Accrued Expenses	0	500
Total Current Liabilities	0	1,500
Note Payable to Bank	20,000	10,000
Due to J. Tarkinton	9,000	9,000
Stockholders' Equity		
Common Stock	5,000	5,000
Retained Earnings	0	10,000
Total Liabilities and	$34,000	$35,500

Shareholders' Equity
Example Loan Proposal
(Page 7)

SOURCE OF FUNDS TO BE INVESTED
IN BUSINESS IN ADDITION TO THE BANK LOAN

Mr. and Mrs. Joseph Smith	
From Savings Bank	$2,000
Sale of Common Stock	3,000
Loan from James Tarkinton	9,000
Total	$14,000

The $9,000 loan from James Tarkinton will be used to purchase a used pickup truck so the Company will have two crews available for lawn care and snow plowing.

The $5,000 from the Andersons will be used to purchase new snow plow attachments and for working capital.

Example Loan Proposal
(Page 8)

NOTE: This section is to attach the bank's standard application form. It will have a section for your personal assets and liabilities.

Example Loan Proposal
(Page 9)

CREDIT REFERENCES

First National Bank, 444 S. Fourth St., Anywhere

National Oil Co., P.O. Box 1111, New Amsterdam, NY 10001

Onion Oil Co., 99 Cooper Lane, Grover, OH 54622

Mesa Department Store, 8th at Love Streets, Anywhere

MacAdams Jewelers, 1234 Pine St., Anywhere

American Express Co., P.O. Box 1984, Old York, NY 10001

Shoppers Charge, P.O. Box 1234, Jaxon, TX 76357

PERSONAL REFERENCES

Rev. James Bardy, 9674 Waverly St., Anywhere 555-6262

Samuel Bloom, MD, 4646 Cotton St., Anywhere 555-9273

Robert Krasner, DDS, 1212 South St., Anywhere 555-3546

Mr. Robert Joyce, 7777 Vegas Lane, Reno, IL 312-555-7777

Mrs. Erica Sloan, 2035 No 47th Place, Anywhere 555-9999

PRESENT AND PAST BUSINESS ASSOCIATES

Mr. T.S. Gardner, Trivial Motors, 22 South St., Anywhere 555-3544

Mr. J.R. Williams, President, Acme Electronics Co., Jackson, NE   33325 333-555-6668

Mrs. Shirley Welsome, Manager, Welsome Parts Store, 2nd at   South Streets, Anywhere 555-2222

Meyer Lobotsky, Manager, Van's Storage and Transfer, 4900 Branch   Ave., Anywhere 555-8932

Example Loan Proposal
(Page 10)

PERSONAL BACKGROUND
JOE & DORIS SMITH

My first job was driving truck for four summers for Van's Storage and Transfer. After graduating from college, I worked four years for the federal government in statistical surveys. From there, I entered the marketing department of the Jones Construction Company and assisted in bidding contracts. After eight years, I moved to Jackson and joined the Acme Electronics Company doing long-term forecasting and planning for this major electronics company.

After completing 20 years service, I decided to come back to Anywhere and get into business for myself. While deciding what type of business to enter and planning this venture, I spent three years selling cars at Trivial Motors. Throughout our moves, Doris has found a job teaching in elementary schools and is currently employed at West Elementary teaching the third grade.

We intend to use our business, sales, mechanical and organizational skills to develop this business opportunity. Until the business demands become excessive, we intend to maintain our current positions.

Example Loan Proposal

(Page 11)

How Loan Is To Be Repaid

Joe and Doris Smith request that their loan of $20,000 be repaid as follows:

PRINCIPAL   Beginning August 1, 20XX their Business Checking Account will be charged $1,000 a month for the next 20 months until the loan is paid.

INTEREST   Beginning on the 1st day of each month following the beginning of the loan that the interest for the preceding period be charged against their business checking account.

It is understood that the interest will be on the unpaid balance of the loan.

ASKING FOR YOUR LOAN

Now that Joe and Doris Smith have completed their Loan Proposal, they are ready to meet with their banker. Prior to this time they had done one other very important thing.

Eight years before they even considered having a business of their own, they opened a joint CHECKING ACCOUNT at the local branch office of the First National Bank of Anywhere.

Over the past eight years, they had taken out two small loans from the bank. The first was to finance their automobile purchase of three years ago. Then last year they had taken out a $5,000 loan to remodel their kitchen and breezeway.

While doing this, they became well acquainted with Ted Benson, the bank's vice-president.

When they first considered going into their Snow Plowing and Lawn Care Service, they casually mentioned to Mr. Benson that they might see him for a business loan. Thus, they had paved the way to set an appointment with their bank for a business loan. If your banking experience has been limited, consider taking all or some of the following steps:

1.   Open a personal checking account with a commercial bank.

2.   Ask to meet a bank officer when you open your account. Even the president is not too high on the ladder. If he is not available, ask to meet a vice president.

---

3.   Ask to see this same person from time to time when you come into the bank to make a deposit or to cash a check. Simply go over and say "HELLO".

4.   If you already have a checking account open, consider opening a savings account.

5.   Take out a loan, even if it is a small one, in order to establish a LOAN HISTORY with your bank.

In short, if at all possible, attempt to establish a personal relationship with a specific individual at your bank. This relationship is best established over a period of time. However, if it is not possible, then when you ask for a loan, you simply have to meet with a loan officer.

Make an appointment to discuss your loan and state that you wish to present your loan proposal. DO NOT DISCUSS THE PROPOSAL AT THIS TIME.

Once you appear at the appointed time, present your loan proposal to the bank officer. At that time he will probably ask you some clarifying questions and then indicate that your loan request will be presented to a loan committee.

Or, if you have a loan history with the bank, you may hear immediately. Naturally, the higher the amount of the loan request, the greater the number of questions you may be asked.

In this chapter you have learned:
1.   *In order to be successful in a Small Business, you have to WANT to MAKE MONEY.*
2.   *In order to be successful in a Small Business, you have to know how to spend money properly in order to maximize your profits.*
3.   *In order to be successful in a Small Business, you have to know how to borrow money.*

---

4. Some of the many sources of loans include:
    -Family or relatives
    -Friends
    -Commercial Banks
    -Savings and Loan Banks
    -Credit Unions
    -Loan Companies
    -SBICs
    -Community Dev Companies
    -Insurance Companies
    -Suppliers
    -Leasing Companies
    -Brokers and Investors

5. Prepare a LOAN PROPOSAL when you need to borrow money. In this way, when you go to a bank to ask for a loan, you are showing the banker that not only are you highly knowledgeable about business but that the money you are borrowing will be spent wisely.

    Further, you are indicating how and when the money is going to be repaid.

6. Get to know your banker or a loan officer at the bank where you do business. Your friendship or personal acquaintance can be just as important to you in receiving the loan as is your LOAN PROPOSAL.

Chapter 13

WHAT ASSISTANCE WILL THEY PROVIDE?

SBA **Learn About SBA**

The Small Business Administration offers a wide variety of services for the entrepreneur. Since 1953 the SBA has helped small businesses succeed from start-up through the many stages of growth. In fact, many big businesses whose names are now household words – FedEx, Intel, Nike, Apple, Ben & Jerry's, Compaq, and AOL, just to name a few – received help from the SBA along the way.

In this chapter you will learn:

1. *The history of the Small Business Administration*
2. *The different SBA loan financing programs that are available*
3. *Other financing programs that are available*
4. *Where to go for business counseling and training*

SBA History

Officially established in 1953, the SBA philosophy and mission began to take shape years earlier in a number of predecessor agencies, largely as a response to the pressures of the Great Depression and World War II.

The Reconstruction Finance Corporation (RFC), created by President

Herbert Hoover in 1932 to alleviate the financial crisis of the Great Depression, was SBA's grandparent. The RFC was basically a federal lending program for all businesses hurt by the Depression, large and small. It was adopted as the personal project of Hoover's successor, President Franklin D. Roosevelt, and was staffed by some of Roosevelt's most capable and dedicated workers.

Concern for small business intensified during World War II, when large industries beefed up production to accommodate wartime defense contracts and smaller businesses were left unable to compete. To help small business participate in war production and give them financial viability, Congress created the Smaller War Plants Corporation (SWPC) in 1942. The SWPC provided direct loans to private entrepreneurs, encouraged large financial institutions to make credit available to small enterprises, and advocated small business interests to federal procurement agencies and big businesses.

The SWPC was dissolved after the war, and its lending and contract powers were handed over to the RFC. At this time, the Office of Small Business (OSB) in the Department of Commerce also assumed some responsibilities that would later become characteristic duties of the SBA. Its services were primarily educational. Believing that a lack of information and expertise was the main cause of small business failure, the OSB produced brochures and conducted management counseling for individual entrepreneurs.

Congress created another wartime organization to handle small business concerns during the Korean War; this time they called it the Small Defense Plants Administration (SDPA). Its functions were similar to those of the SWPC, except that ultimate lending authority was retained by the RFC. The SDPA certified small businesses to the RFC when it had determined the businesses to be competent to perform the work of government contracts.

By 1952, a move was on to abolish the RFC. To continue the important functions of the earlier agencies, President Dwight Eisenhower proposed creation of a new small business agency -- the Small Business Administration (SBA).

In the Small Business Act of July 30, 1953, Congress created the Small Business Administration, whose function was to "aid, counsel, assist and protect, insofar as is possible, the interests of small business concerns." The charter also stipulated that the SBA would ensure small businesses a "fair proportion" of government contracts and sales of surplus property.

By 1954, the SBA already was making direct business loans and guaranteeing bank loans to small businesses, as well as making loans to victims of natural disasters, working to get government procurement contracts for small businesses and helping business owners with management and technical assistance and business training.

Over the past 40 years, SBA has grown in terms of total assistance provided and its array of programs tailored to encourage small enterprises in all areas. SBA's programs now include financial and federal contract procurement assistance, management assistance, and specialized outreach to women, minorities and armed forces veterans. The SBA also provides loans to victims of natural disasters and specialized advice and assistance in international trade.

SBA continues to branch out to increase business participation by women and minorities along new avenues such as the minority small business program, micro loans and the publication of Spanish language informational materials.

Small businesses have become a driving force in the U.S. economy.

Nearly 25 million strong, they now employ 58% of the private work force, produce 51% of the nation's gross domestic product and are the principal source for new jobs.

In the year 2000, there were 25.4 million business tax returns filed. The breakdown is as follows:

Sole Proprietorships	17.9 million
Partnerships	2.0 million
Corporation	5.5 million

In 1999 the breakdown of minority businesses is as follows:

Women-owned	4,600,000
Asian-owned	600,000
Hispanic-owned	800,000
Black-owned	600,000

Small business is where the innovations take place. More flexible and often more daring than big businesses, small firms produce the items that line the shelves of America's museums, shops and homes. They keep intact the heritage of ingenuity and enterprise and they help keep the "American Dream" within the reach of millions of Americans. Every step of the way, SBA is there to help them. You can reach the SBA Information Answer Desk at 1-800-U-ASK-SBA.

SBA PROGRAMS

The U.S. Small Business Administration is dedicated to providing customer-oriented, full-service programs and accurate, timely information to the entrepreneurial community. All of the SBA's programs and services are provided to the public on a nondiscriminatory basis.

Basic Conditions of SBA Financing Programs

1. SBA **DOES NOT** loan money or give grants to small businesses. The SBA guarantees loans for banks or other agencies.
2. A business must be a for-profit entity.
3. Small business must have less than $2 million net profit and fewer than 500 employees.

4. Business owner must be of good character and demonstrate ability to run a successful business.

5. Loan applications must discuss how the loan will be repaid.

6. Typically the SBA requires the business owner to put in monies equal to 1/3 of the total amount of financing.

7. Maximum loan limit is $2,000,000.

8. Maximum SBA loan guarantee is $1,000,000

9. The guarantee fee on the loan is between 2-3.5%

10. Loan may be used for working capital, inventory, machinery and equipment, improvements.

11. Loans can be made for 5-7 years for working capital, 10 years for equipment or 25 years for property.

12. Interest rates are discussed by you and the banker, but can not be more than the SBA guidelines permit.

13. Personal guarantees will be required from owners with 20% or more ownership in the business.

FINANCING

www.sba.gov/financing

7(a) Guaranteed Loan Program

Its function is to provide short- and long-term loans to eligible, credit-worthy start-up and existing small businesses that cannot obtain financing on reasonable terms through normal lending channels. The SBA provides financial assistance through its participating lenders in the form of loan guaranties, **not direct loans**. The SBA **DOES NOT provide grants or loans** for business start-up or expansion. The SBA Office of Capital Access administers the 7(a) Loan Guaranty Program. Loans under the program are available for most business purposes, including purchasing real estate, machinery, equipment, and inventory, or for working capital. The loans cannot be used for speculative purposes. The SBA can guarantee a maximum of $1,000,000 under the 7(a) program.

Those that use this program are start-up and existing small businesses.

Certified and Preferred Lenders

Its function is to designate the most active and expert SBA participating lenders as either Certified or Preferred. Certified lenders receive a partial SBA delegation of authority to approve loans. Preferred lenders receive full delegation of lending authority. A listing of participants in the Certified and Preferred Lenders Program is available from SBA district offices.

LowDoc Loan Program

Its function is to reduce the paperwork involved in loan requests of $150,000 or less. The SBA uses a one-page application for SBALowDoc that relies on the strength of the applicant's character, business experience and credit history. Under the LowDoc Program, the SBA will guarantee 80% of the loan made by a banker to an existing business, a business purchase or business start-up.

SBA Express Program

Its function is to encourage lenders to make more small loans to small businesses. Participating banks use their own documentation and procedures to approve, service and liquidate loans of up to $150,000. In return, the SBA agrees to guarantee up to 50% of each loan. SBA Express can be used as a revolving line of credit up to seven years. An example of a revolving line of credit has the same characteristics of a loan, except you do not have to take all the money at once. On a $10,000 loan, you can borrow $2,000 this month and $3,000 next month and $5,000 in month 3. The interest that you pay on the loan is calculated on the amount of the loan you have borrowed. In the previous example, you would pay interest on $2,000 for one month, $5,000 for two months and $10,000 for the balance of time you make payments.

CAPLines Loan Program

Its function is to finance small businesses' short-term and cyclical working-capital needs. Under CAPLines, there are five distinct short-term working-capital loans: Seasonal, Contract, Builders, Standard Asset-Based, and Small Asset-Based lines. The SBA generally can guarantee a maximum of $1,000,000 or 75% of the amount needed. Owners must meet the same requirements as any other SBA 7(a) business loan.

Those that use this program are start-up and existing small businesses

Export Working Capital Program (EWCP)

Its function is to help small businesses for short term export financing when financing is not available on reasonable terms. The program enables the SBA to guarantee up to 90% of a secured loan, or $1,000,000, whichever is less. Loan maturity may be for up to three years with annual renewals. Loans can be for single or multiple export sales and can be extended for pre-shipment working capital, post-shipment exposure coverage or a combination of the two.

Those that use this program are export-ready small businesses

Defense Loan & Technical Assistance (DELTA), 7(a) Loan Program

Its function is to help defense-dependent small firms that are adversely affected by defense cuts diversify into the commercial market through financial and technical assistance. Loans must be used for the following: to retain jobs of defense workers, create new jobs in impacted communities, or modernize/expand in order to remain in the national technical and industrial base. DELTA uses the following loan programs: 7(a), with a maximum total loan of $2 million; and/or 504, with a maximum guaranteed debenture of $1.3 million. 7(a) loans carry a maximum guaranty of 80%. Federal, state and private-sector resources provide a full range of management and technical assistance.

Those that use this program are defense-dependent small firms adversely impacted by defense cuts. Small businesses must have 25% of their sales from Department of Defense or defense-related Department of Energy contracts.

Funding is established through SBA resource partners.

International Trade Loan (ITL), a 7(a) Loan Program

Its function is to offer long-term financing to small businesses engaged or preparing to engage in international trade, as well as to small businesses adversely affected by import competition. The SBA can guarantee up to $1.25 million for a combination of fixed-asset financing and working capital. The working-capital loan guaranty portion cannot exceed $750,000 and the fixed asset portion cannot be greater than $1,000,000.

Those that use this program are export-ready small businesses

Pollution Control Loan, a 7(a) Loan Program

Its function is to assists businesses that are planning, designing or installing a pollution control facility. This includes most real or personal property that will reduce pollution. The program has a maximum loan amount of $2 million with an SBA guaranty of $1 million, less any outstanding balance due the SBA on other loans.

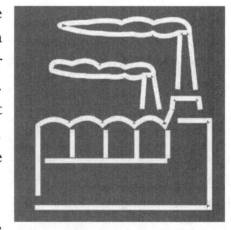

Those that use this program are businesses

building, installing, or servicing a pollution control facility

Certified Development Companies (CDCs), a 504 Loan Program

Its function is to provide long-term, fixed-rate financing to small businesses to acquire real estate, machinery or equipment to expand or modernize. Typically at least 10% of the loan proceeds are provided by the borrower, at least 50% by a non-guaranteed bank loan, and the remainder by a SBA-guaranteed debenture. The maximum SBA debenture is $1 million for meeting the job creation criteria or a community development goal. Generally, a business must create or retain one job from every for $35,000 provided by the SBA. The maximum SBA debenture is $1.3 million for meeting for meeting a public policy goal.

Those that use this program are small businesses requiring "brick and mortar" financing

Funding is established through certified development companies (private, nonprofit corporations set up to contribute to the economic development of their communities or regions). To find a certified development company go to:

http://www.sba.gov/gopher/Local-Information/Certified-Development-Companies/cdcall.txt

Community Adjustment and Investment Program (CAIP), a 7(a) Loan Program

Its function is to create new sustainable jobs and preserves existing jobs in businesses at risk due to changed trade patterns with Canada and Mexico following the National American Free Trade Agreement (NAFTA) was signed. Business applicants must be located in a CAIP-eligible community. They also must demonstrate that within 24 months and as a result of the loan they will create or preserve at least one job per $70,000 of federally guaranteed funds they receive. CAIP is a partnership between the federal government (primarily the SBA and U.S. Department of Agriculture) and the North American Development Bank.

Those that use this program are Businesses in communities with significant job losses related to the North American Free Trade Agreement.

Funding is established through Certified Development Companies.

MicroLoan, a 7(m) Loan Program

Its function is to provide short-term loans of up to $35,000 to small businesses for working capital or the purchase of inventory, supplies, furniture, fixtures, machinery and/or equipment. Proceeds cannot be used to pay existing debts or to purchase real estate. Loans are made through SBA-approved nonprofit groups. These lenders also receive SBA grants to provide technical assistance to their borrowers. Additional entities also receive grants to provide technical assistance to other businesses selecting non-SBA-backed financing.

Those that use this program are small businesses needing small-scale financing and technical assistance for start-up or expansion

Funding is established through intermediary lenders (nonprofit organizations with experience in lending and technical assistance).

The Facts About . . . The MicroLoan Program for Entrepreneurs

The MicroLoan Program combines the resources and experience of the U.S. Small Business Administration with those of locally based nonprofit organizations to provide small loans and technical assistance to small businesses.

Under the MicroLoan Program, the SBA makes funds available to qualified nonprofit organizations, which act as intermediary lenders. The intermediaries use these funds to make loans of up to $35,000 to new and existing small businesses. The intermediaries also provide management and technical assistance to help ensure success.

Eligibility Requirements

Virtually any type of for-profit small business is eligible for the MicroLoan Program. The form of the business, whether a proprietorship, partnership or corporation, is not a determining factor. It must, however, meet the SBA's size standards at the time of application. Generally, businesses applying for this type of loan will fall well within these standards. Not-for-profit child-care centers are also eligible to apply.

Use of Loan Funds

MicroLoan funds may be used for working capital or to purchase inventory, supplies, furniture, fixtures, machinery and equipment. Funds may not be used to purchase real estate or to provide a down payment on real estate.

Loan Terms

The maximum MicroLoan is $35,000. The average-sized loan is around $10,500. The maximum term allowed for a loan is six years. Terms may vary according to the size of the loan, the planned use of funds, the requirements of the intermediary lender, and the needs of the borrower. MicroLoans are direct loans from the intermediary lenders and are not guaranteed by the SBA. Interest rates vary, depending upon the intermediary lender.

Credit Requirements

A MicroLoan applicant must meet the credit requirements of the local intermediary lender. Generally, the applicant will be expected to have good character, a strong commitment to his/her business idea, and a credit history that provides reasonable assurance that the loan will be repaid. In addition, the applicant should have some management expertise or be willing to participate in training designed to strengthen management skills.

Collateral Requirements

As with credit standards, collateral requirements for the MicroLoan Program are set by each local intermediary lender. In most cases, loans are at least partially collateralized by equipment, contracts, inventory or other property. Lenders may also require personal guaranties.

Applying for a MicroLoan

The first step in applying for a MicroLoan is to contact your local intermediary lender. The intermediary lender will provide information on applying for a loan and receiving technical assistance. To find an intermediary in your area check:

http://www.sba.gov/financing/microparticipants.html

INVESTMENT
www.sba.gov/inv

Small Business Investment Companies (SBICs)

Its function is to provide equity capital, long-term loans, debt-equity investments and management assistance to small businesses particularly during their growth stages. The SBA's role consists of licensing the SBICs and supplementing their capital with U.S. government-guaranteed debentures, participating securities or low-interest loans. SBICs are privately owned and managed, profit-motivated companies, investing with the prospect of sharing in the success of the funded small businesses as they grow and prosper.

Those that use this program are small businesses seeking long-term capital. Almost 75% of the businesses that were funded in 2001 were in the manufacturing, information, or professional, scientific or technical services. Over 75% of the businesses received $25 million or greater.

Funding is established through small business investment companies. To find a small business investment company go to:
http://www.sba.gov/gopher/Local-Information/Small-Business-Investment-Companies/sbicall.txt

Angel Capital Electronic Network (ACE-Net)

Its function is to provide an Internet-based secure listing service for entrepreneurs seeking equity financing of $250,000 to $5 million from accredited "angel" investors. The "angels" using ACE-Net can negotiate directly with listed companies to provide equity capital funding and advice for a stake in the entrepreneur's corporation. ACE-Net is operated as a partnership between the SBA's Office of Advocacy and a number of nonprofit organizations nationwide. It will ultimately be turned over to a private nonprofit organization.

Those that use this program are entrepreneurs and "angel" investors.

SURETY BONDS
www.sba.gov/osg

Surety Bond Guarantee

Its function is to guarantee bid, performance and payment bonds for contracts up to $1.25 million for eligible small businesses that cannot obtain surety bonds through regular commercial channels. By law, prime contractors to the federal government must post surety bonds on federal construction projects valued at $25,000 or more. In addition, many states, counties, municipalities, and private-sector projects and subcontracts also require surety bonds. Contractors must apply through a surety bonding agent, since the SBA's guaranty goes to the surety company.

Those that use this program are small construction and service contractors; surety and insurance companies, and their agents; federal and state agencies; state insurance departments -- federal, state and other procurement officials

Funding is established through surety and insurance companies and their agents; four SBA area offices: Atlanta, Denver, Philadelphia, and Seattle. To find out which office to call go to:
http://www.sba.gov/osg/contacts.html

FEDERAL PROCUREMENT
www.sba.gov/gc and pronet.sba.gov

The function of the SBA in federal procurement that all small businesses have the maximum practicable opportunity to participate in providing goods and services to the government. Each year the SBA negotiates procurement goals with each Federal agency.

The most current goals are as follows:
1. 23% of prime contracts for small businesses;
2. 5% of prime and subcontracts for small disadvantaged businesses;
3. 5% of prime and subcontracts for women-owned small businesses;
4. 3% of prime contracts for HUBZone small businesses;
5. 3% of prime and subcontracts for service-disabled veteran-owned small businesses.

To identify Federal opportunities that may be available, go to: http://www.fedbizopps.gov/ or http://www.pronet.sba.gov/

Natural Resources Assistance Program

Its function is intended to help small businesses receive a fair share of the large quantities of natural resources and surplus real property that the Federal Government sells on an annual basis. The program covers timber and related forest products, strategic materials (go to: http://www.gsa.gov/Portal/home.jsp to get a list of products), royalty oil, leases involving rights to minerals, coal, oil and gas and surplus real and personal property.

Certificate of Competency (CoC)

Its function is to help small businesses secure government contracts by providing an appeal process to low-bidder businesses denied government contracts for a perceived lack of ability to perform satisfactorily. SBA is authorized by the Congress to certify as to a small company's "capability, competency, credit, integrity, perseverance and tenacity" to perform a 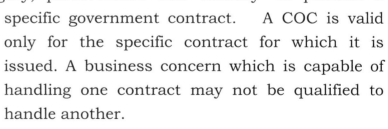 specific government contract. A COC is valid only for the specific contract for which it is issued. A business concern which is capable of handling one contract may not be qualified to handle another.

Those that use this program are small businesses that have been denied government contracts for perceived lack of ability.

Office of Federal Contract Assistance for

Women-Owned Business Owners (CAWBO)

Its function is to use a multifaceted outreach and educational program to teach women business owners to market to the federal government.

This program is for women-owned businesses. To find out more or if you qualify as a women-owned business go to: www.womenbiz.gov

Procurement Marketing & Access Network (PRO-Net)
www.pronet.sba.gov

Its function is to serve as a search engine for contracting officers, a marketing tool for small firms, and a "link" to procurement opportunities and other important information. Pro-Net; contains business information on almost 200,000 small firms. The Pro-Net project is a cooperative effort among SBA's offices of Government Contracting, Minority Enterprise Development, Advocacy, Women's Business Ownership, Field Operations, Marketing & Customer Service, the Chief Information Officer, and the National Women's Business Council. Registration for this database is free.

HUBZone Empowerment Contracting

Its function is to encourage economic development in historically underutilized business zones — "HUBZones" — through the establishment of federal contract award preferences for small businesses located in such areas. After determining eligibility, the SBA lists qualified businesses in its PRO-Net database.

Those that use this program are Small businesses located in historically underutilized business zones

See the SBA Office of HUBZone Empowerment Contracting Program, www.sba.gov/hubzone

---

RESEARCH & DEVELOPMENT

Small Business Innovation Research (SBIR)

Its function is to provide a vehicle for small businesses to propose innovative ideas in competition for Phase I and Phase II awards, which represent specific R&D needs of the participating federal agencies. These awards may result in commercialization of the effort at the Phase III level.

Small businesses must meet certain eligibility criteria to participate in the SBIR program.

- American-owned and independently operated
- For-profit
- Principal researcher employed by business
- Company size limited to 500 employees

Each year, ten federal departments and agencies are required by SBIR to reserve a portion of their R&D funds for award to small business.

- Department of Agriculture
- Department of Commerce
- Department of Defense
- Department of Education
- Department of Energy
- Department of Health and Human Services
- Department of Transportation
- Environmental Protection Agency
- National Aeronautics and Space Administration
- National Science Foundation

For more information on SBIR go to:
http://www.sba.gov/sbir/indexsbir-sttr.html#sbir

Small Business Technology Transfer (STTR)

Its function is to require each small firm competing for an R&D project to collaborate with a nonprofit research institution. This program is a joint venture from the initial proposal to the project's completion. STTR's most important role is to foster the innovation necessary to meet the nation's scientific and technological challenges in the 21st century.

Small businesses must meet certain eligibility criteria to participate in the STTR Program.

- American-owned and independently operated
- For-profit
- Principal researcher need not be employed by small business
- Company size limited to 500 employees

Funding is established through five federal agencies with extramural research and R&D budgets of $1 billion: NASA, the National Science Foundation, and the departments of Defense, Energy, and Health & Human Services.

Tech-Net is an electronic gateway of technology information and resources for and about small high tech businesses. It is a search engine for researchers, scientists, state, federal and local government officials, a marketing tool for small firms and a potential "link" to investment opportunities for investors and other sources of capital. To learn more about Tech-Net, go to: http://tech-net.sba.gov/index2.html

BUSINESS COUNSELING & TRAINING

The SBA provides most business counseling and training programs through its resource partners.

Small Business Development Centers (SBDCs)

Its function is to provide high quality, low-cost management and technical assistance, counseling and training to current and prospective small business owners. Administered by the SBA, the program is a cooperative effort of the private sector, the educational community, and federal, state and local government.

Those that use this program are pre-business, start-up and existing small businesses

There are more than 1,000 locations, including universities, colleges, state governments, private-sector organizations. To find an office near you, go to: http://www.sba.gov/gopher/Local-Information/Small-Business-Development-enters/

Business Information Centers (BICs)

Its function is to provide information, counseling and technical assistance designed to help entrepreneurs start, operate and grow their businesses. BIC counseling and training are provided by the SCORE Association (SCORE), other community organizations and SBA resource partners. Services also include High-tech computer hardware, copier and fax, DSL access to the Internet, up-to-date business software, reference library and videotapes.

To find a Business Information Center close to you, go to: http://www.sba.gov/gopher/Local-Information/Business-Information-Centers/Bics/

SCORE Association (SCORE)

Its function is to offers counseling and training for small business owners who are starting, building or growing a business. SCORE services also include going into business seminars, and specific business topic seminars, including sales and marketing, finance, or international trade. Most seminars and one-on-one counseling is either free of charge or a small nominal fee.

There are more than 12,000 volunteers in 389 chapters with 700 locations, www.score.org

To find a SCORE office near you or to sign up for e-mail counseling, go to: http://www.score.org/

BUSINESS INFORMATION SERVICES

Answer Desk

Its function is to help callers with questions and problems about starting and running businesses. The computerized telephone message system is available nationwide 24 hours a day, seven days a week. Counselors are available Monday through Friday, 9:00 a.m. to 5:00 p.m. Eastern Time.

This is open to the general public

Toll-free telephone number: 1-800-U-ASK-SBA

Publications

SBA field offices and the Answer Desk (see above) offer free publications that describe the SBA's programs and services. The SBA also produces and maintains a library of business-management publications, videos and computer programs. These are available by mail for a nominal fee (to defray reproduction and shipping costs). A complete listing of these products can be found in the Resource Directory for Small Business Management (SBA no. CO-0042).

These are available to the general public

Available at SBA field offices, Answer Desk and SBA resource partners, the federal Consumer Information Center, etc., www.sba.gov/library

SBA Online

Its function is to provide fast and easy help to the small business community via a computer-based electronic bulletin board. Operating 23 hours a day, 7 days a week, SBA OnLine offers relevant, current information to the public. SBA OnLine services include: SBA publications, access to SBA programs and services, points of contact, calendars of local events, on-line training, access to other federal agency on-line services and data, electronic and Internet mail, information exchange by special-interest groups, and down-loadable files.

This is open to the general public

Limited access: 1-800-697-4636

Full access: 1-900-463-4636

SBA home page: www.sba.gov

U.S. Business Advisor: www.business.gov

U.S. Business Advisor

Its function is to provide a one-stop electronic link to the government's business information and services. With the U.S. Business Advisor, small businesses no longer have to contact dozens of agencies and departments to access applicable laws and regulations, or figure out on their own how to comply. They can download business forms and conduct a myriad of other business transactions through this web site.

Those that use this program are the General Public

Accessible through the Internet at web site www.business.gov

ADVOCACY

www.sba.gov/advo

Office of Interagency Affairs

Its function is to monitor regulatory and other policy proposals of more than 20 federal agencies to assess their impact on small business and suggests alternatives for consideration. The office provides information to Congress on legislative issues and drafts testimony on public policy issues of concern to small business. Monitors regulatory agencies' compliance with the Regulatory Flexibility Act, as amended by the Small Business Regulatory Enforcement Fairness Act, and reports annually to Congress on the agencies' activities.

Those that use this program are small businesses, regulatory agencies, and Congress.

Office of Economic Research

Its function is to produce the annual report to Congress, "The State of Small Business: A Report of the President"; oversees research on small business issues, banking and the economy; and compiles and interprets statistics on small businesses according to size, industry and geographic distribution.

Those that use this program are Congress, the media, academic institutions, government agencies, foreign governments

Funding is established through the White House, federal agencies, Congress, state and local governments, the media, and independent researchers

Office of Public Information

Its function is to publicize and disseminate information on small business issues, statistics, research and advocacy publications; prepares printed material for Office of Advocacy-sponsored economic research, policy and conferences; and provides outreach to small businesses, trade associations, the legal community and others interested in small business policy.

Those that benefit from this program are small businesses, Congress, state legislatures, the media, government agencies, economic-research organizations

See Office of Advocacy, the SBA home page, under Offices & Services. www.sba.gov/advo

Regional Advocates

Its function is to serve as the SBA chief counsel's direct link to local communities. Regional advocates monitor the impact of federal and state regulations and policies on communities within their regions. They also work with state officials to develop policy and legislation that shape an environment in which small companies can prosper and grow.

Those that use this program are local business owners, state and local government agencies and legislatures

Small Business Regulatory Enforcement Ombudsman

Its function is to receive comments from small businesses about the regulatory enforcement and compliance activities of federal agencies and refers comments to the appropriate agency's Inspector General on a confidential basis. Coordinates the efforts of the 10 small business regulatory fairness boards and reports annually to the SBA Administrator and to the heads of the affected agencies on the boards' activities, findings, and recommendations.

Those that use this program are small businesses, federal agencies

For more information see SBA ombudsman, 10 SBA regional fairness boards, SBA Office of Field Operations, toll-free number: 1-888-REG-FAIR. www.sba.gov/regfair

DISASTER ASSISTANCE

www.sba.gov/disaster

Administered by the Office of Disaster Assistance, the SBA Disaster Assistance Program is the primary federally funded disaster assistance loan program for funding long-range recovery for private-sector, nonagricultural disaster victims. Eligibility is based on financial criteria. Interest rates fluctuate according to statutory formulas. A maximum interest rate of 4 percent is provided to applicants without credit available elsewhere; a higher maximum of 8 percent is for those with credit available elsewhere.

In addition to presidential declarations, the program handles disaster loans when a declaration is made by the SBA Administrator. There are two disaster loan programs: physical disaster loans for permanent rebuilding and replacement homes and personal property for homeowners and non-farm businesses, and economic injury loans to small businesses for working capital until normal operations resume.

After the terrorist attacks on the World Trade Center in 2001, the SBA has guaranteed over $885 million in low interest loans to small businesses affected by the attacks. These loans went to more than 9,300 businesses employing over 148,000 employees.

Economic Injury Disaster Loans (EIDLs)

Its function is to provide up to $1.5 million in working-capital loans for businesses that suffer economic injury as a direct result of a disaster, regardless of whether the property was damaged. The loans are made to help small businesses pay ordinary and necessary operating expenses that they would have been able to pay if the disaster had not happened. NOTE: The maximum loan amount is $1.5 million for EIDL and physical disaster business loans combined, unless the business meets the criteria for a major source of employment. This was a very active type of loan after the September 11, 2001 disaster in New York City. Small businesses around the country were hurt by this disaster.

ASSISTANCE FOR ARMED FORCES VETERANS

www.sba.gov/vets

Veterans' Business Outreach Program (VBOP)

The Veterans Business Outreach Program (VBOP) is designed to provide entrepreneurial development services such as business training, counseling and mentoring to eligible veterans owning or considering starting a small business. Workshops include accounting, marketing, computer training, business-plan preparation and loan packaging. To find a VBOP center near you, go to:

http://www.sba.gov/vets/vbop.html

Veterans Business Development and Procurement Conferences

Its function is to assist veteran-owned businesses and start-ups, primarily in areas impacted by military downsizing. Start-ups receive information on how to market and finance their businesses; existing businesses seeking to sell products and services can network with federal procurement representatives. The conferences are co-sponsored by the Department of Veterans Affairs.

Technology Transfer Conferences

Its function is to provide assistance to defense-dependent firms adversely affected by reductions in defense spending and non-defense-dependent small firms interested in buying or selling technology.

Those that use this program are high-tech, veteran-owned small businesses and defense-dependent and non-defense-dependent small firms

Funding is established through the SBA Office of Veterans' Affairs and small business development centers

ASSISTANCE FOR EXPORTERS
www.sba.gov/oit

U.S. Export Assistance Centers (USEACs)

Its function is to combine the trade-promotion and export-finance resources of the SBA, the U.S. Department of Commerce, the Export-Import Bank and, in some locations, the Agency for International Development. Designed to improve delivery of services to small- and medium-sized businesses, USEACs work closely with other federal, state and trade partners in local communities.

Those that use this program are export-willing, export-ready and exporting small businesses

Export Legal Assistance Network (ELAN)

Its function is to provide free initial legal consultations to export-willing and exporting small businesses. Under an agreement among the SBA, the U.S. Department of Commerce and the Federal Bar Association, experienced trade attorneys volunteer their time to answer exporters' legal questions.

Those that use this program are export-willing and export-ready small businesses

Strategic Partnerships

Its function is to foster improved cooperation and business opportunities for small businesses in international markets. The partnership agreements are between the SBA and its counterparts in other countries.

Those that use this program are export-willing, export-ready and exporting small businesses

ASSISTANCE FOR NATIVE AMERICANS

www.sba.gov/naa

Native American Affairs

Its function is to develop initiatives that ensure native individuals have access to business-development resources, training and services in their communities. The primary focus of the Office of Native American Affairs is economic development and job creation through small business ownership and education. The office works with the following: individual and tribally owned organizations; other federal, state and local agencies; nonprofit organizations; and national Native American organizations.

Those that use this program are American Indians, Alaskan Natives and Native Hawaiians.

Funding is established through the SBA field offices, small business development centers, and reservation-based tribal business information centers (TBICs).

Tribal Business Information Centers (TBICs)

Its function is to provide access to state-of-the-art computer software technology, individualized business counseling services and business management workshops. TBICs serve Native American reservation communities in the states of Montana, North Dakota, South Dakota, California, Minnesota, North Carolina and the Navajo Nation. TBICs are SBA resource partners.

ASSISTANCE FOR SMALL & DISADVANTAGED BUSINESSES

Small Disadvantaged Business (SDB) Certification

Its function is to ensure that small businesses owned and controlled by individuals claiming to be socially and economically disadvantaged meet the eligibility criteria. Once certified, the businesses are eligible to receive price evaluation credits when bidding on federal contracts.

8(a) Business Development

Its function is to utilize the SBA's statutory authority to provide business development and federal contract support to small disadvantaged firms. The 8(a) Program has also implemented a mentor/protégé program that helps small companies learn from more experienced businesses in the Federal contracting arena.

Funding is established through the SBA and other federal contracting officers, small business specialists at federal procurement activities.

For more information on the 8(a) Development Program, go to:
http://www.sba.gov/8abd/

7(j) Management & Technical Assistance

Its function is to authorize the SBA to provide grants and enter into cooperative agreements with service providers for specialized assistance in areas such as accounting, marketing and proposal/bid preparation. (This program does not provide grants to start or expand a business.) Industry-specific technical assistance and entrepreneurial training also are available.

Those that use this program are small disadvantaged businesses, low-income individuals, firms in either labor-surplus areas or areas with a high proportion of low-income individuals

Funding is established through service providers (including small businesses and educational institutions), and SBA Office of 8(a) Business Development.

ASSISTANCE FOR WOMEN

www.sba.gov/womeninbusiness

Women's Business Centers

Its function is to provide long-term training and counseling in all aspects of owning or managing a business, including financial, management, marketing and technical assistance, and procurement.

Those that use this program are women-owned small businesses, start-ups, pre-business start-ups

Online Women's Business Center

Its function is to serve as an interactive, state-of-the art web site that offers the information an entrepreneur needs to start and build a successful business. The center is a public-private partnership between the SBA and several major U.S. corporations. The numerous features of the center include training, mentoring, individual counseling, and topic forums and newsgroups. Information is available in several languages.

Those that use this program are women-owned small businesses, start-ups, pre-business start-ups

Women's Network for Entrepreneurial Training (WNET)

Its function is to provide a vehicle for established women business owners to serve as mentors, passing on knowledge, skills and support to protégées who are ready to expand their businesses. WNET roundtables offer support and guidance in a group setting. Sponsors include small business development centers, local business leaders, government representatives and SCORE.

Funding is established through the SBA field offices, women's business and professional organizations, SBDCs, women's business centers, SCORE, the WNET roundtables around the country

EMPOWERMENT ZONES/ENTERPRISE COMMUNITIES
www.sba.gov/onestop

One Stop Capital Shops (OSCSs)

Its function is to provide centralized access to the full range of a community's small business resources, including entrepreneurial development, access to capital and federal procurement. Clients can do the following: access a range of small business information resources (through the Business Information Center located in the OSCS); receive counseling (from SCORE volunteers) and training (from a local SBDC); learn to develop a business plan or mend damaged credit; and apply for financing (typically under the SBA's MicroLoan Program). An OSCS is a partnership between the federal government — primarily the SBA — and a local community designed to offer small business assistance from a single, easy to access, retail location. Created through the federal government's Empowerment Zone (EZ) Initiative, an OSCS is located in a distressed area, and is generally targeted to under served communities.

Small Business Welfare to Work Initiative

Its function is to help small businesses gain access to a new pool of workers by connecting them to local service providers and job-ready workers. Targets efforts toward small businesses in industries that are experiencing labor shortages. Provides entrepreneurial counseling and training to persons currently or formerly on welfare who are interested in starting a business as a means to self-sufficiency. The Welfare to Work Initiative is a function of the SBA Office of Entrepreneurial Development.

Provided through the SBA headquarters, field offices, resource partners, and service providers

HOW CAN THE SBA HELP YOU?

Can the SBA help you get started in business?

The U.S. Small Business Administration provides a wealth of information on starting a business at the SBA home page (www.sba.gov). You can take advantage of SBA's resource partners; the SCORE Association and the Small Business Development Centers (SBDC) provide free one-on-one counseling to those interested in starting and expanding a business. This includes, critiquing your business plan, legal requirements, marketing, and licenses needed for your business. To find the SBA district location nearest you, please visit www.sba.gov/regions/states.html and click on your state.

Business Information Centers (BICs), supported by local SBA District Offices, can assist you by providing access to state-of-the-art computer hardware and software, and through counseling by SCORE Association volunteers. BICs have resources for addressing a broad variety of business start-up and development issues. You can receive help with writing a comprehensive business plan, evaluating and improving your marketing and sales techniques, diversifying into a new product and/or service areas, pricing your products, or exploring exporting opportunities. The BIC web

site is: www.sba.gov/bi/bics

How do you get a small business loan from the SBA?

The SBA does not lend money. It guarantees loans for the bank. The loan is actually provided by your local lender.

You should prepare a business plan, including your loan proposal and submit it to a local lender. If the lender is unable to approve your loan, you may request that your application be submitted, by the lender, to the SBA. The SBA can guaranty up to 85% of a small business loan; however, the lender must agree to lending the money with the SBA guaranty. The lender will then forward your loan application and a credit analysis to the nearest SBA District Office. Upon SBA approval, the lending institution closes the loan and disburses the funds.

How do you get a small business grant from the SBA?

At this time, Congress has not set aside any monies for grants to start and/or expand a small business.

How do I write a business plan?

The Business Plan Chapter will assist you in writing a business plan, also, at the SBA's home page select "Starting," you will find information on starting a business and writing a business plan.

How do you get a business license?

Licensing is generally handled through your state or local government. You will need to consult your local telephone directory in the

"Government" section for an office that will assist you with a license or permit. See www.sba.gov/hotlist/license.html

How do you get a tax identification number?

For a Federal Tax ID number, please contact the Internal Revenue Service for Form SS-4. This form is available through their web site at http://www.irs.gov/pub/irs-pdf/fss4.pdf. You may call the IRS at 1-866-816-2065 to apply over the phone or you can mail you completed form to the IRS Service Center for your area. You will need a filled out copy of your Form SS-4 prior to applying over the phone.

You will need to contact your state Department of Revenue for state taxes (if any). Please consult your local telephone directory in the "State Government" section for the office in your state.

What type of collateral do you need for a loan?

Repayment ability from the cash flow of the business is a primary consideration in the SBA loan decision process but good character, management capability, collateral, and owner's equity contribution are also important considerations. All owners of twenty percent (20%) or more of the business are required to personally guarantee SBA loans.

The SBA does not deny approval for an SBA Guaranty Loan solely due to lack of collateral. However, it can be used as a reason, in addition to, other credit factors.

What SBA business assistance is available in your area?

There are 12,400 SCORE Association chapters and approximately 1,000 Small Business Development Centers (SBDC) nationwide. SCORE provides free, expert advice based on many years of firsthand experience and shared knowledge, on virtually every aspect of business. The SBDC provides a variety of management and technical assistance services to small businesses and potential entrepreneurs.

You may also want to visit one of the Business Information Centers (BICs) that have various books, videotapes, and training workshops on starting and expanding your business. This includes marketing, business planning, legal requirements, bookkeeping, etc.

What classifies a business as "small?"

There is no "official" certification process to be determined as a small business. The U.S. Small Business Administration (SBA) uses Standard Industrial Classification (SIC) codes in determining size standards. To see if your business is considered small by the federal government, or to determine which SIC code(s) is applicable to your business, please go to www.sba.gov/regulations/siccodes/.

It is considered a self-certifying process; therefore, no paperwork needs to be filled out.

How can you get your business certified as a woman or minority owned?

On a Federal level, Congress considers a minority-owned business as generally anyone other than white. The business MUST be owned and at least 51% controlled by one or more minorities. Women are not considered minorities. It is a self-certifying process and no paperwork needs to be filled out.

However, your state and local government may have different rules and regulations regarding their contracts and what their definitions are. Consult your state and local government for rules and requirements.

There is a certification process to be considered a Small Disadvantaged Business (SDB). The SDB certification ensures that small businesses are owned and controlled by socially and economically disadvantaged individuals meeting SDB eligibility criteria. If you are considered an SDB, you may receive a price evaluation credit of up to 10% when you bid on a federal contract. For more information on this program, please go to: www.sba.gov/sdb

The HUBZone Empowerment Contracting Program encourages economic development in historically underutilized business zones, through the establishment of federal contract award preferences for small businesses located in such areas. To learn more about this program, please go to www.sba.gov/hubzone

---

In this chapter, you have learned:

1. *The SBA was created in 1953 and has helped many small businesses.*
2. *The different programs the SBA has established to enhance small businesses.*
3. *Where is information for women-owned, veteran-owned and native American-owned businesses?*

Chapter 12

Bookkeeping Made Easy

More mental than fun

Depending on whom you ask, the subject of accounting is likely to produce one of three responses: Great! or Huh? or Yuk!

Too many entrepreneurs are less than enthusiastic about accounting, and that's unfortunate. They view it as a necessary evil -- to satisfy tax reporting requirements. And we all have varying views of taxes, don't we -- most of them unfavorable!

Accounting is nothing more than a process of organizing and recording financial activities in a **disciplined** manner. "Disciplined" is emphasized to stress the need for a thoughtful, deliberate approach.

Back to attitudes about accounting; why do so many view it negatively? In most cases, it's probably because they haven't recognized the full value of knowing where they are and where they've been (financially). You see, good accounting is a little like good navigation of ships and airplanes -- financial "fixes" are just as important to the entrepreneur as good navigational "fixes" are to the ship captain or the aircraft commander. If you know where you've been, and where you are now, you have a much better chance of arriving at your chosen destination. This chapter will focus on ideas which can help you establish financial "fixes" as you "navigate" to economic security.

Many bookkeeping and accounting courses offered in high schools and colleges emphasize the technical aspects while appearing to ignore the practical side. To overcome this problem, we will concentrate on converting the technical to the practical.

> *In this chapter you will learn:*
>
> 1. *Understand basic accounting terms and procedures and why they're so important;*
> 2. *Organize your financial activities into an understandable form;*
> 3. *Calculate the value of your business; and*
> 4. *Determine whether or not you're making money.*

When we're finished, while you may not be qualified to hang out your public accountant's shingle, you will have a reasonable understanding of the fundamentals of accounting, and an appreciation of their value.

So much for the preamble -- let's get to the meat of accounting fundamentals! We'll start off with some of the more obvious items so we can build a foundation.

First of all, why even start a business? Usually, it's: a) to make money (increase wealth); b) to satisfy an ego drive; or c) some combination of the two. Please understand; there is nothing wrong with giving in to a healthy ego -- it's what makes us all tick deep down inside. At the same time, unless a person is blessed with an unending supply of funds, chances are that he or she will want to make a reasonable profit from the venture at the same time as feeding the ego.

What happens all too frequently is that some business people (perhaps you've known one or two) overlook the little details of keeping good business records in their enthusiasm to satisfy the ego. In fact, they might have made a better income if they had merely put their funds in a passbook savings account! Others may be operating at a loss and don't even know it, much less know what to do about correcting the situation.

The function of accounting could be defined as the creation and organization of records about a business's financial activities and transactions. We can subdivide this rather broad definition into four components:

1. **Documenting** -- The individual documents pertaining to each activity, sometimes called Source Documents.

2. **Recording** -- Listing each activity (transaction) in an orderly manner (usually chronologically) on individual pages or in books commonly called journals.

3. **Organizing** -- Placing these transactions into workable categories in order to provide meaningful summaries, usually in a book called a ledger.

4. **Development of reports** which provide the overall pictures of a company's financial activities and health.

The owner/manager needs reliable information about the company's financial activities in order to guide its growth and development. While a shoebox full of receipts and bills may be considered to be reliable **data** it certainly will not qualify as **information** for the effective management of the firm.

Another definition is necessary -- something called the Accounting Equation: Assets = Liabilities + Owner's Equity -- or:

$$A = L + OE$$

Assets (the value of the things owned by the company) equal Liabilities (the amounts owed to others) plus Owner's Equity (the net value or worth of the company). From this it becomes obvious that if we know two of the values, we can solve for the third. For example, given Assets and Liabilities, we can compute Owner's Equity merely by turning the equation around to:

$$OE = A - L$$

Assets, Liabilities, and Owner's Equity are commonly combined into a report called a Balance Sheet which reflects the financial position of the company at a given point in time.

Another equation deals with day-to-day activities and has no specific name: Revenues (the monies we've collected or are scheduled to collect) = Expenses (the amounts we've paid or are obligated to pay) + Net Income (whatever is left over). It, too, can be turned around to:

$$NI = R - E$$

These three components are usually combined into a report called the Income Statement and reflect the profitability of a company during the period for which the report was prepared.

These two reports -- Balance Sheet and Income Statement -- are intimately tied together because at the end of each accounting period (a month, quarter, year -- whatever is desired) the Net Income is added to Owner's Equity. It becomes obvious, then, that Owner's Equity goes up and down with the fortunes of Net Income!

Now that we have established some basic definitions, let's look at the situation facing Ed Entrepreneur.

Ed has been a machinist for most of his life and takes a great deal of pride in his work. The pay is satisfactory, and the company for which he works has been good to him over the years.

At the same time, he is a tinkerer -- the kind of individual who has a good imagination and who enjoys putting ideas to work. He has developed some miscellaneous devices for use around the home which have been quite useful and, most recently may have discovered the pot of gold at the end of the rainbow! It seems that Ed has invented a new household gadget (he calls it a "Widget") which performs just about any function desired by the householder. Further, Ed has discovered a special technique which makes it easy and simple to shape and assemble the Widget, cutting manufacturing time to about 15 minutes.

When Ken, his neighbor, saw and tried the Widget, he asked Ed to make one for him, insisting on paying $5 for it since it was so useful. Ed didn't mind doing it for a couple of reasons. First, he enjoyed the work. Second, Ken was a highly respected doctor and Ed enjoyed the compliment. Third, he had the necessary materials in his scrap drawer. And, fourth, he could always find some good use for the $5! It wasn't until a couple of weeks later that Ed discovered his new device should have been called the "Tiger" (as in 'by the tail').

At a neighborhood barbecue, Ken told Ed that he had shown the Widget to some of his medical friends who instantly saw great value in it not only as a household device but also as a medical instrument if he could make it out of stainless steel. And, to top it off, the other doctors would be willing to pay $100 for one of stainless steel because it was extremely useful and they had never before seen anything like it for any price! Could he deliver 20 in the next two weeks?

That evening, Ed started doing some serious thinking. The cost of stainless steel would be several dollars compared to a dollar or so for the cold rolled steel he had been using. Machining would be more time consuming; so it might take a half-hour to make this new version.

The biggest problem was that his lathe was old and rather worn. It was good enough to do his home jobs, but when it came to handling stainless steel, it wouldn't be able to provide the precision he needed. The machine shop had the equipment, but Ed didn't want the boss to know he was moonlighting because others had gotten into trouble before.

Then he remembered that his brother-in-law George had a first class shop in the garage. While George wasn't much of a machinist, he had been smart enough to buy top-of-the-line equipment.

He called George, explained the situation, and asked if he could use the shop.

"Sure," said George, "for $50 per hour."

Ed thought briefly about George's offer, and said he would call him back.

Giving himself time to cool off, Ed did some more figuring. First, he knew how to do the work and do it well. Second, he could probably make two Widgets per hour; so the cost of George's equipment would be only $25 per unit. Third, if he were going to collect $100 per Widget, he could still make about $65 per unit after subtracting another $10 for the costs of the materials. Fourth, in spite of George's outrageous charge, Ed was still excited about the possibilities.

20 widgets at $100 each	A	$2,000
Garage charges 2 widgets per hour @ $50/hour	B	500
Cost of materials at $10 each widget	C	200
Net Income for 20 widgets (A-B-C)	D	$1,300
Revenue per widget (D/20)		$35

He called Ken to see if his doctor friends were really serious.

"Absolutely," said Ken.

Ed took a deep breath and told Ken he would do it.

Then Ed called George, agreed to the $50 hourly charge, and set up a

---

schedule to use the equipment.

On Friday he took a day's vacation and went to several suppliers, buying raw materials, rivets, nuts and bolts, along with the special cutters he would need for the lathe and bits for the drill press. Altogether, he spent nearly $350, musing that it was a mere pittance compared to the $2,000 he would make in this venture. Over the weekend he completed 15 of the stainless steel Widgets (SSW). He could have done all of them, but decided to put some extra care into them since Ken's reputation was also at stake. By the end of the next week, he had finished the lot and called Ken. When Ken arrived and looked at the finished SSW's, he was genuinely excited. Since he was meeting with his doctor friends on Monday, he said he would take them along and deliver them.

On Tuesday Ken called Ed and said his associates were really pleased with the SSW's and would promptly send their checks as soon as Ed sent invoices for their records.

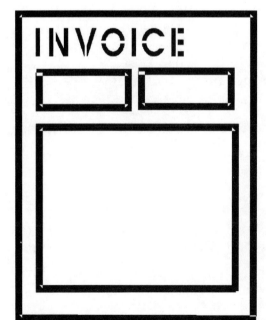

Ed had an old beater of a typewriter at home, so he bought some packaged forms at the local stationery store and laboriously pecked out the 20 invoices. When he was done, he mused to himself that it seemed to take nearly as long to prepare the invoices as it had to manufacture the SSW's.

By the end of the month, he had received checks from 12 of the doctors and deposited them in the bank, feeling rather smug. The $1,200 would help him make the down payment on the new Olds 98 he wanted, and the $800 coming later would pay for his summer vacation.

Then, he remembered George -- and winced as he gave him a check for $750 for the 15 hours spent using George's shop.

Now he was faced with another problem. His phone was ringing every evening when he arrived home from work -- other doctors had learned about SSW's and wanted to order them. Before he knew it, he had agreed to make another 35 units.

He called George again and arranged a new schedule.

Over the next couple of weeks (or weekends), Ed worked diligently on SSW's -- producing and delivering all 35 finished units. There was a little more scrap than he had expected, and it took a little longer for each one than he had planned. Still, Ed thought to himself that he was making money -- in fact, more than he had ever made!

He began to resurrect an old dream of having his own machine shop where he could turn out first-class goods at a fair profit instead of the boring activities he did at his current job. The only problem was his concern over continuing to make a reasonable living -- he realized there were a lot of things he didn't know about running a business.

At the next neighborhood barbecue, he found himself chatting with Alice Accountant and he discussed his dilemma with her. She asked him some rather serious questions, such as how much did a finished SSW really cost and how many could he produce in a given time, and was he really making a profit.

Ed commented that things seemed to be going quite well but admitted that he didn't really have the precise answers. He asked Alice if she could help him over the weekend, offering to pay her $25 per hour to get the financial records straightened out.

By Saturday, Ed had found all the sales slips from his purchases, along with the duplicates of the invoices sent to the doctors. He and Alice began organizing things.

"The first thing to remember," Alice emphasized, "is to keep all of your original sales slips and invoices, the source documents. From them we organize and record the financial activities in a logical manner. Let's begin with purchases -- we will create a Purchases Journal."

She took the sales slips from the first purchases, broke the items into categories, and posted them to the journal using Ed's check numbers as a reference. Then she added the cost of renting George's equipment as another item. When she was done, it looked like this:

PURCHASES JOURNAL

Date	Purchased From	Description Ref.	Materials	Tools	Rental
5/10	Jones Steel Co.	Steel 3012	$250		
5/10	Jones Steel Co.	Bolts, Rivets	50		
5/10	Smith Mach Tool	Cutters, Bits		50	
5/30	George	Shop Rental			750
5/31	Monthly Totals		$300	$50	$750

Then she took the duplicate invoices from the first order and, assigning a number to each as a reference, posted them -- this time to another sheet she called a Sales Journal:

SALES JOURNAL

Date	Sold To	Description	Ref	Dr. Amt.	Cr. Amt
5/20	Doc #1	Widget	101		$100
5/20	Doc #2	Widget	102		100
5/20	Doc #3	Widget	103		100
5/20	Doc #20	Widget	120		100
5/31	Total Month				$2,000

Alice stressed that each transaction should be posted separately to minimize the chance of missing something. She also urged that the items be posted chronologically, in date order.

Then, since Ed was selling Widgets on credit, she set up a journal to reflect the amounts owed to him by others, and also to record the payments received from these same people. She placed the ones for which Ed had been paid in a **closed** file and the remainder in an **open** invoices file.

ACCOUNTS RECEIVABLE JOURNAL

Date	In Acct With	Description	Ref	Dr. Amt	Cr Amt
5/20	Doc #1	Sale on Acct	101	$100	
5/20	Doc #2	Sale on Acct	102	100	
5/20	Doc #3	Sale on Acct	103	100	
5/20	Doc #20	Sale on Acct	120	100	
5/20	Doc #6	Recd on Acct	106		$100
5/20	Doc #7	Recd on Acct	107		100
5/20	Doc #8	Recd on Acct	108		100
5/20	Doc #12	Recd on Acct	112		100
5/31	**Month Totals**			**$2,000**	**$1,200**

Another journal was set up to record the cash transactions.

CASH JOURNAL

Date	Name	Description	Ref	Dr. Amt	Cr. Amt
5/10	Jones Steel	Materials	3012		$300

5/10	Smith Mach Tool	Tools	3013		50
5/22	Doc #1	Recd on Acct	101	$100	
5/24	Doc #2	Recd on Acct	102	100	
5/24	Doc #3	Recd on Acct	103	100	
5/29	Doc #11	Recd on Acct	111	100	
5/31	George	Shop Rental	3025		750
5/31	Doc #12	Recd on Acct	112	100	
5/31	**Month Totals**			**$1,200**	**$1,100**

As she went along with the various journals, Alice explained that each item was of significant importance if Ed wanted to know how his business was really doing. She stressed that credits of $100 in one journal required complementing total debits of $100 in another journal (or journals) -- she called it **double entry bookkeeping.**

Alice pointed out that as Ed recorded a sale (she called it a **Credit**) in the Sales Journal, he either was or was not paid for it at the time the sale was made. If he received payment on the spot, it would be directly recorded (as a **Debit**) in the Cash Journal; if not, then it must be recorded as a debit in the Accounts Receivable Journal.

Similarly, as Ed purchased materials, they must be recorded as Debits in the Purchases Journal and as Credits in the Cash Journal (if he paid for them at the time of purchase), otherwise, in an Accounts Payable Journal. In this way, Ed would always know the balance of outstanding accounts as well as his cash position.

"Great Scott!" Ed exclaimed. "I didn't know that you had to do all these things just to run a small operation like mine. Is it all really necessary?"

Alice smiled. "Well," she replied, "I've already taken a few shortcuts in order to keep things as simple as possible. For example, if you had lots of cash transactions, such as a retail store, we would set up separate journals for cash receipts and cash disbursements. I just didn't feel that was necessary at this time.

"However," she went on, "your purchases tend to fall into different categories; so I decided to spread them out to allow you to see more accurately just how you're spending your money.

"Now that we've summarized your activities for May, we need to prepare a couple of reports which will really put things in perspective. First, though, we'll do a worksheet which will help us.

ED ENTREPRENEUR

TRIAL BALANCE WORKSHEET ENDING MAY 31

Account Title	Opening		Adjustments		Closing	
	Debit	Credit	Debit	Credit	Debit	Credit
Sales				2,000		
Materials			300			
Tools			50			
Shop Rental			750			
Net Income			**1,100**	**2,000**		
Cash			1,200	1,100	100	
Accts Rec			2,000	1,200	800	
Accts Pay						
Owner's Equity			1,100	2,000		900
Totals			**4,300**	**4,300**	**900**	**900**

"Here, too," Alice explained, "I've taken a few shortcuts. If your activities were more complicated, I would have to enter more detail -- but the result would be the same.

"The idea here is to transcribe the activity from each journal and, when we balance, we can be pretty sure that we've covered all the details. You will note that once we determined the Net Income, we then posted it to the Owner's Equity account -- that's the one which tells you how much your business is worth at the end of each accounting period."

"You mean my business is already worth something?" asked Ed.

"Sure, by an amount equal to the Net Income. If you had opened a separate checking account at the very beginning and put the same $350 into it that you used to buy the materials and tools, the Balance Sheet would have been a little different. You merely would have posted a $350 debit to Cash and a corresponding credit of $350 to Owner's Equity; and the value of your business would now be $1,250. Our situation here is the same as if you had then taken the $350 back out of the business account and returned it to your personal account. Now, let's prepare the Income Statement."

ED ENTREPRENEUR -- INCOME STATEMENT FOR MAY

REVENUES:		
Sales of 20 widgets	$2,000	
		$2,000
EXPENSES:		
Raw Materials/Cost of Goods Sold	300	
Tools	50	
Shop Rental	750	
Total Expense		$1,100
NET INCOME		**$900**

"Let's see," said Ed rather thoughtfully, "if I sold 20 Widgets for a $900 profit, that's $45 per Widget. Not too bad!"

"Looks pretty good," responded Alice. "Just how much time did it take you to earn the $900?"

"Well, I spent more time than I had expected -- about 15 hours, I guess."

"Yes," she acknowledged, "but how about the time you spent getting the materials and preparing the invoices?"

"Oh! I forgot about that. There's probably another 15 hours tied up there, too. Still, $900 for 30 hours isn't bad, is it?"

"Not at all," she agreed. "Let's finish up the first month by preparing one more report -- something we call a Balance Sheet. It will give you a bird's eye view of where you stand as of the close of each monthly period. Once again, all we have to do to prepare this report is to pick the numbers right off the worksheets."

ED ENTREPRENEUR -- BALANCE SHEET AS OF MAY 31

ASSETS		LIABILITIES	
Cash in Bank	100	Accts Payable	0
Accts Rec	800		
		Total Liabilities	0
		Capital Paid In	0
		May Earnings	900
		Total Equity	900
Total Assets	900	**Total Liabilities & Owner's Equity**	900

"Well," said Ed, "I can see one thing for sure -- my Cash is low and my Receivables are high! In fact, most of my value is sitting in someone else's pocket. I'll call Ken and see if he can push on his doctor friends a little."

"Before we do that," advised Alice, "let's go to work on June's activities." She glanced at the source documents. "You go ahead and post these transactions as I watch over your shoulder."

Ed took the first one, the sales slip for the materials to make the second group of Widgets, and began to post the details, following that with the postings of cash received and the 35 new sales he had made, along with the Widget returned by Doctor #18. Oh, yes, and $1,000 of the $1,200 he owed to George for the month's use of the machine shop.

PURCHASES JOURNAL

Date	Purchased From	Description Ref.	Materials	Tools	Rental
5/31	Month Totals		$300	$50	$750
6/3	Jones Steel Co.	Steel 3033	500		
6/3	Jones Steel	Bolt/Rivets	100		
6/30	George	Shop Rental			1,200
6/30	Month Totals		$600		$1,200

CASH JOURNAL

Date	Name	Description	Ref	Dr. Amt	Cr. Amt
5/31	Month Totals			$1,200	$1,100
6/3	Jones Steel	Materials	3033		600
6/4	Doc #13	Recd on Acct	113	$100	
6/5	Doc #15	Recd on Acct	115	100	
6/7	Doc #16	Recd on Acct	116	100	
6/8	Doc #17	Recd on Acct	117	100	
6/28	Doc #44	Recd on Acct	144	100	
6/28	Doc #48	Recd on Acct	148	100	
6/30	George	Shop Rental	3057		1,000
6/30	Doc #53	Recd on Acct	153	100	

6/30	Month Totals			2,000	1,600

SALES JOURNAL

Date	Sold To	Description	Ref	Dr. Amt.	Cr. Amt
5/31	**Total Month**				**$2,000**
6/17	Doc #21	Widget	121		$100
6/17	Doc #22	Widget	122		100
6/17	Doc #23	Widget	123		100
6/26	Doc #55	Widget	155		100
6/27	Doc #18	Return	118	100	
6/30	**Total Month**			**$100**	**$3,500**

ACCOUNTS RECEIVABLE JOURNAL

Date	In Acct With	Description	Ref	Dr. Amt	Cr Amt
5/31	**Month Totals**			**$2,000**	**$1,200**
6/3	Doc #13	Recd on Acct	113		100
6/4	Doc #15	Recd on Acct	115		100
6/5	Doc #16	Recd on Acct	116		100
6/7	Doc #17	Recd on Acct	117		100
6/17	Doc #21	Sale on Acct	121	100	
6/17	Doc #22	Sale on Acct	122	100	
6/17	Doc #23	Sale on Acct	123	100	
6/26	Doc #55	Sale on Acct	155	100	
6/27	Doc #18	Return	118		100
6/28	Doc #44	Recd on Acct	144		100
6/28	Doc #48	Recd on Acct	148		100
6/30	Doc #53	Recd on Acct	153		100
6/30	**Month Totals**			**$3,500**	**$2,100**

Oh yes, Ed had to set up a new journal, Accounts Payable, to handle the amount which he still owed George for the June shop rent.

ACCOUNTS PAYABLE JOURNAL

Date	Acct With	Description	Ref	Dr. Amt	Cr Amt
6/30	George	Balance of Rent	3057	$200	
6/30	Month Total			$200	

It took them the better part of another hour to pull all of June's figures together and get them properly posted.

"Whew," Ed sighed, "isn't there an easier way to do all this?"

"Sure," laughed Alice, "hire someone else to do it! The point remains, however, that it does need to be done."

"But aren't there more shortcuts I could take? How about that Accounts Receivable Journal -- of the 35 sales I recorded, I received payment for 16 of them during the month. Do I really have to go through all that effort?"

"If you're especially careful, you can probably put all of June's invoices in a separate file and pull them out as you receive the checks. Those which remain in the file at the end of the month will still have to be posted to Receivables if you're going to keep track of things."

"Oh, by the way," Ed suddenly remembered, "what happens if I don't use all the raw materials I bought? I'm getting better as I do each Widget, and I've got about $120 in unused materials left over."

"Then we'd better set up another journal -- we'll call it Inventory.

"We'll handle this one a little differently because we have to 'back' into the figure we need for the Operating Statement. At the same time, we will include the approximate value of the Widget returned by Doctor #18 because at the end of the month it's unsold. Let's assume its worth is $50."

INVENTORY

Date	Description	Begin	+ Purch	- End	=Used
6/30	Stainless Steel		500	100	400
6/3	Bolts, Rivets		100	20	80
6/27	Widget (finished)			50	-50
6/30	Cost of Goods		600	170	430

"You see," Alice commented after preparing the journal, "what we need is the Cost of the Goods which you sold during the month. We determine that figure by taking the balance of the Inventory at the beginning of the month -- in this case zero -- adding to it the amounts you purchased during the month, and then subtracting the value which remains at the end of the month.

"Now, let's do the worksheet for June. Note that we ignore the Opening and Closing columns when we transcribe the Revenues and Expenses. But, for the Balance Sheet accounts, we first transcribe the Closing figures from the previous month into the Opening column. This way, we assure ourselves of staying in balance. Remember, Net Income is the remainder after we subtract Total Expenses from Total Revenues."

ED ENTREPRENEUR
TRIAL BALANCE WORKSHEET
ENDING JUNE 30

Account Title	Opening Debit	Opening Credit	Adjustments Debit	Adjustments Credit	Closing Debit	Closing Credit
Sales			100	3,500		
Materials			430			
Tools			0			
Shop Rental			1,200			
Net Income			**1,730**	**3,500**		
Cash	100		2,000	1,600	500	
Accts Rec	800		3,500	2,100	2,200	
Inventory			600	430	170	
Accts Pay				200		200
Owner's Equity		900	1,730	3,500		2,670
Totals	**900**	**900**	**7,830**	**7,830**	**2,870**	**2,870**

"Oh, I see!" exclaimed Ed. "We use the worksheet to verify the month's transactions. We took the $100 Cash from last month's closing, added the $2,000 received this month, then subtracted the $1,600 paid this month, to arrive at a closing Cash balance of $500."

"Good! I think you've got the idea! Now, let's prepare the month's Income Statement and Balance Sheet."

ED ENTREPRENEUR -- INCOME STATEMENT FOR JUNE

REVENUES:		
Sales of 35 widgets	3,500	
Less: Return of 1 widget	100	
		$3,400
EXPENSES:		
Cost of Goods Sold	430	

Tools	0	
Shop Rental	1,200	
Total Expense		1,630
NET INCOME		**1,770**

ED ENTREPRENEUR -- BALANCE SHEET AS OF JUNE 30

ASSETS		LIABILITIES	
Cash in Bank	500	Accts Payable	200
Accts Rec	2,200		
Inventory	170	**Total Liabilities**	200
		Capital Paid In	0
		May Earnings	900
		June Earning	1,770
		Total Equity	2,670
Total Assets	**$2,870**	**Total Liabilities & Owner's Equity**	**$2,870**

"Whew," sighed Ed, "that's a lot of work, but I do have to admit that it gives me a good view of the activity in June and where I am now. The only problem is, what happens when I get a big bunch of these reports? It seems to me that I can get buried in numbers and paper, and still not know which way I'm heading."

"For example, I've had this idea about leaving my present company and going into the Widget business full-time. How can I do a better job of determining whether or not this business can support me?"

"An excellent observation and a worthwhile question," Alice replied. "While there's probably nothing which will answer all your questions, there are **some** things you could do to help reduce the uncertainty."

"For example, you should probably get some more knowledge about the industry in which you're selling your products -- perhaps some kind of market research to determine the need for Widgets, the competition you're likely to encounter, and the price you'll be able to charge over the long run. Unfortunately, the things we've done here won't help you with this part of the decision making process."

"There are some ways, however, to use the results of your accounting efforts to help you in your decisions. One good approach is to develop ratios which, in turn, can help you figure out the trends. In other words, the idea is to establish comparisons to see if things are improving, staying pretty much the same, or getting worse.

"For example, let's compare Expenses as a percentage of Revenues. Using the May and June figures, we can set up a little chart -- something like this:

ED ENTREPRENEUR -- EXPENSES VS. REVENUES

	Month of May		Month of June		Year-to-date	
Account Title	**$**	**%**	**$**	**%**	**$**	**%**
Net Sales	2,000	100	3,400	100	5,400	100
Cost of Goods	300	15	430	12.65	730	13.52
Tools	50	2.50	0	0	50	.93
Shop Rent	750	37.50	1,200	35.29	1,950	36.11
Net Income	900	45	1,770	52.06	2,670	49.44

"Now," Alice invited, "what can you see from this?"

"Hey, that's easy! My Cost of Goods Sold is going down -- I'm getting more done with less scrap. Likewise, my costs of Shop Rent are declining -- it's not taking me as long to make a Widget. Now, I can see not only that my profit is improving, but I can also see which factors are affecting the improvement."

"Right!" she acknowledged. "And, one of the reasons we took the effort to add that returned Widget to Inventory was to avoid distorting the Cost of Goods Sold. Oh, sure, CGS would have still improved, but the results of your work wouldn't have been as obvious."

"But," Alice continued, "We've got one more step which will further help us to see how things are going. Remember, you commented earlier that you could get buried in the numbers? Well, here's a method which can help turn the numbers, the data, into truly useful information. I'll add a few hypothetical values for purposes of illustration," she said graphically, as she took out a piece of paper and began to plot some data points.

"Keep in mind, Ed, while this graph reflects Cost of Goods Sold as a percentage of Sales, it could have shown CGS in dollars per unit."

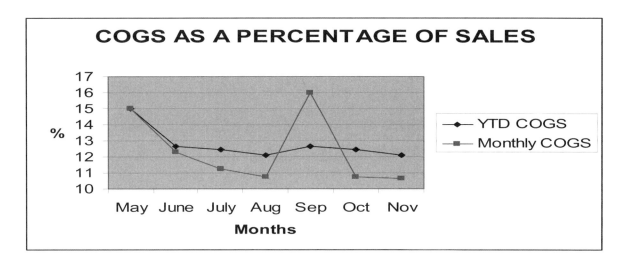

As Alice finished her efforts she asked, "What would this chart tell you, Ed?"

"Holy cow!" Ed exclaimed. "Everything looks great except for that big jump in September."

"If this were your company and you saw this chart, what would you do?" Alice asked.

"I'd be looking very seriously to see what happened -- could be an increase in the price of materials or, more likely, an increase in scrap. If I had a number of people working for me, I'd also check into labor costs. As long as I'm fairly small, though, I'll probably know about these things as they occur."

"Still, it makes sense to put things in this form so I can focus on the important items without being overwhelmed by all the data. Now I understand why the boss at the shop has all those charts on his wall.""

"Ed, my friend and neighbor," Alice smiled as she stood up and stretched, "you've just graduated with flying colors from Alice's beginning school of accounting and financial management!"

"I'm truly pleased with what you've taught me this afternoon. And, looking at the clock, I think I owe you about $125 for the education."

"I'll tell you what, Ed. Make it $100 even, and a steak on the grill, and I'll call it even."

"Done!" And Ed started the grill.

As they relaxed on the patio after dinner, Alice decided to give Ed some additional food for thought.

"Earlier, Ed, you mentioned that you had made about $30 per hour in May. What do you feel your hourly earnings were in June?"

"Let's see," he said thoughtfully, "I spent about 24 hours in manufacturing, an hour getting raw materials, about six hours preparing the invoices, and another hour delivering the Widgets -- say, 32 hours altogether." He punched his calculator quickly. "That's a little over $55 per hour!"

"Now," challenged Alice, "if I correctly understand what you've said, you have an interesting problem facing you." Taking another worksheet from her pad, she put down some more figures.

ED ENTREPRENEUR -- HOURLY LABOR EXPENSES

	Month of June		Month of June		Year-to-Date	
Account Title	**Hours**	**$/Hr**	**Hours**	**$/Hr**	**Hours**	**$/Hr**
Manufacturing	15	30	24	55	39	45.38
Pickup/Delivery	5	30	2	55	7	37.14
Administration	10	30	6	55	16	39.38
Totals	**30**	**30**	**32**	**55**	**62**	**43.06**

"Now, Ed, as a businessman, what does this set of figures tell you?"

"If I owned a company and saw figures such as these, I'd blow my stack! Fifty-five dollars an hour for these jobs is just as outrageous as $50 per hour for George's shop!"

"And," Alice continued, "your labor costs for this month are going to have to include another four hours of bookkeeping."

"What I hear you saying is that I should allocate an appropriate value to these jobs, and then decide which ones I'm going to do, and which ones are better done by someone else." Ed paused, then said, "A good machinist should earn about $15 per hour. Jones Steel will deliver my materials for $15 per load. What should I expect to pay a good assistant to handle the paperwork?"

"Probably about $10 to $12 per hour for, say, three hours per month," she responded. "Add another one-third for fringe benefits and payroll taxes if the person is an employee, or pay him or her the same additional amount if the work is done as an independent contractor."

Ed worked furiously with his calculator for a few minutes.

"If I were to redo these figures to

allocate costs directly to each of the functions, they would begin to make more sense. For example, I'll use $12 plus 1/3 for administrative work, and $15 plus 1/3 for machinist's labors."

ED ENTREPRENEUR
REVISED HOURLY LABOR EXPENSES

Account Title	Month of May			Month of June		
	Hours	$/Hr	Total	Hours	$/Hr	Total
Manufacturing	15	20	300	24	20	480
Pickup/Delivery			15			15
Administration	3	16	48	3	16	48
Management- Ed			537			1,227
Totals			**900**			**1,770**

"Now I can see what my profit line is, or at least what the value of my management efforts are -- because I separated them from the other jobs."

"If I were to keep track of my hours spent in management tasks, such as planning, and allocate an hourly value to that work, I'd get a much better idea of whether or not my business is really making any money," he concluded.

Ed was quiet for several minutes. When he finally spoke, there was a gleam in his eye. "I've been planning on taking off for a couple weeks of vacation. It's time for my annual fishing trip. Orders are down for the moment -- guess all the doctors are on vacation, too.

"This time it's going to be a working vacation. I hear that the fish aren't biting too well right now anyway; so I'll have plenty of time to do some thinking.

"What I really need now is a business plan. But, I need another bit of information before I can put one together. If I were to purchase my own equipment, how would I handle the bookkeeping?"

"Quite simply," Alice responded. "Equipment, such as the kind used in a machine shop, should have a useful life of at least five years and is considered a capital investment, rather than an expense. One way to handle it is to expense a fraction, say 1/60 of the equipment's value, each month. This would be similar to a charge for rent, but it's called depreciation. It's a method of writing off the equipment's value over a period of time to compensate the owner for wear and tear."

"But," she cautioned, "There are several different ways of handling depreciation -- I've only mentioned one. When you come to the point of making a decision about a purchase of this magnitude, I suggest that we get together first to discuss it. In that way, you will be more informed and can pick the one most appropriate for you."

"That really makes some sense," agreed Ed. "I'm going to work on my business plan while I'm waiting for the big ones to bite. This should be a fascinating fishing trip."

When Ed returned from his vacation, he had his plan fairly well organized. He went over it with Alice, who helped him smooth out a few wrinkles.

Realizing that he could keep better track of his business cash if he separated it from his household finances, he opened a business checking account, depositing the current business cash balance. He also added the original $350 as capital paid in.

He retained Alice's accounting firm to handle his firm's books and prepare invoices. The charges would be $100 per month which included not only the bookkeeping services and preparation of invoices, but also periodic consultation with Alice to help him as questions arose.

On Ken's recommendations, he also contracted with Mike to promote the sales of SSW's. Mike was a seasoned medical supplies salesman who represented several manufacturers, and who had earned Ken's respect. The understanding was that Mike would receive a 10% commission only when the payments for SSW's were received by Ed.

Over the next couple months, Accounts Receivable dropped to about $1,000 and Sales increased to about 50 units per month. Ed was able to concentrate his time on the manufacturing, a long time love, along with the new excitement of being a manager.

Ed's current financial statements were as follows:

ED ENTREPRENEUR
INCOME STATEMENT FOR OCTOBER

REVENUES:		
Sales of 50 widgets	5,000	
Less: Returns	0	
		$5,000
EXPENSES:		
Sales Commissions	500	
Cost of Goods Sold	600	
Tools	25	
Shop Rental	1,500	
Accounting Services	100	
Total Expense		2,725
Net Income		**2,275**

ED ENTREPRENEUR
BALANCE SHEET AS OF OCTOBER 31

ASSETS		LIABILITIES	
Cash in Bank	7,470	Accts Payable	
Accts Rec	1,000	Commission Payable	250
Inventory	350	**Total Liabilities**	250
		Capital Paid In	350
		May Earnings	900
		June Earnings	1,770
		July Earnings	500

		August Earnings		1,000
		September Earnings		1,775
		October Earnings		2,275
		Total Equity		8,570
Total Assets	**8,820**	**Total Liabilities & Owner's Equity**		**8,820**

One problem remained -- that $50 per hour Ed had to pay George for the use of the shop.

By sheer luck, Ed found out that he could purchase some nearly new shop equipment from an estate for $24,000. Further, the estate would rent that portion of the building where the equipment was installed for $375 per month if he bought the equipment.

He went to see his favorite banker, Larry Lender, to find out what kind of financing they would suggest. Larry told Ed that based on the reputation Ed had established together with the financial reports Ed had the foresight to bring with him; the bank would be willing to lend 80% of the funds necessary to purchase the equipment. The loan would be amortized (paid off) over three years, with interest at a rate of 15% on the unpaid balance. Monthly payments would be $666.

Ed hurried over to Alice's office to get the benefit of her insight.

"What should I do?" he asked.

"I'm not in a position to tell you what to do, Ed," she responded, "but I can help by showing you how last month's financial statements would appear if you had owned the equipment at that time."

She took another worksheet and began to make some adjustments to last month's reports. "I'm going to include only those accounts from the Operating Statement which will change as a result of a purchase."

ED ENTREPRENEUR
ADJUSTMENTS TO OCTOBER FOR NEW EQUIPMENT

Account Title	Actual Debit	Actual Credit	Adjustments Debit	Adjustments Credit	Projected Debit	Projected Credit
Shop Rental				A 1,500		
Depreciation			C 400			
Building Rent			D 375			
Interest Exp			E 240			
Net Income Adj			**1,015**	**1,500**		
Cash	7,470		A 1,500	B 4,800		
				D	} 3,129	
				375		
				E 666		
Accts Rec	1,000				1,000	
Inventory	350				350	
Machinery		B	24,000		24,000	
Depreciation			C (400)		(400)	
Comm Payable		250				250
Bank Loan			E 426	D 19,200		18,774
Owner's Equity		8,570	1,015	1,500		9,055
Totals	**8,820**	**8,820**	**26,541**	**26,541**	**28,079**	**28,079**

As Alice made the adjustments, she labeled each one and discussed it with Ed:

    A.   represented not having to pay the $1,500 for shop rental;

    B.   was the addition of the machinery as a capital asset and required corresponding credits to Cash of $4,800 (the down payment) and Bank Loans of $19,200;

    C.   was the allowance for Depreciation for the month, treated uniquely as a negative Debit so that it makes more sense when printed on the Balance Sheet;

    D.   was the monthly Rent for the new building; and

E.   was the monthly payment to the bank, split between the interest which would have been due on the loan, and the remainder of the payment which would have been applied to the reduction of the loan.

"Are you saying," Ed challenged, "that by buying the equipment my Net Income would have gone up by $485?"

"Yes," she confirmed, "as a result of decreasing costs. In addition, if we can set the down payment aside for a moment, your monthly cash flow would have improved by $451 -- the $1,500 saved on rent to George minus the new charges for the rent on the building and the payment on the loan."

"I think you can already see the results of this opportunity," she remarked. "We'll finish the financial statements anyway, just so there is no confusion."

ED ENTREPRENEUR
ADJUSTED INCOME STATEMENT FOR OCTOBER

REVENUES:		
Sales of 50 widgets	5,000	
Less: Returns	0	
		$5,000
EXPENSES:		
Sales Commissions	500	
Cost of Goods Sold	600	
Tools	25	
Depreciation	400	
Building Rent	375	
Interest Expense	240	
Accounting Services	100	

Total Expense		2,240
Net Income		**2,760**

ED ENTREPRENEUR
ADJUSTED BALANCE SHEET AS OF OCTOBER 31

ASSETS		LIABILITIES	
Cash in Bank	3,129	Accts Payable	
Accts Rec	1,000	Commission Payable	250
Inventory	350	Bank Loans	18,774
Machinery	24,000	**Total Liabilities**	19,024
Less: Depn	(400)		
		Capital Paid In	350
		May Earnings	900
		June Earnings	1,770
		July Earnings	500
		August Earnings	1,000
		September Earnings	1,775
		October Earnings	2,760
		Total Equity	9,055
Total Assets	28,079	**Total Liabilities & Owner's Equity**	28,079

"Remember, though, that the rent for George's shop has varied in the past depending on how many Widgets you were making. These new payments will be there even if you have no orders."

"Alice, I really want to go ahead with this change. How do you see my chances of success?

"There's no way I can forecast any company's success," she reminded him. "You still need to survey the marketplace and draw conclusions as to the likelihood of continuing increases in sales. Once you've done this, you can use your newly acquired skills in accounting to predict the results. "And, by the way, now that you have a sales rep, you can use him for valuable feedback from the marketplace. Ask him to keep his eyes open for information, especially regarding opportunities for new products or accessories.

"There will always be some uncertainty - that's what we call **business risk**. And, because of this risk, the entrepreneur deserves to make a profit."

There you are -- an overview of the world of bookkeeping and accounting. You should now have a reasonable understanding of the fundamentals and an appreciation of their value

We have covered the basics -- the Balance Sheet categories of Assets, Liabilities, and Owner's Equity, along with the Income Statement categories of Revenues, Expense and Net Income. And, we've shown how the periodic Net Income affects the Balance Sheet.

We have also demonstrated how diligence and thoroughness are keystones in the accounting process. We've discussed how each posting to one journal requires a corresponding entry in another journal (or journals) in order to keep things in balance. Discipline is an absolute **must**!

We've learned that Revenue accounts are those which reflect our earnings, whether we received the cash at the time of sale or merely the right to receive payment in the future. Revenues are considered **Credits** (abbreviated Cr.).

Expense accounts, we found, were those to which we posted the costs of day-to-day operations. Once again, this was true when we had made payment immediately, and also when we had incurred the obligation to pay later. Expenses are called **Debits** (abbreviated Dr.).

To keep things in balance, we discovered that Assets (the value of the things which we own) are normally Debits, and both Liabilities (the amounts we owe to others) and Owner's Equity (the remaining value) are Credits.

Further, we have explored some methods of using and interpreting the results of your accounting efforts as devices for management of a business. You see, the figures are not an end unto themselves. Instead, they are tools which are there for your use as you seek ways of establishing your business on a firm foundation and guiding it toward your goals.

In this chapter you have learned:

1. *The definitions for basic accounting terms including: assets, liabilities, owner's equity, net income, balance sheet.*
2. *The differences between the journals that you need to keep in running a profitable business. Even though accounting software packages keep these journals for you, you need to understand how they get created.*
3. *How to manage your cash flow and tell if you are making money and where you may be short on cash to pay bills.*
4. *How to use the financial information to make better decisions as you grow your business.*
